Beyond Calvin

European History in Perspective
General Editor: Jeremy Black

**European History in Perspective
Series Standing Order
ISBN 0–333–71694–9 hardcover
ISBN 0–333–69336–1 paperback**
(outside North America only)

You can receive future titles in this series as they are published by placing a standing order. Please contact your bookseller or, in the case of difficulty, write to us at the address below with your name and address, the title of the series and the ISBN quoted above.

Customer Services Department, Palgrave Ltd
Houndmills, Basingstoke, Hampshire RG21 6XS, England

Beyond Calvin
The Intellectual, Political and Cultural World of Europe's Reformed Churches, *c.* 1540–1620

GRAEME MURDOCK

palgrave
macmillan

First published 2004 by
PALGRAVE MACMILLAN
Houndmills, Basingstoke, Hampshire RG21 6XS and
175 Fifth Avenue, New York, N.Y. 10010
Companies and representatives throughout the world

PALGRAVE MACMILLAN is the global academic imprint of the Palgrave Macmillan division of St. Martin's Press, LLC and of Palgrave Macmillan Ltd. Macmillan® is a registered trademark in the United States, United Kingdom and other countries. Palgrave is a registered trademark in the European Union and other countries.

ISBN 0–333–69138–5 hardback
ISBN 0–333–69139–3 paperback

This book is printed on paper suitable for recycling and made from fully managed and sustained forest sources.

A catalogue record for this book is available from the British Library.

A catalog record for this book is available from the Library of Congress.

10 9 8 7 6 5 4 3 2 1
13 12 11 10 09 08 07 06 05 04

Printed in China

In loving memory of Callum
You will always be in our hearts

Contents

List of Abbreviations

AFR   *Archiv Für Reformationsgeschichte*

AHR   *American Historical Review*

BHR   *Bibliothèque d'Humanisme et Renaissance*

BSHPF   *Bulletin de la Société de l'Histoire du Protestantisme Français*

HJ   *Historical Journal*

JEH   *Journal of Ecclesiastical History*

JMH   *Journal of Modern History*

PHS   *Proceedings of the Huguenot Society*

PP   *Past and Present*

SCJ   *Sixteenth Century Journal*

Acknowledgements

There is a vast and ever-growing literature on Calvinism and the Reformed churches of early modern Europe. This book by no means attempts to offer comprehensive coverage of all aspects of Reformed religious life from the emergence of the movement to around the outbreak of the Thirty Years' War. Rather it investigates some of the ways in which Calvinism operated as an international form of religion, and the successes and failures of international Reformed co-operation. I have tried to include consideration of churches across the Continent in this study, although inevitably some areas have probably fared better than others. In thinking about aspects of this book I have benefited greatly from the wisdom of any number of colleagues and friends, and would like to register thanks to Phil Benedict, Diarmaid MacCulloch, Howard Hotson, Bill Naphy, Andrew Spicer, Judith Pollman, Maria Crăciun, Penny Roberts and Katalin Péter. This is, of course, not intended to distribute blame for my mistakes. I would like to thank all my family for their love and support. Thanks also to Brigid, Helen, Matthew and to many friends and colleagues at Birmingham, which has proved to be such a great place in which to research, teach and live.

Introduction

Europe's Reformed churches had no formal international organisation during the sixteenth and seventeenth centuries. There was no accepted primate who held authority across the Continent, nor any international agreement on a single confession or statement of doctrine. The connections between Europe's Calvinists and Reformed churches were therefore decentralised, unofficial, and could often be disorganised and ineffective. However, many Reformed clergy and ordinary members of congregations consistently expressed their support for, and participated in, a wider international community which is the focus of this study. Establishing and maintaining the ties that bound the Reformed world together held an ideological and emotional significance for many Calvinists, even among those with no first-hand experience outside their own locality. For one thing, if Reformed religion was true, then its truth claims looked more convincing if they were shared across the Continent. However, gaining consensus on key points of Reformed doctrine proved difficult to achieve. Chapter 1 highlights the emergence and development of the shared ideas, in particular on the sacrament of Holy Communion, which underpinned all the connections between Reformed churches. Reformed theology was based not only on the work of John Calvin but was also developed from the insights of a range of leaders of Swiss and south German centres of reform. Much time and effort was spent trying to obtain and maintain international harmony on doctrine. Calvinists were, however, far from wholly united on some issues, and Reformed orthodoxy also changed over time. This was particularly the case over ideas about aspects of God's plan for salvation and decrees of predestination.

The international strain within Reformed ideology and culture can be traced right back to the roots of Reformed churches, which were often

1

founded despite persecution and the forced exile of tens of thousands of Calvinists. The common Calvinist experience of life as a refugee, or of being part of a host community that received refugees, led to lasting international connections between individuals and communities. Chapter 2 examines these exchanges as refugees gathered from the 1540s in centres including Geneva, Emden and London. As churches became established in Switzerland, the Palatinate, Scotland, England and Béarn, and the churches in the Netherlands, France, Hungary and Poland battled for legal recognition and survival, princely courts, noble houses, universities and colleges also became locations for interaction between many Calvinists. Theologians, clergy, students, booksellers, merchants, diplomats, courtiers and military officers became involved in networks of personal contacts, correspondence, teaching and negotiation. International connections were most common among the social and intellectual elite, although the engagement of ordinary people in the international Reformed world, while less likely at first hand, should not be overlooked. There were also persistent attempts to build political alliances between Reformed states, which tested princely commitment to the cause of religion from the French civil wars to the Thirty Years' War. By 1620 the limited achievements of international Reformed diplomacy were brought into sharp relief, and Calvinist churches faced renewed threats of persecution in France, the Empire and central Europe.

The level of involvement by different churches in this wider international community varied depending on geography and local circumstances. While Calvinists from the Carpathians to the Grampians could make long journeys to study at cosmopolitan universities, there was a geographic heart to the international Reformed world which stretched from the south of England through the Netherlands and the Rhineland to Swiss cities, and on through the Huguenot crescent to the Atlantic coast. A network of Reformed churches, communities and individuals from across the Continent coalesced during the second half of the sixteenth century around these key cities and territories. This Reformed movement had dominant personalities, but although Calvin's reputation later came to dominate the landscape, this should not be allowed to obscure the variety of intellectual sources for Reformed Protestantism. Neither should Geneva be seen as the natural and constant centre of this network of Reformed churches, as Zurich played a greater role in international affairs than did Geneva at the beginning of the period considered here. Geneva's role as a centre of activity also lessened during the latter decades of the sixteenth century, and academic centres such as

Heidelberg in the Palatinate and the university towns of the Dutch Republic had become the intellectual engines of the international Reformed world by the end of the sixteenth century.[1]

Chapter 3 considers the political outlook of this international Reformed community, detailing how exchanges between writers and intellectuals informed the development of a distinctive tradition of political thought. While leading reformers stressed the normal obligation of obedience towards civil magistrates, where Calvinists faced persecution from Catholic authorities they debated how far, and in what circumstances, resistance to lawful rulers could be permitted. Suggestions about when, and why, magistrates and nobles could oppose the commands of their sovereigns spread from the Empire to France, England, Scotland, the Netherlands and central Europe. While Calvinists applied these ideas to their particular political circumstances, striking similarities appeared between arguments which were deployed about rights of resistance. The connections between Reformed works on politics therefore demonstrates the significance of intellectual communication between Calvinist activists.

Chapters 4 and 5 focus on the impact of Calvinism on the religious life and culture of communities across Europe. Both chapters acknowledge variety between the ways in which churches were structured, and differences between forms of church services and religious ceremonies. International contacts could lead to intense disagreements over the best way to implement reforms and to organise the government of the church. However, there were also many comparable elements to religious life across Reformed Europe. Common ideas about the need for discipline informed the use of similar institutions and tactics in campaigns to enforce orthodox beliefs and moral behaviour on Reformed communities. Chapter 4 considers the work of consistories, presbyteries and kirk sessions in many Reformed parishes. It traces the development of a hierarchy of synods in territorial churches, and examines the often difficult relationship which emerged between churches and Reformed civil authorities. Despite disputes over the powers of consistories and synods, there was broad support for the role of elders in monitoring the behaviour of congregations. This chapter will compare the intentions, values and moral agenda of Calvinist discipliners, and discuss how the impact of Reformed disciplinary campaigns differed between communities.

Chapter 5 reviews key aspects of the worship and church life of Reformed communities, and builds up a portrait of what it meant to belong to a Reformed church. It looks at patterns of education through catechising, use of the Psalms, sacramental rituals and forms of church services. Calvinists worshipped God in plain buildings which deliberately had very limited decoration. Reformed ministers abandoned wearing traditional vestments which they associated with unnecessary ostentation and with superstition. Clergy normally led church services in simple, dark clothing, similar to academic dress, which was intended to represent values of decent sobriety and intellectual authority to congregations. In England, however, traditional vestments were retained which led to a prolonged debate involving reformers across the Continent, which highlights the role of international opinion about best practice in a local dispute. Finally, this chapter examines the importance for Reformed communities of drawing comparisons between their experiences and the history of Old Testament Israel, and considers Calvinists' expectations about the future.

Using both the terms Reformed and Calvinist, although preference is given here to Reformed, this book examines the international character of this religious movement from its emergence during the 1540s up to around the outbreak of the Thirty Years' War. While the label Calvinist has come to be very widely recognised and is commonly adopted by historians, its sole use can give rise to the mistaken impression that all Reformed churches ultimately owed their existence, ideas and identity to the inspiration of one man, John Calvin. The term Calvinist was first used by Calvin's opponents at Bern in 1548, and there was understandable reticence even among his most enthusiastic supporters to adopt a label which would allow opponents to ask Reformed Christians if their faith had its origins in Calvin.[2] The name Reformed on the other hand was commonly applied to churches across the Continent during the sixteenth and seventeenth centuries, and it offers a better sense of the broad nature of the movement and reflects the important contribution made by other reformers, and in particular by Zurich's Heinrich Bullinger. However, this term is also somewhat problematic as it suggests acceptance that the declared objective of Reformed religion to restore a lost purity to the Christian Church was in fact accomplished. This was of course not a view shared by opponents. As the French Catholic authorities liked to remind Huguenots, their church was not 'the Reformed church of France' but in fact a 'so-called reformed religion'. In Transylvania meanwhile a new sect was first labelled in a 1558 law as 'Sacramentarians', but as this group grew in strength it was later offered legal privileges as a Hungarian church, a Calvinist church, a Reformed church, and in the 1653 summary of the principality's laws was called the 'Evangelical Reformed (or Calvinist)' church.[3] In recognising these problems of terminology, and by using both terms of Reformed and Calvinist but by favouring use of Reformed, this book seeks to depict a emerging religious tradition which, despite its debt to John Calvin, was always very much more than a product of his life and work in Geneva.

Chapter 1: Reformed Ideas

Fraternal relations between Europe's Reformed churches were grounded in broad agreement about the fundamentals of true Christian doctrine. There were strong similarities between the confessions of faith and catechisms which were adopted by different Reformed churches. Many churches also recognised the 1566 *Second Helvetic Confession* written by Zurich's Heinrich Bullinger, and used the 1563 *Heidelberg Catechism* which was composed by Zacharias Ursinus from Breslau in Silesia and by Caspar Olevian from Trier. While it would therefore be incorrect to see John Calvin as the single, authoritative theological voice behind the European Reformed movement, his personal contribution to the emergence and development of Reformed theology was undoubtedly immense. Calvin's ideas about the nature of God, the Church, salvation and the sacraments spread across the Continent through his published works. These texts included dogmatic works, polemic tracts, Biblical commentaries, and written versions of the sermons which Calvin delivered at Geneva on the books of the Old Testament during weekday services and his exegesis of New Testament passages on Sundays. Calvin's intellectual authority within the Reformed world rested above all on his *Institutes of the Christian Religion*. Calvin declared that this book was intended to help readers to understand the Bible correctly by providing them with an orderly 'sum of religion in all its parts'. The first edition of the *Institutes* appeared in 1536, it was first published in French in 1541, and Calvin produced a final version of the text in 1559. The *Institutes* then appeared in 25 different published editions between 1559 and 1578 in Latin, French, and in Dutch, English and German translations. Calvin himself acknowledged that the *Institutes* was 'received by almost all godly men with an acclaim which I would never have ventured to hope for'.[1]

Both Calvin and other Reformed theologians called for urgent reform of the erroneous doctrine and fraudulent religious practices which they perceived in the Catholic church. Reformed writers rejected alternative reform projects as inadequate or heretical, and condemned the faults of Anabaptists and anti-Trinitarians. A profound gulf also opened between Reformed and Lutheran leaders by the 1550s, and Calvinists pressed forward with their own plans to build a true Church, which was to be cleansed of all idolatry, superstition and false doctrine. This true Church was also a universal Church, and repeated efforts were made to bring uniformity between the statements of faith adopted by different Reformed churches. These efforts to build an international consensus aimed to demonstrate the degree of harmony which existed between the fundamental beliefs of churches across the Continent. However, the lack of much concrete achievement from all the discussions and debates held about doctrinal unity highlights some variety within Reformed thought, diversity in ceremonial practices and forms of church government, and local pride in domestic arrangements.

This chapter will examine the Calvinist agenda for reform of Catholic religious life, then discuss attempts to build international unity between Reformed churches, and highlight key areas of debate within the Reformed camp about the sacrament of Holy Communion and God's plan for salvation. In the first case, a consensus was reached during the mid-sixteenth century on the question of how the elements of bread and wine in Communion related to Christ's body and blood. However, Calvin's ideas about salvation, election and predestination were not only challenged during his lifetime but remained highly controversial into the early seventeenth century. While Calvin was prepared to describe some aspects of God's plan for salvation as a divine mystery, other writers attempted to resolve any areas of uncertainty. Theodore Beza, and the Italian reformers Peter Martyr Vermigli and Girolamo Zanchi, all attempted to provide more systematic explanations of salvation theology.[2] Their efforts to support all aspects of Reformed doctrine with logically consistent statements in a coherent structure have been described as a drift back towards scholasticism among Reformed theologians. Later Reformed theology was also marked by greater attention to more speculative questions, particularly relating to the exact order and nature of divine decrees of predestination. However, later Reformed orthodoxy should not be thought of as a distorted version of Calvin's Bible-based theology, but marked the evolution of a theological tradition. Reformed theology changed over time, partly in response to polemic attacks from

other churches, partly in reaction to arguments within the Reformed
movement, and partly as a reflection of the pastoral experience of ministers. This chapter will therefore reflect both the shared ideas which
united the international Reformed community, but also chart the development of Reformed orthodoxy, and note variations and divisions
between different theologians and churches.[3]

The True Church and False Churches

According to Calvin, 'the Church universal is a multitude gathered from
all nations; it is divided and dispersed in separate places, but it agrees on
the one truth of divine doctrine and is bound by the bond of the same
religion'.[4] While the community of those saints whom God would receive
into heaven was not visible on earth, reformers identified clear marks by
which God's true Church could be recognised. For Theodore Beza these
marks were the true preaching of the Gospel, the right administration of
the sacraments, and the application of ecclesiastical discipline.[5] While
the 1559 French *Confession of Faith* only referred to the preaching of God's
word and proper administration of the sacraments as the marks of the
true Church, the 1561 *Confession* adopted by the Dutch church, and the
1560 Scottish *Confession* added the third mark of 'ecclesiastical discipline
uprightly ministered', so that 'vice is repressed and virtue nourished'.[6]

There could be no compromise between the true Church and the
Catholic church, and Reformed writers insisted that individuals could
not find salvation in any church where there was false preaching and idolatry. This left no room for so-called Nicodemites, who were denounced
by Calvin for privately supporting reform while continuing to attend
Catholic services and partaking of the 'abominable sacrilege' of the Mass.
According to Calvin, such people were involved in a 'miserable sub-
terfuge', remained contaminated with idolatry, and should show greater
courage in their convictions.[7] Reformed confessions and catechisms
across the Continent taught that Christians could have nothing to do
with the Roman church, and should certainly not participate in the Mass.
The *Heidelberg Catechism* described the Catholic Mass as 'a complete
denial of the once for all sacrifice and passion of Jesus Christ (and as such
an idolatry to be condemned)'. This absolute condemnation of Catholic
ritual, and especially of the idea of transubstantiation of the host during
the Mass, was also reflected in more popular language as some Calvinists
ridiculed Catholics' adoration of their 'god of paste'.[8]

However, the Mass was not the only problem which reformers identified among the practices of Catholic religion. A wide variety of aspects of
the 'new form of worship' introduced by the Roman church were
rejected as entirely false and devices of Satan. The French *Confession*
listed inventions thought up in Rome to deceive Christians which
included praying to dead saints, purgatory, pilgrimages, auricular confession, the prohibition on clerical marriage and rules on eating meat.[9]
The *Bee-Hive* written by Philip Marnix van St Aldegonde, a Brabant noble
who had been educated in Geneva, also ridiculed all sorts of Catholic
errors. Marnix satirically pretended that his text had been written by a
Catholic, who revealed how the personal opinions of Popes were in fact
the only basis for Catholic ideas on the Mass, salvation, purgatory, confession, worshipping saints, the use of images in churches and the powers ascribed to priests. In his discussion of the alleged virtues of
pilgrimages to holy sites, Marnix's thinly disguised Catholic writer
explained how

> a good honest man of Paris, who could have no children by his wife,
> and in hope of help, did vow diverse pilgrimages: And first he went to
> seek Saint James of Compostella, and from thence he went to Rome to
> visit the holy Apostles, Peter and Paul: and then on forward to our holy
> and blessed lady of Loreto, and from thence to Jerusalem: and last of
> all, to Saint Catherine of Siena: in fine, so as he was about three years
> from home: And when he came home again, he found his wife merry,
> and had in the mean space three pretty children, with help of the good
> Saints, which he so devoutly had sought.[10]

Marnix concluded by describing how Catholic priests were like honey-
bees, who 'cease also from work in the winter time, and when it is foul
weather'. However, he noted that Catholic honey, shipped to the
Netherlands from Spain, was the colour of blood, poisonous, and had
recently very much gone out of fashion.[11]

The tone of much Reformed writing aimed to ridicule Catholic forms
of worship, and to expose fraud and corruption in the Catholic church.
However, Catholicism was at the same time seen as a well-organised
threat to true religion, headed by a Pope commonly identified as a manifestation of Antichrist. These potent fears of an imagined Catholicism
staffed by wily, disciplined and ruthless agents did not lessen with physical distance from actual centres of Catholic power. Safe in England in
1598, William Perkins wrote of the risks to delicate Protestant consciences

of even travelling through Catholic countries.[12] This pervasive fear of Rome also inspired the 1581 *Negative Confession* in Scotland. This *Confession* added to the original church articles of the 1560 *Confession* with a long list of Catholic errors and false practices. The *Negative Confession* denounced Papistry, the 'usurped authority of the Roman Antichrist' and 'his five bastard sacraments'. It was hoped that by requiring people to subscribe to this *Negative Confession*, secret followers of Rome would be unmasked to ensure the safety of both the Reformed church and of Scotland.[13]

Placing trust in the power of material objects rather than in the spiritual power of God was one of the chief charges laid by Calvinists and other reformers against Catholic forms of worship. Hostility towards the traditional forms of devotion offered by believers to images and statues in churches was shared by some humanists and early reformers as well as Zwinglians and Calvinists. Zwingli wrote that

> faith is from the invisible God and it tends toward the invisible God, and is something completely apart from all that is sensible. Anything that is body, anything that is of the senses, cannot be an object of faith.[14]

Statues and images were also condemned on the grounds that they were greedy recipients of money which ought rather to be donated to the poor who were the true 'living images of God'.[15] Calvin argued that pictures and statues could not be tolerated in church buildings, although he offered greater latitude for objects of devotion in private homes. For Calvin, God was too glorious and remote from men's understanding to be depicted in any way which did not lead to idolatry. Calvin wrote that images bore no resemblance to God, held no sacred power, and fostered a false relationship between God and men. Calvin also attacked the physical appearance of some statues, suggesting on one occasion that 'brothels show harlots clad more virtuously' than some statues displayed in churches. Calvin also commented that Catholic churches were 'stuffed with dolls' and 'idols of wood and stone'. However, a Catholic visitor to Geneva in 1549 was equally outraged by the abominable state of its 'synagogues', in which the altars had been 'shattered and broken, the images destroyed ... the sacred vessels polluted, the holy oil poured out, the precious relics burned ... [and] no images of the saints in paradise'.[16]

In 1543 Calvin published a devastating critique of the use of relics in Catholic religion, which was soon translated into German, Dutch and

English. Calvin listed alleged surviving pieces of the true cross, sufficient he claimed to make a large boat, and enough body parts to make four corpses for each Apostle. Calvin argued against the evident fraudulence of Catholic relics, but also suggested that whether the relics were true or false, the worship of relics remained an execrable idolatry.[17] Guillaume Farel had also argued that Christ must be worshipped in spirit and truth, and that placing crosses, images and paintings in churches was directly contradictory to God's commands. For Farel, crosses and images led both to idolatry and to superstition, as they were used to try to effect miracles, to bring healing to people and animals, and to combat the effects of storms.[18] Pierre Viret wrote against the superstition, idolatry and blasphemy which he perceived in the Catholic cult of Mary. For Viret, Catholic depictions of Mary had turned her into something akin to the pagan goddess Diana.[19] The *Heidelberg Catechism* also warned that 'we must not try to be wiser than God who does not want his people to be taught by means of lifeless idols, but through the living preaching of his Word'.[20]

Reformed theologians and preachers were therefore clear that statues, crosses and images of God and the saints had to be removed from church buildings to allow for true worship. While this was seen as the responsibility of civil magistrates, the spread of Zwinglian and Calvinist reform in the 1520s and 1530s was accelerated by the destruction of the objects of Catholic worship by ordinary people in Zurich, Strassburg, Neuchâtel and Geneva. In Basel, three years of prolonged discussion in the council over the need for reform in the church was abruptly curtailed by one hour's work by a crowd of iconoclasts on 9 February 1529. Within two months the council had caught up with popular sentiment, and issued ordinances to reform the practice of religion in the city.[21]

In Bern the previous year a public disputation between Catholics and reformers ended in favour of reform. All the images, statues and altars were ordered to be removed from the city's churches within eight days. However, popular impatience for change again ran ahead of the magistrates' planned steps towards reform, and a mob set on Bern's central church. On the second day of this riot against the objects of Catholic belief and ritual in Bern, Huldrych Zwingli spoke to the crowd amid the wreckage of the church:

> There you have the altars and idols of the temple! ... now there is no more debating whether we should have these idols or not. Let us clear out this filth and rubbish! Henceforth, let us devote to other men, the

living images of God, all the unimaginable wealth which was spent on
these foolish idols. There are still many weak and quarrelsome people
who complain about the removal of the idols, even though it is clearly
evident that there is nothing holy about them, and that they break and
crack like any other piece of wood or stone. Here lies one without its
head! Here another without its arms! If this abuse had done any harm
to the saints who are near God, and if they had the power which is
ascribed to them, do you think you would have been able to behead
and cripple them as you did? ... now, then, recognise the freedom
which Christ has given you, stand fast in it, and ... be not entangled
again with the yoke of bondage.[22]

Zwingli offered encouragement to the Bernese crowd that their actions
had shown the lack of power in Catholic cultic objects. They had
unmasked the deception of Roman religion, and the people of Bern
could now worship God in true Christian freedom.

This pattern of preaching in favour of reform, official hesitation and
popular action to ensure the success of reform by physically testing the
power of Catholic objects, was followed in other Swiss towns. Despite the
role which iconoclasm played in speeding the implementation of reform
measures, Calvin continued to condemn ministers who led their congregations in destroying images, crosses and statues in France. Calvin wrote
that 'God has never commanded the destruction of idols, except to each
one in his own house and in public to those he arms with authority'.[23]
However, when books attacking Catholic forms of worship spread to
France and the Netherlands, or when ministers preached about the idolatry of Catholic objects of worship in Scotland, such words, whether
intentionally or not, often led to the physical destruction of images and
icons by ordinary men and women. In 1559 crowds responded to calls for
reform by attacking churches in Perth, Stirling and Edinburgh. When
John Knox preached in St Andrews on the cleansing of churches, the
cathedral and monastic houses soon came under attack, and statues,
images, altars and screens were destroyed.[24]

There had been iconoclastic incidents in the Netherlands from the
1520s. Reformed voices only became more numerous and distinct within
the diversity of early Dutch Protestantism by the 1550s and early 1560s.
The iconoclastic riots which broke out in Flanders and Brabant in August
1566 were still far from the result of a co-ordinated and well-organised
campaign orchestrated by Reformed clergy. Nevertheless, as crowds in
1566 attended hedge-preaching events, or marched through towns and

villages singing Psalms, or attacked images and statues in churches, they claimed space for Reformed preaching and worship, and marked out territory in which Calvinist churches could be organised.[25] Reformed clergy in the Netherlands and sympathetic nobles were very reluctant to claim that the rebellious acts of violent destruction by ordinary people in 1566 had anything to do with them. In 1567 Philip Marnix described iconoclasm as sedition, and asserted that the Reformed church had always taught that only public authorities could remove idols. Marnix claimed that only some of the iconoclasts were in fact supporters of reform. He suggested that in some parishes, priests had hidden all their statues and images, that elsewhere magistrates had ordered the destruction, while in some places Marnix suggested that 'only women and children were involved'. However, even Marnix could not help but wonder whether

> God Himself intervened to lead the whole action and carry it out, and men cannot resist God's power. How else could women, children and men without authority, without arms, in small numbers, for the greater part poor and humble people, pull down and destroy nearly everywhere in the country so many images, altars and church ornaments in only four or five days?[26]

The suggestion that priests had destroyed objects in their churches to try to get civil officials to take action against reformers could certainly not be used again in 1572. When the Beggar rebels took over towns in Holland and Zeeland there were subsequent attacks on monasteries, iconoclastic riots in churches, and the expulsion and some murders of Catholic clergy.[27]

Some of the most dramatic popular riots against Catholic churches, priests and material objects related to Catholic religion took place in France. There was a similar pattern to that in the Netherlands of early incidents of popular violent action claiming space for Reformed preaching and church services. During the late 1550s and early 1560s at least 1000 Reformed congregations were established, particularly in the southern Huguenot crescent and in Normandy. Although French synods repeatedly warned that only local magistrates could act to cleanse church buildings, this dramatic spread of support for Calvinism was marked by a wave of iconoclasm. For example, at La Rochelle a small congregation had been set up with a consistory from 1558, and in 1561 the city authorities permitted public preaching by Reformed clergy. With the Reformed community growing in confidence and support, Catholic power was soon physically challenged in La Rochelle. In May 1562 a Reformed crowd attacked and destroyed the images, statues and altars in the city's churches.[28] However, by no means all of those who participated in iconoclastic riots in France or elsewhere can be counted as fervent Calvinist ideologues. Resentment against local clergy and nobles, economic hardship, and the breakdown of law and order during war, all played some part in causing disturbances. Nevertheless, Reformed ideas were the essential element which inspired the desecration of objects viewed as polluting agents of idolatry which had previously been revered as conduits of divine power.[29]

By the 1560s many local communities in France had divided confessional loyalties. This led to ongoing popular religious violence as the royal authorities struggled to find a political and legal settlement which could offer rights to satisfy both Catholics and Huguenots. The *Discipline* of the French church strictly warned the Reformed community against using violent language or causing injuries to Catholic priests or believers. However, when Calvinist parties seized control over cities such as Montauban in 1561, churches were cleansed and Catholic clergy were attacked, and at Nîmes in 1567, Catholic citizens and clergy were murdered.[30] In areas where Catholics remained in the majority they fought back against the heretics who turned their back on the host in Corpus Christi processions, refused to participate in traditional festivals, and who attended their own sinister meetings. Catholic mobs often mirrored official sanctions against heretics in their torture, execution and desecration of their Huguenot victims' corpses. However, it was the inability or unwillingness of the crown authorities to maintain order and to control religious passions which was primarily responsible for the spiral of violence across France up to, and beyond, the terrible events of St Bartholomew's day in 1572.[31]

The removal of images from Catholic churches was not everywhere a signal of popular enthusiasm for Calvinist preaching. In 1556 Polish Calvinist and Bohemian Brethren ministers discussed a gradual strategy to remove images so as not to antagonise local people. It was suggested that noble patrons of churches organise that images were first covered or turned to face the wall, then moved to less important areas of church buildings, before finally being eased out of sight altogether.[32] The removal of images was imposed by law in England, although many objects were hidden rather than destroyed after Edward VI's 1547 injunctions against shrines, and against pictures and statues in church buildings.[33] Instructions issued by magistrates also commanded the removal of images, statues and altars from churches in Béarn, and from Lutheran churches in states of the Empire which underwent a second reformation. In the Palatinate, Nassau, Bremen, Anhalt, Hesse and Lippe churches were cleansed of 'leftover papal dung', as Abraham Scultetus put it. Scultetus was court preacher to Johann Sigismund, the Hohenzollern convert from Lutheranism who attempted to cleanse the churches of Brandenburg in the face of resistance from Lutheran clergy and popular opinion. Images and statues were also removed from churches in territories where Reformed rulers came to power, as at Prague in 1619 when St Vitus cathedral was made fit for Reformed worship on the orders of Frederick V of the Palatinate.[34]

International Unity

Since reformers claimed that churches which were committed to preaching the Gospel, to rightly administering the sacraments and to living under Christian discipline, formed part of a true, universal Church, then it seemed to many that Reformed churches ought to adopt a single confession of faith. Doctrinal unity was also sought in order to combat more effectively the threat which Rome was thought to pose to the future of the Church. The most active support for international unity came from France, where clergy were particularly keen to secure allies to assist in their struggle for survival at home. However, as early as March 1552 archbishop Thomas Cranmer had written to Calvin and to Philip Melanchthon, suggesting that a council of godly men should meet to reach harmony over doctrine and to 'unite the churches of God'. Calvin responded by declaring himself willing to come to England to agree articles of faith with others, and to 'hand down to posterity a definite form of doctrine according to their united opinion'.[35] This initiative from England, and many later projects for international union, extended beyond the Reformed world and addressed the possibility of reaching agreement with Lutherans. These irenic appeals were, however, rarely marked by any serious intention to compromise on key issues which divided the two confessions. While the ideal of a pan-Protestant alliance continued to be promoted into the early seventeenth century by David Pareus at Heidelberg and by John Dury, attention remained mostly focused on achieving unity among Reformed churches across the Continent.[36]

One means of promoting unity was by getting territorial churches to recognise the same confessional statement. Theodore Beza wrote in September 1566 to the general assembly of the church in Scotland requesting that they accept Bullinger's *Second Helvetic Confession*. The assembly examined the text, and only questioned the list of approved festivals of Christ's birth, circumcision, passion, resurrection and ascension, and of Pentecost. The assembly reported that in Scotland the church followed the instructions of the Bible and only set apart Sundays from other days. Despite showing native pride in their 'pure worship of religion in the farthest corners of the earth', the assembly decided 'most willingly' to embrace Bullinger's *Confession*. In time, the *Second Helvetic Confession* was not only accepted by the church in Scotland, but also by churches in France, Hungary, Poland and the Netherlands, and became the most widely recognised statement of shared Reformed doctrine.[37]

A less successful strategy to bring uniformity to Reformed churches was through calls for a general council to agree on a new statement of faith. Theodore Beza's 1558 *Confession of Faith* expressed the hope that Christian magistrates would call a general council made up of representatives of national and territorial synods.[38] This project was taken up by German, French and Dutch Calvinists from the 1570s, partly in response to the success of Lutherans in agreeing their own *Formula of Concord* in 1577. Johann Casimir, the younger son of Frederick III of the Palatinate, sponsored an assembly at Frankfurt in 1577 which aimed to produce a unified statement of Reformed beliefs. Delegates at Frankfurt represented churches from the Empire, the Netherlands, Hungary, Poland, Béarn, France and England. An agreed confession was prepared by the delegates, with the hope of meeting again the following year to finalise the document. However, no further meeting took place, and the only concrete product of the Frankfurt assembly was the 1581 publication of a *Harmony of the Confessions* by Jean-François Salvard, a French minister living in exile in the Palatinate. This text reflected the ambitious programme of the assembly to unify Europe's Reformed churches, and then also to seek unity with Lutherans. Salvard's text published the confessions of churches in France, England, the Netherlands, Basel and Bohemia, as well as the *First* and *Second Helvetic Confessions*, and the Lutheran confessions of Augsburg, Saxony and Württemberg.[39]

In the preface to Salvard's text there was a declaration by the French and Dutch churches of their desire to 'knit all the churches of Christ together with one bond of brotherly love'. The two churches also expressed their hope that

> it will come to pass that not so much the several names of the French, Belgic, and other Confessions shall hereafter be heard, as that one only

universal, simple, plain, and absolute Confession of all Churches (speaking as it were with one and the same tongue of Canaan) shall be seen.[40]

The French national synod in 1578 had also taken up the challenge to unify all Reformed churches and all Protestants. The French synod envisaged a conference at which representatives from Protestant churches would agree on a single confession and on terms of union. Four ministers led by Antoine de Chandieu were chosen to work on the project on behalf of the church. At the 1579 synod, the French church repeated its commitment to seek ways to unify all Protestant nations under one confession. The synod also agreed to a practical gesture towards this ideal by subscribing to the 1561 Belgic *Confession* compiled by Guy de Brès. This *Confession* had been adopted by the 1571 Emden synod of the Dutch church, which had also recognised the 1559 French *Confession*.[41]

Further co-operation between Calvinists from France and the Netherlands followed during the early 1580s. In 1581 representatives from French-speaking churches in England were sent to the Middelburg synod of the Walloon churches as 'testimony to the friendship and union' with 'their brothers'. While the French wished to exchange information and gain advice from the Walloon churches, they however clearly stated that they did not intend to follow any statutes agreed by the synod.[42] In 1583 the French synod decided, as evidence of their mutual conformity with the Dutch church, to recognise their confession and order of church discipline. Another sign of the 'holy union and concord' between the French and Dutch churches was the agreement of both churches to send ministers and offer other assistance when it was required.[43] The French also responded to the request of the Dutch church that the two national synods should send representatives to each other's assemblies. These exchanges followed, and when Dutch representatives failed to turn up at the 1598 synod at Montpellier, the French synod wrote with regret at their absence.[44]

In 1603 the French church renewed its efforts to encourage a European Reformed union, seeking responses to their initiative from the Dutch, German and Swiss churches. In 1607 the French synod assessed the replies it had received, which offered general support for unity and complete approval of the French *Confession*.[45] Enthusiasm was sustained in the French church for union projects in the 1610s. In 1614 the synod at Tonneins thanked those of its members who were working for union, and encouraged them to continue in their 'pious and necessary' efforts to establish a general assembly of French, English, German, Dutch and Swiss churches. The synod looked for support to achieve 'perfect uniformity of doctrine' from Reformed princes, and especially from the British king James I. James offered the synod a letter of support, and the synod wrote back to James encouraging action. Initially the synod hoped for a conference of Reformed churches to be held in Zeeland to gain agreement on a single confession, while allowing for different churches to abide by their own ceremonial practices and forms of church government. At that stage, the French hoped that Reformed princes would then invite Lutherans to a second assembly to discuss theological divisions between the churches over sacramental theology and predestination.[46] These grand plans for Reformed union and Protestant irenicism failed to get off the ground. However, the next French synod at Vitré in 1617 tried to give further impetus to international agreement among Calvinists, and four ministers, including André Rivet and his brother-in-law, Pierre du Moulin, were delegated to continue work on plans for union.[47]

When an international gathering of Reformed theologians finally did meet to ratify a common platform of beliefs, the context was not the idealised setting imagined by the French national synod. Rather the 1618/19 synod of Dordrecht was sanctioned as a result of a political battle between Maurice of Nassau and the States of Holland. Delegates were called from churches across the Dutch Republic and beyond to discuss theories about predestination advanced by Jacobus Arminius and his followers from the 1590s, which had been tolerated by the States of Holland, but were condemned by mainstream Reformed opinion.[48] The synod at Dordrecht demonstrated both the strengths and limits of international Reformed unity. Delegates travelled to Dordrecht from Britain, the Palatinate, Hesse, Nassau, Bremen, Emden, Geneva, Zurich, Bern and Basel. After their years of endeavour to get an international synod, representatives from the French synod were forbidden by Louis XIII to travel to Dordrecht. However, Pierre du Moulin appealed to the British ambassador in the Dutch Republic to support their efforts to get the synod to agree to a general confession for all Reformed churches. The French proposal was taken up by the president of the Dordrecht synod, Johannes Bogerman, and discussed with delegates from Britain and the Palatinate. From the outset of negotiations the British theologians were concerned about the content of any statement on the issue of church government, and in the end no progress was made at Dordrecht towards agreeing a single confession.[49]

Nevertheless by May 1619 the Dordrecht synod had agreed on a statement on the doctrine of predestination, and had issued a condemnation of the Arminian or Remonstrant party. Some of the foreign delegates at Dordrecht expressed concern that Dutch Counter-Remonstrants showed little regard for the judgement of outsiders.[50] However, when the States General of the Dutch Republic confirmed the resolutions of the synod, they claimed to hold nothing more dear than 'the preserving of correspondence and communion between the churches within these countries, and all other foreign Reformed churches'.[51] The French synod also saw the outcome of Dordrecht as an affirmation of their project to achieve 'union with all Reformed churches'. In 1623 the French church formally endorsed the conclusions agreed at Dordrecht and required all those appointed to church offices in France to subscribe to them, but it was the only church outside the Dutch Republic to do so.[52]

Holy Communion

Reformed churches managed to find consensus about how to understand the sacraments of baptism and Holy Communion. Calvin had expressed his desire for fraternity with others who shared his rejection of the Mass as a diabolic forgery. However, Calvin's experience of conferences with Lutherans in Germany in the late 1530s and early 1540s only revealed insurmountable obstacles to any potential agreement with Lutherans. From Calvin's perspective, the major stumbling block to agreement was the Lutheran insistence that Christ was really present in the elements of bread and wine in Holy Communion. In the *Institutes*, Calvin argued that the sacraments were instead an opportunity provided by God to partake in visible signs of his grace. The water of baptism represented a sign of forgiveness and of acceptance within the community of the Church, and the bread and wine of the Lord's Supper were visible symbols of Christ's body through which believers could enter into a spiritual communion with Christ. As the bread and wine were distributed to the congregation, Calvin argued that Christ was offered to believers through a spiritual mystery. Calvin added that only those who believed in Christ should take part in Communion, and that it was not only useless but also dangerous for non-believers to participate in the sacrament.[53]

From Calvin's return to Geneva in 1541, his attention turned to negotiations over Communion theology with the leaders of the Zurich church. Bullinger and Calvin entered into prolonged discussions and private negotiations before agreement was finally reached in 1549. Their Zurich agreement was a set of convoluted statements on Communion, which

marked a compromise between language which only described the bread
and wine as external signs of God's promises and the view that the elements were signs through which God offered believers spiritual communion with Christ. There were deep local sensitivities about any
changes to doctrine implied by the terms of the Zurich agreement, and
at Bern the text was not even published until 1551. However, over time
the successful outcome to these negotiations, Theodore Beza claimed,
'knit Bullinger and Calvin, and the churches of Zurich and Geneva in the
closest ties'.[54] While Beza endorsed the terms of the Zurich agreement,
his *Confession of Faith* argued that since Communion was a sacrament, it
had to involve a conjunction between the signs of bread and wine and the
reality of Jesus Christ signified by those signs. According to Beza, the
bread and wine were offered to the participant's external senses, while by
faith through the power of the Holy Spirit the bread and wine became
signs and seals of the believer's spiritual communion with Christ in
heaven.[55]

The 1549 Zurich agreement therefore drew the Swiss churches
together, but without requiring either Calvinists or Zwinglians to abandon their own versions of what they thought the agreement meant. The
agreement certainly hardened divisions between the Swiss Reformed and
German Lutheran or Evangelical churches. Arguments between
Reformed and Lutheran theologians on the sacraments continued during the second half of the sixteenth century in various debates and
printed exchanges, and the issue remained the clearest point of theological difference between the two emerging Protestant traditions.[56] In 1577
the Lutheran *Formula of Concord* clarified an agreed explanation of the
articles of the 1530 Augsburg *Confession* which insisted that in the 'Holy
Supper the body and blood of Christ are truly and essentially present',
and that believers received the body and blood of Christ 'not only spiritually, by faith, but also orally'.[57]

Meanwhile the confessions of faith adopted by some Reformed
churches during the second half of the sixteenth century followed
Calvin's ideas, and agreed that while Christ was not physically present in
the bread and wine, these visible symbols of the sacrament offered
unseen spiritual benefits to the believer. According to the 1559 *Confession*
of the French church, which was based on a draft written by Calvin, while
Christ is in heaven

> still we believe that by the secret and incomprehensible power of his
> Spirit, he feeds and strengthens us with the substance of his body, and

of his blood. We hold that this is done spiritually, not because we put imagination and fancy in the place of fact and truth, but because the greatness of this mystery exceeds the measure of our senses and the laws of nature. In short, because it is heavenly, it can only be apprehended by faith.[58]

The 1560 *Confession* of the Scottish church also explained that the elements of Communion were seals of God's promises to his people, and so 'we utterly condemn the vanity of those who affirm the sacraments to be nothing else than naked and bare signs'. Rather the faithful 'have such union with Christ Jesus as the natural man cannot apprehend', and 'true faith carries us above all things that are visible, carnal and earthly, and makes us feed upon the body and blood of Christ Jesus'.[59] The 1561 Belgic *Confession* agreed that by receiving bread and wine believers also received by faith the 'true body and blood of Christ' in a manner which 'surpasses our understanding'. The *Confession* also asserted that although Christ remains at the right hand of his Father in heaven, 'we err not when we say that what is eaten and drunk by us is the proper and natural body and the proper blood of Christ'.[60]

While the French, Scottish and Dutch churches closely followed Calvin's ideas on Communion, other Reformed confessional statements and catechisms reflected the compromises of the Zurich agreement and the Zwinglian inheritance to the Reformed movement. This was particularly the case in churches which had strong connections with Bullinger's Zurich as well as Calvin's Geneva, or where Reformed churches emerged in formerly Lutheran territories and writers were keen to stress the different positions of the two churches. In Hungary, Reformed clergy did not accentuate the spiritual presence of Christ in the elements of Communion. Péter Méliusz Juhász, one of the authors of the 1562 *Confessio Catholica*, completed a catechism which simply explained how the bread of the sacrament was 'neither Christ's body in form, nor changed into becoming Christ's body, but was bread given in the name of Christ's body'.[61] Bálint Szikszai's 1574 catechism agreed that 'there is a different use for the bread and wine in the Lord's Supper than at your home because here it represents the body of Jesus Christ'. According to Szikszai, the bread and wine were certain pledges, seals, and signs of salvation, without any 'change or combination' to their substance.[62]

Heinrich Bullinger's 1566 *Second Helvetic Confession* used language which stopped just short of fully accepting a spiritual presence of Christ in the elements of Communion. Bullinger described how the bread and wine were 'holy signs' which 'outwardly represented' those things which God inwardly performs in the sacrament.[63] The answers to the questions on Communion in the 1563 *Heidelberg Catechism* attempted to balance both Zwinglian and Calvinist traditions.[64] To the question, 'What does it mean to eat the crucified body of Christ and to drink his shed blood?', the answer was given that it was to

be so united more and more to his blessed body by the Holy Spirit dwelling both in Christ and in us that, although he is in heaven and we are on earth, we are nevertheless flesh of his flesh and bone of his bone, always living and being governed by one Spirit, as the members of our bodies are governed by one soul.[65]

Reformed churches were in complete agreement that Catholic ideas about transubstantiation of the host, and Lutheran ideas about the ubiquity of Christ's body and its real presence in the sacrament, were wrong. While some different accents were retained in doctrinal statements on Communion, enough was held in common between Reformed churches on this vital area to sustain unity between them.

Salvation and Predestination

The starting point of Calvin's theology in the *Institutes* was that God is a perfect, all-mighty, all-knowing, transcendent power who created the universe, holds sovereign authority over the world, and judges the life of each individual. God set out divine laws for people to follow in the Bible. These laws were necessary because, through their sin, people had become estranged from God. Tainted by the corruption of sin, none could perfectly follow God's laws and all deserved eternal destruction in hell. However, God offered a mediating sacrifice in Christ to reconcile man to God. Through Christ's death and resurrection, sinners who believed in Christ could be saved by God's grace. God alone determined, through his sovereign will, the fate of the souls of all humanity, choosing to grant grace and a saving faith in Christ to those whom he wished to save from a fallen humanity. No one could do anything to alter God's decisions, which were 'founded upon his freely given mercy without regard to human worth'.[66]

Calvin advised against trying to search the 'hidden recesses of the divine wisdom' to discover God's judgement about the fate of individual souls. He suggested that this should certainly not be a matter which ministers focused on in sermons and teaching, warning of the potential consequences if people began to examine their lives for signs of their fate:

> But what proof have you of your election? When once this thought has taken possession of any individual, it keeps him perpetually miserable, subjects him to dire torment, or throws him into a state of complete stupor.[67]

Rather, Calvin encouraged Christians to trust in the justice of their creator, and to look to their saviour Jesus Christ for the hope of salvation. Faith in Christ would turn their hearts from sin, and lead them to live by God's commands and according to the 'appointed duties' which God provided for their lives. Calvin also stressed that God was engaged in ceaseless activity in the world, and Christians should give thanks for his providence over their lives, and even see persecution as a special badge and honour bestowed by God on his soldiers.[68]

Calvin's view of God's plan for salvation was attacked by opponents outside the Reformed camp, and criticised by figures within the Reformed tradition from Jerome Bolsec to Jacobus Arminius. Such challenges often dealt with the operation of the divine decrees of predestination of some to salvation which left others to their destruction. Thus, the area which Calvin had advised should not become a focus of teaching became a keenly contested area of polemic writing. The first major challenge to Calvin's explanation of salvation came in 1551 when Jerome Bolsec stood up in a Friday meeting in a Genevan church and attacked the notion that some people were predestined to damnation, arguing that Calvin had portrayed God as the author of sin. Bolsec's attack brought a vehement response from Guillaume Farel, who claimed Bolsec was 'about as versed in sacred things as the filthiest pig, profanely overturning everything with his utterly vile snout'.[69] The Genevan council agreed to banish Bolsec in December 1551, but the other Swiss churches were less certain about the Genevan church's condemnation of Bolsec as a Pelagian. Bullinger expressed some reservations about Calvin's 'harsh' understanding of predestination, and Bolsec found refuge in Bernese territory. In 1552 Calvin produced a formal response to the whole controversy on predestination raised by Bolsec. Calvin argued that those who did not acknowledge that the reprobate were damned to hell could not affirm the election of the saints to heaven. He then elaborated on God's decisive role in the salvation of believers. Calvin rejected the idea that God's decisions were in any way conditional on human behaviour, or were swayed by God's foresight of human faith. According to Calvin, this would render man's faith as the effectual cause of election to salvation, whereas he argued that all sovereignty over humanity must belong to the 'perpetual governor' of the world.[70]

The Bolsec dispute illustrated how attacks on Calvin's ideas tended to lead to more detailed explanations of predestination and to more rigid expressions of the boundaries of acceptable orthodoxy on the issue among Reformed theologians.[71] However, according to Beza, the main result of the Bolsec controversy was that the idea of predestination, 'which was formerly most obscure, became clear and transparent to all not disposed to be contentious'.[72] Beza's desire to clarify theology on salvation still further led him to develop a coherent system of ordered rational statements about the decrees of predestination, capable of being defended in the heat of polemic debate. To this end, in 1555 Beza produced a chart which depicted the process of salvation as a series of chronological and logical steps, and placed God's decree for some to be saved and others to be damned to hell as occurring even before the creation of man.[73]

Despite the Bolsec controversy, the confessions of faith adopted by Reformed churches during the mid-sixteenth century did not particularly highlight the issue of predestination. The *Confession* of the French church limited comment on the subject to stating that God chose to call some to salvation

> without consideration of their works, to display in them the riches of his mercy; leaving the rest in this same corruption and condemnation to show in them his justice.[74]

Bullinger's *Second Helvetic Confession* agreed that God predestined from eternity 'the saints whom he wills to save in Christ', and that God's grace was not given because of any prior knowledge of the faith or good works of individuals. However, Bullinger also cautioned that 'we must hope well of all and not rashly judge any man to be a reprobate'. Repeated warnings were made against anyone seeking proof of their election to salvation. Bullinger found fault with those who sought assurance that they were counted among the elect, recommending, as had Calvin, that people should look to Christ as 'the looking glass, in whom we may contemplate our predestination'.[75] In his *Confession of Faith* Beza too warned of the dangers of introspection into whether a believer was among the elect or not. Beza offered the reassurance that any believer who once 'had a sure testimony of true faith' could not lose that faith even though 'for a while, it is neither felt nor perceived'.[76]

Leading Reformed writers were therefore concerned on the one hand to defend ideas about salvation and predestination from polemic attacks by rival theologians, but they were equally concerned that drawing too much attention to predestination would lead to pastoral problems in their communities. It was feared that some might think they were elect and become arrogant, or even think that no matter how they behaved God would save them. Meanwhile others might be driven to anxious self-examination in seeking proof of their election, or conclude that God had not chosen them and that there was therefore no point in trying to believe or to behave. In many Reformed churches across the Continent, clergy heeded these warnings, and predestination did not become a central feature of preaching or of printed literature aimed at ordinary believers.

However, in England some writers identified a need among believers for practical advice about predestination, but their responses only opened up further problems and questions on election and damnation. Some theologians developed the notion of a covenant of grace established between man and God which explained the responsibility of each individual in working out their salvation.[77] For example, in 1592 William Perkins wrote *A case of conscience, the greatest that ever was: how a man may know whether he be the child of God or no*. In this tract Perkins argued that the covenant of grace was God's

> contract with men, concerning the obtaining of life eternal, upon a certain condition. This covenant consists of two parts: God's promise to man, and man's promise to God. God's promise to man, is that, whereby he bindeth himself to man to be his God, if he performs the condition. Man's promise to God, is that, whereby he voweth his allegiance unto his Lord, and to perform the condition between them.[78]

Alongside this greater accent on individual action in the scheme of salvation, Perkins also suggested that believers could gain assurance that they were among the elect by looking for the signs of the operation of this covenant of grace leading them to live according to God's commands.

Such attempts to reassure believers that they could in fact know whether they were counted among the elect under a covenant of grace only generated other pastoral difficulties. Believers' sense of assurance of election needed to be fed by constant pious and moral activity. Attention to monitoring personal conduct and commitment to spiritual exercises for signs of the fruit of the covenant of grace became an obsession for some Calvinists in England from the latter decades of the sixteenth century. The division between those God was going to save and those he was going to damn even began to seem apparent to some as social divisions hardened in England between those who were known to each other as 'the godly' but who were labelled by their detractors as pharisaic Puritans. The intense personal commitment shown by Puritans to their own piety and morality was often matched by highly critical attitudes towards signs of lukewarm religiosity or lax moral discipline in the Elizabethan church. Puritans were also often vehemently anti-Catholic, and extremely sensitive to any remaining Catholic influences in the ceremonies and rituals of the English church.[79]

Many of 'the godly' in England anxiously searched for signs of election in their daily lives. They did so without the benefit of any congregational framework for the regulation of moral discipline. Patterns of self-regulation and group-regulation filled this vacuum, which at its worst led to endless and despairing private battles against sin. Such concerns filled the spiritual journals kept by some Puritans, such as the Essex minister, Richard Rogers, and the London artisan, Nehemiah Wallington. Rogers' endless concern about his commitment to piety and morality was played out in the pages of his journal. In 1587 he noted sadly that 'even the most zealous do somewhat in time decline and wax remiss in caring for the matters of God', and he fought again and again to purge his heart of the love of worldly things.[80] Wallington's notebooks from 1618 recorded his preoccupation to find evidence of his response to God's grace. When Wallington could only see failures and sin, and he became convinced that he was among the reprobate, it led him on several occasions to attempt to take his own life.[81]

These were admittedly exceptional characters, but their experiences marked a particularly intense reaction to popular preaching and writing about God's providence and constant activity in the mundane affairs of daily life which made a significant impact on the beliefs of English Protestants well beyond the ranks of 'the godly'.[82] Ideas about salvation were also a key focus of a growing body of literature on practical theological questions. Influential, for example, was *The plaine mans path-way to heaven* of 1601 by Arthur Dent, another Essex preacher. Dent set up a dialogue between four characters which allowed him to discuss how 'every man may clearly see, whether he shall be saved or damned'. Dent listed and discussed eight signs of salvation which were love for God's people, delight in reading the Bible, frequent prayer, zeal for God's glory, selflessness, bearing suffering with patience, faithfulness in following callings, and honest dealing with others. He also noted nine marks of condemnation which included pride, lying, swearing, drunkenness, idleness and covetousness. Dent suggested that signs of salvation offered certain assurance to the faithful:

> For when once we feel the work of grace within us, ... then we are sure and out of all doubt, that we are predestinate to life. And it is even as much as if God had personally appeared unto us, and whispered us in the ear, and told us that our names are taken, and written in the book of life.[83]

However, for those who could not see these signs in their lives Dent wondered, 'what hope can you have to be saved?' Dent advised that those who did not yet feel themselves to be counted among the elect should live honestly, and wait patiently for God to grant them 'the true touch'.[84]

This Puritan reception of Reformed teaching on salvation from the latter decades of the sixteenth century provided the basis for Max Weber's discussion about the long-term impact on Calvinism on Western society. In *The Protestant ethic and the spirit of capitalism*, Weber noted how some Calvinists began to create a conviction about their salvation through systematic self-control which was thought to be a fruit of election. As Weber put it, 'the God of Calvinism demanded of his believers not single good works, but a life of good works combined into a unified system'.[85] Weber described this as a 'rational asceticism' in which all aspects of life were subjected to examination as to whether or not they were in accordance with God's will. According to Weber, ideas of being called to a particular vocation in this context had the effect of sacralising worldly activity. Weber also suggested that Calvinists were not encouraged to struggle against the rational acquisition of wealth but were instead told to restrict their consumption of goods to rational and moral uses.[86] For Weber, these beliefs structured patterns of sober, disciplined behaviour which eventually helped to form the character of the Western bourgeoisie. He concluded that Calvinism more than any other religion held an elective affinity with the spirit of capitalism. However, evidence supporting any such long-term affinity with Puritanism, let alone Calvinism, remains at best rather doubtful.[87]

Puritan zeal to live by precise standards of moral behaviour in an effort to confirm a personal sense of assurance of salvation was not only influential among Calvinists in England, but also made an impact in Scotland, among some Hungarian clergy during the early seventeenth century, and

among supporters of 'further reformation' in the Dutch church.[88]
English influences can often be found behind the spread of Puritanism,
as in the Dutch Republic. By the early seventeenth century some English
Puritan writers avoided censorship at home by publishing their tracts at
Amsterdam and Leiden. A number of English-speaking congregations in
the Netherlands were also served by exiled radical ministers from
Thomas Cartwright to William Ames. Many Dutch proponents of further
reform were directly influenced by English practical theological literature and had personal connections with English exiles in the Dutch
Republic. For example, Willem Teellinck had lived for some time in
England, was married to an English woman, and was pastor from 1613
until 1629 at Middelburg, which hosted a substantial English exile congregation. Teellinck's tracts followed the pattern of English piety literature in stressing the importance of godly living and avoiding all sorts of
immorality to gain assurance of salvation.[89]

There were also domestic reasons within the Dutch Republic which
encouraged the desire among some clergy during the early seventeenth
century for further reform. The status of the Reformed church as the
public church of the Dutch state was uncomfortable for some who
desired to belong to a community of faith committed to a disciplined
moral life. Opponents attacked this concern to display piety and morality as a hypocritical formalism. However, Gisbert Voetius at Utrecht
defended the attention which he paid to issues such as dancing, extrava-
gant hairstyles, sumptuous clothing, and to the use of jewellery and
make-up. He claimed that only ignorance and malice about the motives
of supporters of reform led to them being labelled as 'Precisionists,
Puritans, Roundheads, or shorthairs, foolish-wise, joyless, sad-humoured,
clothed in melancholy, Sabbatarians, salty-sour Zeelanders. ... '[90]

The Dutch church sustained a broader variety of opinions among its
clergy than most other Reformed communities, partly related to the history of reform in the Netherlands and partly because of the political
organisation of the Republic's provinces. So while Puritanism made some
headway among Dutch supporters of further reform, other Reformed
clergy within the Dutch church, and to a lesser extent in France and
England, developed a very different view about salvation and predestination. Jacobus Arminius, who taught at Leiden university from 1603,
maintained that Christ was sent by God to save all those who believed and
provided the means by which all sinners may believe. According to
Arminius, this universal grace was only rejected by those who did not seek
forgiveness for their sins and refused to believe in Christ.[91]

Fear of the spread of this Arminian infection of Reformed orthodoxy caused rigidly defined statements to be composed which defended established views on predestination. In 1595 a sermon preached against the idea that believers could gain assurance of salvation provoked Cambridge theologians to agree with archbishop John Whitgift on a rigorous definition of predestination in the Lambeth Articles. Only Elizabeth's intervention prevented these articles from being accepted as the official doctrine of the church in England.[92] In 1615 an assembly of Irish clergy did agree a revision of the 1563 *Thirty-Nine Articles*. The revised *Articles of Religion* of the Irish church set out an unambiguous statement that some were predestined to be saved while others were reprobate and destined for destruction. The Irish *Articles* denied that this scheme of salvation made God the author of sin, rejected the view that God's grace was sufficient for all to be saved, and refuted the opinion that believers could entirely lose true faith. Rather, assurance of election for believers was a 'sweet, pleasant and unspeakable comfort to godly persons', who could 'feel in themselves the working of the Spirit of God'.[93]

Jacobus Arminius died in 1609, but in 1610 Johannes Uytenbogaert and 43 other Dutch ministers presented a Remonstrance to the States of Holland which advocated Arminius' ideas on salvation. Opposition in the Dutch church to this Remonstrant party increased after the appointment of one of Arminius' supporters, Conrad Vorstius, to replace Arminius at Leiden university. When the Dordrecht synod was eventually called in 1618, the Remonstrant view that God's decree of election was dependent on foreknowledge of an individual's faith was bitterly condemned, and the synod concluded that Remonstrant clergy were guilty of corrupting Reformed religion. Conrad Vorstius was also removed from Leiden university and banished from Holland.[94] However, the synod also brought to the surface divisions between delegates over various issues about predestination. Representatives from Germany and England were wary of judging that Christ had not died for all. Some Dutch hardliners insisted that the decrees of election and damnation came before the Fall.[95] However, the synod eventually agreed that after creation and God's permission of man's Fall, God predestined some to be saved in Christ while others were left to a just judgement of their sins. People could gain assurance of their salvation

not by searching curiously, into the depths and secrets of God, but by observing in themselves, with spiritual joy and holy pleasure, the infallible fruits of election.[96]

The conclusions reached at Dordrecht on predestination were vigilantly defended by later Reformed theologians. Writers such as Johannes Wolleb at Basel restated the orthodoxy agreed at Dordrecht of twin decrees of salvation and condemnation determined by the absolutely free will of God. When the French minister Moses Amyraut wrote in favour of the view that although only the elect were saved, Christ's death offered salvation to all, he was subjected to a heresy trial at the 1637 French national synod.[97] Reformed churches encountered difficulties in securing and maintaining consensus on questions about salvation and predestination. However, when challenges were issued by Bolsec, Arminius and Amyraut, churches responded by trying to impose ever more rigorous and detailed statements of orthodoxy on these issues. Where attention to predestination also spread into popular preaching and writing, views on gaining assurance of election to salvation which were distant from Calvin's own opinions informed a distinctive Puritan religious culture within the international Reformed community.

Chapter 2: International Connections

This chapter will explore the ways in which Reformed churches and states established and retained close contacts with one another. It will first focus on the significance of communities of Reformed exiles, who abandoned their homes to avoid persecution. The social mobility of early Calvinists, and the experiences of many who went into exile, strengthened commitment to Reformed religion as a trans-national movement, led to many personal and practical connections across the Continent, and significantly impacted on the development of Reformed churches. Calvinist refugees gathered together in some key bases, from where they planned missionary campaigns and political resistance back in their home countries. The presence of many refugees was not always warmly received by host communities, but many Calvinists offered financial and spiritual support to foreigners and exiles through collections, prayers and fasting.[1] Connections between different Reformed churches were later bolstered by the education of clergy in cosmopolitan academic centres. Universities and academies became crucial centres of international activity and contacts. Personal links were built between foreign students and professors, many of whom also travelled around the Continent during their careers. Connections between this network of intellectuals often facilitated the spread of theological orthodoxy across the Continent, but contacts could also reveal differences over understanding of doctrine, patterns of ceremonies and forms of church government.

International connections between Calvinists were also sustained through correspondence between both clergy and laity. In particular, some of the Continent's leading figures received a wide range of requests and pleas for help and advice on any number of different theological and practical issues. Leaders in Geneva, Zurich and Strassburg attempted to use such connections to try to influence local churches. However, the degree to which these leading figures within the Reformed movement were in fact in control of these exchanges is difficult to ascertain. Apparently innocent appeals to Calvin, Beza or Bullinger for wise counsel could disguise planned efforts to push or prevent specific changes in a local church. International connections could also reflect and even exacerbate disharmony among Calvinists as the different beliefs and attitudes among members of Reformed churches were played out in an international context. There was some degree of resentment of any outside interference in local affairs, and there could certainly be tension between domestic priorities and the claims of the international community. This was the case in relations between Reformed courts, where, despite a clear rhetoric of international co-operation, expectations of financial and military aid were often dispelled by pragmatic self-interest. This chapter will therefore set out some of the ways in which an international community was forged between Calvinists, but also point out how appeals to the Calvinist international were utilised in different contexts, and suggest limits to the degree of international influence over local churches and states.

Exile and Migration

The experience of exile, being a refugee, and of internal displacement was common to many Calvinists and Reformed communities. Persecution certainly disrupted the spread of Reformed religion across the Continent. However, the imprisonment and martyrdom of Calvinists failed to silence dissent, as stories of martyrs were advertised by propagandists as examples of men and women of true faith. Equally, tales of Calvinists forced into exile were recorded as evidence of individual courage and commitment, and as proof of providential guidance over the lives of believers. Life on the run was also often seen to place Calvinists in the footsteps of Biblical Israel and of the early Apostles. Jan Utenhove, a nobleman from Ghent who was one of the leaders of the Dutch exile church in London under Edward VI, described how his community was thrown out of England by the new Marian regime. In the autumn of 1553 a group of 175 people led by Utenhove, the Pole Johannes à Lasco (taski), and Martin Micron also from Ghent, went ahead of the main body of the London exile congregation of between 3000 to 4000 people. Two boats left Gravesend bound for Denmark to the sound of tears and Psalms sung by the rest of their community. However, the refugees' petition to the Danish king for sanctuary from the 'persecution of the Antichrist' was rejected after a debate revealed differences between the refugees and local Lutheran clergy over Communion theology. The London refugees then tried to gain entry to a number of Baltic ports over the winter of 1553, but were turned away from Rostock, Wismar, Lübeck and Hamburg, before finally reaching a safe haven at Emden in East Friesland. Most of the rest of the congregation left London in far less dramatic circumstances in 1553, and many moved to Flanders and Brabant.[2]

Individuals also wrote accounts of their dramatic flight from Catholic persecution. John Bale, for example, recorded his departure as bishop of Ossory from Kilkenny in 1553 as Irish priests plotted to have him killed. Bale recounted how he retreated to Dublin, and then boarded a ship bound for England. He narrowly escaped capture when the ship arrived in Cornwall, and Bale compared his experiences at St Ives with those of the apostle Paul at Malta. Bale bribed the ship's captain to take him on to Flanders, where he was still in danger of being captured by the Catholic authorities. He finally reached safety at Wesel in the Rhineland, able to give thanks to God for his miraculous delivery 'from the greedy mouths of devouring lions'.[3] Divine providence had also directed Calvin to Geneva when he fled from France in 1536. Calvin was trying to reach the safety of Strassburg or Basel, but to avoid conflict on his route he was forced to travel to the south through Geneva, 'having himself no thought of this city'. However, Guillaume Farel from Dauphiné, who was leading reform in the city demanded that he remain in Geneva, claiming that if Calvin did not remain, 'the Lord will punish you for seeking your own interest rather than his'. Suitably 'struck with this fearful denunciation', Calvin accepted an office to preach in Geneva.[4] Theodore Beza, who provided this narrative of Calvin's arrival in Geneva, left France voluntarily in 1548 after a dramatic conversion during a bout of illness. For Beza, the physical experience of moving to an environment in which he could worship freely provided a powerful parallel with his spiritual journey of personal redemption. Beza recalled not knowing 'what to do with my wretched life', before God offered consolation to his troubled spirit. According to Beza, 'the vision of death threatening my soul awakened in me the desire for a true and everlasting life'. Beza renewed his oath to serve the church, and

> burst asunder every chain, collected my efforts, forsook at once my native land, my kinsmen, my friends, that I might follow after Christ,

and accompanied by my wife, betook myself to Geneva in voluntary exile.[5]

In the early years of the spread of Reformed ideas, cities such as Geneva, London and Emden became crucial havens for the physical survival of Calvinists, and served as stations for mission efforts and political activity. Beza recalled that on Calvin's return to Geneva in 1541, people 'flocked from all parts of the Christian world, some to take his advice in matters of religion, and others to hear him'.[6] Geneva also became an important base for publishing, and from the late 1550s served, along with Lausanne, as a crucial centre for training clergy for service in congregations in France. Between the mid-1550s and 1570 over 200 clergy were trained in Geneva, Lausanne and Neuchâtel, and sent to France. Between 1555 and 1562, the Genevan Company of Pastors offered letters of official accreditation to 88 ministers dispatched to fill specified vacancies serving churches in France. These ministerial candidates were tested on their ability to preach and subjected to examinations of their personal conduct before they were permitted to leave Geneva. These missionaries also required considerable courage and commitment, and ten of this group were martyred in France.[7]

Geneva also saw thousands of religious refugees stream in and out of the city. In 1530 Geneva's population had stood at over 10 000, but by 1560 refugees had roughly doubled the number of people in the city. Between September and December 1572, 1300 adult males alone fled to Geneva. However, many refugees also returned back to France during periods of peace, and by 1585 the city's population had returned to a total of 15 000. French refugees also set up bases in the Rhineland, and close relations developed between exile churches in the Palatinate and Geneva.[8] Geneva in time sustained not only large numbers of French exiles but also Italian, English and Spanish communities. By the late 1560s the Italian church in Geneva was more than 1000 strong, including many skilled artisans in the silk and velvet trades.[9] Enthusiasts came to see the city as more than a temporary place of safety. When John Bale made his way there, he thought that Geneva was a 'miracle' and a 'sanctuary', adding

> is it not wonderful that Spaniards, Italians, Scots, Englishmen, Frenchmen, Germans, disagreeing in manners, speech and apparel, sheep and wolves, bulls and bears, being coupled only with the yoke of Christ, should live so lovingly and friendly... like a spiritual and Christian congregation.[10]

Opponents were certainly less convinced about the idealism of some of the refugees who moved to Geneva. Jerome Bolsec claimed that thieves and all sorts of criminals from France, Flanders and Italy travelled to Geneva under the pretext of seeking reform, but in reality he believed went there to commit adultery and sodomy.[11]

England provided refuge for perhaps as many as 50 000 foreigners across the sixteenth century. By no means all of this total can be counted as committed members of the Reformed cause, and many moved to London and other towns in the south-east of England in search of economic opportunities. Some exiles were to settle in England, but the vast majority only remained in the country for a short period of time. Waves of migrants arrived in England in the wake of persecution on the Continent and during periods of the long-running wars in the Netherlands and France. Some of the Continent's leading reformers had sought refuge in Edward VI's England after Charles V tried to impose Catholic forms of worship in the Empire through the 1548 Interim. Peter Martyr Vermigli, originally from a Florentine noble family, had moved from Strasbourg to England in 1547 and worked at Oxford until 1553, while Martin Bucer also moved from Strasbourg to Cambridge between 1549 and 1551.

Most refugees remained in London, where the government of Edward VI had granted exiles the use of Austin Friars. Edward's royal charter permitting use of the church identified one the duties of Christian princes as the need 'to take thought also for religion and for exiles, who for the sake of religion are broken with calamity and afflicted'.[12] Johannes à Lasco was appointed superintendent of this strangers' church in 1550. Although the London church had strong connections with Zurich, Lasco followed the models provided by Geneva and the French community at Strasbourg in the form of liturgy and church government which he established.[13] The Dutch exiles remained in close contact with their home communities through a network of connections and by correspondence, using commercial links between ports in England and the Netherlands. Underground churches at home were supported with money and books, and in 1550 Martin Micron wrote to Heinrich Bullinger that the London church was going 'to attack our Flanders with fiery darts, and, I hope, take it by storm, that Antichrist being put to flight or at least weakened, our Saviour may reign there'.[14]

After 1553 around 800 English religious and political opponents of the Marian regime were forced to seek refuge on the Continent in Emden, the Rhineland, in Swiss cities, and as far south as Venice. Around 4000 foreign residents also left London, and Peter Martyr Vermigli was among prominent leaders to leave, in his case for Strassburg.[15] In 1555 Edmund Grindal offered Nicholas Ridley encouraging news of the success of communities of English exiles in Zurich, Strassburg and Frankfurt. Ridley replied by expressing the hope that 'ye, blessed by God, are enough through his aid, to light and set up again the lantern of his word in England'. However, the exiles were far from being a united group, and disputes over the conduct of services saw a group of reformers leave the church at Frankfurt for Geneva, which increased the English-speaking community there to around 230 people.[16]

On Elizabeth's accession most of the exiles hurried back to England to gain places in the new church order. England also soon played host once again to foreign Reformed communities. When the strangers' churches were allowed to worship again in 1559 they were placed under the authority of the bishop of London. In 1560 Nicolas des Gallars was sent from Geneva to be one of the ministers at a French-speaking church of Walloons and French exiles in London. In 1561 des Gallars published a new church order, which marked an increase in the direct influence of Geneva on the London exile community.[17] From the 1560s to the end of the sixteenth century the total numbers of members of the French- and Dutch-speaking congregations in London fluctuated with the movement of people to and from the Continent. Towards the end of the 1560s there were around 3800 members of the two churches at Austin Friars and Threadneedle street. By 1593 there were around 7000 foreigners resident in London, which formed around 3–4 per cent of the city's total population. Substantial communities of French- and Dutch-speaking exiles had also been permitted to settle in Norwich, Sandwich, Colchester, Canterbury and Southampton.[18] The arrival of such large numbers of foreigners led to tensions between the exiles and local authorities. However, George Abbot, archbishop of Canterbury from 1611, saw England's reception of religious refugees as a blessing that 'this little island of ours should not only be a temple to serve God for ourselves, but a harbour for the weatherbeaten, a sanctuary to the stranger'.[19]

The survival of the fledgling Reformed movement in the Netherlands was heavily reliant on the support of exile communities until the early 1570s. The scale of the exodus of people from the troubles, wars and Catholic persecution of the Netherlands was vast. Estimates suggest that between the 1530s and 1590s perhaps up to 150 000 people from a variety of religious groups left the southern Netherlands, which formed around 5 per cent of the total population of the region. Around two-thirds of that number settled in the northern Dutch provinces from the 1570s, and the rest moved to parts of the Empire or to England.[20] Again, however, it would certainly be mistaken to ascribe purely religious motivations to all the exiles from the Netherlands. Productive and skilful weavers from Flanders were deliberately sought out by Sir Philip Sidney for a plantation in Ireland. In 1582 Sidney wrote that

> I caused to plant and inhabit there about forty families of the Reformed churches of the Low Countries, flying thence for religion's sake, in one ruinous town called Swords; and truly, sir, it would have done any man good to have seen how diligently they wrought, how they re-edified the quite spoiled old castle of the same town, and repaired almost all the same, and how godly and cleanly they, and their wives, and children lived.[21]

Calvinist refugees were by no means so warmly welcomed everywhere. For one thing, the sheer numbers involved created problems for host communities. When exile communities grew to form a substantial proportion of the local population, or when there was no immediate prospect of the migrants returning to their home countries, then resentment could build. Short-term migrants also often failed to make much effort to integrate into their new communities, and some congregations went together in exile, as for example when the Reformed community of Maastricht moved to Aachen. Migrants to the Rhineland also encountered difficulties with Lutheran urban and state authorities. The English, French, and eventually also the Walloon congregations at Frankfurt were all expelled by the city authorities. Some moved on to the Palatinate in the 1560s, and settled in new towns such as Frankenthal. However, on the succession of Frederick III's Lutheran son Ludwig VI in 1576, some Calvinist refugees in the Palatinate were forced to move yet again to areas of the Palatinate under the control of Frederick's younger Reformed son, Johann Casimir.[22]

Emden was another crucial station for Dutch exiles, and by the 1560s and early 1570s between one-third and one-half of the city's population was made up of refugees. There had been a continuous Reformed presence at Emden from the early 1540s, when Countess Anna invited Johannes à Lasco to lead reform of the town's church. Lasco returned to Emden in 1553, but moved back to Poland in 1556 to become superintendent of the Reformed church there. Emden's Reformed church became a crucial centre of Dutch printing from the 1550s for the growing churches of Flanders and Brabant. Attention switched to these provinces in 1566, when ministers and laymen in the underground churches rather than exiles took the lead in hedge-preaching meetings and incidents of iconoclasm. From 1567 the duke of Alva's repression sent tens of thousands of Calvinists into exile once again to Emden and the Rhineland. Emden was subsequently chosen as the site for the Dutch church's founding synod in October 1571. Although the London church was forbidden by the English government from sending representatives to Emden, other Dutch- and French-speaking delegates arrived from communities in the Rhineland and from some churches in the Netherlands. The Emden synod adopted the 1561 *Confession* of Guy de Brès, endorsed use of the Genevan and Heidelberg catechisms, and agreed on a structure for the church based on parish consistories and district synods. Emden's vital role for the Reformed movement in the Netherlands was brief, and from 1572 many exiles moved to the northern Dutch provinces. When the churches of the southern Netherlands were forced into exile once again in 1585, most this time also fled to Zeeland and Holland.[23]

Exile communities sent money to support underground churches, provided bases for publishing activity and sites for church synods to meet, and organised collections of money for distribution to newly arrived destitute refugees. Exile congregations were also involved in political and military resistance against their former Catholic rulers. The London Dutch church provided 1400 pounds to equip 200 soldiers to fight at Flushing in 1572, and William of Orange demanded greater sacrifices from the exiles in London with frequent requests for men, arms and money.[24] Some fighters also took refuge in England. Sea Beggar privateers operated out of some southern ports, before Elizabeth lost patience with their activities in the Channel and threw them out in 1572. Bands of Wood Beggars who attacked Catholic clergy, sacked churches, and attempted to inspire revolt in west Flanders between 1566 and 1568 had one of their bases for operations in Sandwich. These guerrilla fighters or terrorists also received financial help from the large exile community at Sandwich, which by the mid-1570s was made up of 2900 Flemings and Walloons and formed around two-thirds of the population of the town.[25]

From the 1580s there was a flow of religious exiles from Britain to the Dutch Republic. English and Scottish congregations emerged around communities of merchants and military garrisons at Amsterdam, Leiden, Delft, Utrecht, Flushing, Middelburg and Rotterdam. These congregations were served by some Puritans and radical separatists. For example, the English-speaking church at Middelburg was served over time by

Presbyterians and Congregationalists including Thomas Cartwright, Walter Travers and John Forbes. This later generation of British exiles did not seek refuge from Catholic persecution but moved in search of a purer reformation and tested their ideas about church government and ceremonial reform. The force of this drive for further reform later propelled some ministers and congregations out of European degeneracy altogether and across the Atlantic Ocean.[26]

Close connections had also developed between foreign congregations in London and Puritans in the city. The foreign churches in England enjoyed a wide degree of autonomy over their own affairs, worshipping according to their own orders of service, and living under the discipline of their own governing consistories. These churches provided models of best Reformed practice in the eyes of some reformers in the Elizabethan church.[27] These connections between the strangers' churches and the reform-minded party of English clergy encouraged conservatives to question whether the French and Dutch congregations ought to be brought to conformity with the government and ceremonies of the English church. Eventually the long-standing protection offered to foreign Reformed communities in England was challenged by archbishop William Laud, who launched a campaign in the 1630s to restrict attendance at the strangers' churches only to those who had been born abroad.[28]

International Charity

In December 1621 James I gave permission for a voluntary collection to be taken in Scotland and England for French Calvinists displaced from their homes by Louis XIII's armies. In February 1622 a collection was taken up at the congregation of St Cuthbert's in Edinburgh. The kirk session of St Cuthbert's drew up a list of 265 members of the church who contributed a total of 800 pounds for France. The list was headed by Sir William Nisbet who gave 100 pounds, and included other merchants in the parish, as well as artisans and servants. The greatest financial sacrifice for unknown brethren in distant France was offered by some of the servants who worshipped at St Cuthbert's. Bessie Murdoch gave four shillings, which certainly represented more than a day's wages, and Agnes Moore managed to find twelve shillings to send to her brothers and sisters in France. These poor women in Edinburgh were among many ordinary people who donated money to help foreign co-religionists in their time of trouble. What motivated their actions? Perhaps they were making an unwilling response to the collection under social pressure to do so. However, more likely the elders at St Cuthbert's represented a common view when they declared that the congregation gave the money as a pledge of their mutual communion with the church in France as members together of one body. This was certainly much more than windy rhetoric given the sacrificial donations made by ordinary members of the congregation. The presbytery of Haddington, which raised over two thousand pounds that year for France, also spoke of a 'mutual communion' and a 'holy and strict obligation' to help the French. The collection made across Scotland in 1622 hoped to sustain the Huguenot church which was believed to be facing extermination 'to the unspeakable hurt and detriment of the whole Reformed church, whereof we are a part'. Collectors were sent out to parishes across the land to make 'a true declaration of the great necessity of our poor afflicted brethren, [and] to receive and collect what it shall please God to move their hearts to bestow'.[29]

The extension of practical support to foreign Reformed Christians in need had long been a feature of church activity in Scotland. In 1576 the general assembly was 'inwardly touched with the sorrow of their brethren' from France living in exile in London, and not only offered them 'all hearty and tender affection' but also sent money.[30] In December 1587 the St Andrews kirk session took up another collection for French Calvinists exiled in England, contributing part of the 10 000 merks raised in Scotland that year for the refugees.[31] A collection was also organised in the presbytery of Ellon in north-eastern Scotland for Geneva during its battle for survival against Savoy in 1603. However, the money raised was later returned to the area for unknown reasons, showing at least that the organisation of these international charitable collections was far from a simple matter.[32]

Giving money to foreign brethren was not, however, free from polemic use in Scotland. Solidarity with French Calvinists was seen by some as a demonstration of their true Reformed credentials. According to David Calderwood, those in the church in Scotland who rejected the Articles of Perth proved their honesty and virtue in giving most generously to support the French in 1622. These Articles, which were ratified in 1621, introduced controversial liturgical changes which brought the Scottish church into conformity with England. They included allowing people to kneel to receive Communion, and recognised Christian festivals which the Scottish church had previously abandoned.[33] In England too activists with strong foreign connections or a deep commitment to Reformed internationalism also tended to be most heavily involved in charitable collections for foreign churches. However, when appeals were organised they drew in support from a wider range of donors, as when money was raised for the Genevan church in 1583 and 1589.[34]

Exile communities were often particularly generous in offering assistance both to fellow refugees and to other churches in trouble. In Geneva funds were set up for the relief of poor French, Italian and English religious refugees in the city. From the 1550s the *bourse française* collected money to support refugees in the city with temporary housing and loans, and financial support was distributed to widows and orphans. Wealthy French residents in Geneva and congregations across France contributed to the fund which was administered under the control of the city's Company of Pastors.[35] The exile churches in London and Emden also organised funds which their deacons distributed to help impoverished refugees.[36] Empathy with the suffering of co-religionists, and a particular commitment to internationalism, also helps to explain the money sent by the French and Dutch exile churches in London to Geneva in 1583 and 1602. In 1624 the Dutch church in London took up a collection for Protestants in the Valtelline, and sent 140 pounds to Bohemian Brethren exiles at Leszno in Poland in 1641.[37] The first two collections held in Britain in 1628 and 1630 for German Calvinist refugees from the Palatinate were administered by the elders of the Dutch church at Austin Friars. The suffering of Irish Protestant exiles after the massacres of 1641 also met with an impressive response from the Dutch church in London, which donated help for the citizens of Coleraine in 1642. The church in the Dutch Republic also raised the vast sum of 30 000 pounds for their Irish brethren, and tried to ensure that this money was spent on food and relief and not diverted to support the Parliament's army in Ireland.[38]

Universities and Clergy Education

The education of Reformed students at cosmopolitan universities and academies, particularly at Geneva and Swiss cities, in the Empire and in the Dutch Republic had important consequences for the development of, and for relationships between, the Continent's Reformed churches. In 1559 Theodore Beza became the first rector of the Genevan Academy. Around one-third of the Academy's students in its early years were trained for the ministry in France, and Beza later claimed that the

Academy was 'the nursery-garden' of the ministry not only in France, but also in England and Flanders.[39] The role of the Genevan Academy, however, lessened in importance over time for the French church, as other Reformed academies and colleges were set up at Nîmes, Montpellier, Castres, Montauban, Saumur, at Orthez in Béarn, and at Sedan under the duke of Bouillon. In other Reformed states, students could turn to universities and academies during the sixteenth century in Scotland and England, and at Heidelberg, Basel, Herborn, Leiden and Franeker.[40]

These universities and academies became international centres of the Reformed world, and many teachers migrated between different colleges. The sort of cosmopolitan Reformed academic who worked in these institutions included, for example, François du Jon (Junius). Du Jon was born at Bourges in France, studied in Geneva between 1562 and 1565, then worked as a minister in Antwerp, before serving the French exile congregation at Schönau in the Palatinate. He taught theology at Neustadt from 1578, and then at Heidelberg from 1584, before moving to Leiden in 1592. Another was François Gomaer (Gomarus) who was born in Bruges in 1563. Gomaer studied at Strassburg, Neustadt in the Palatinate, Oxford, Cambridge and Heidelberg, before becoming minister to the Walloon community at Frankfurt. When this community was thrown out of the city by the Lutheran authorities, Gomaer left to teach at Leiden university in 1594. In 1611 he moved to Middelburg, before teaching at the Saumur academy in 1614, and finally moving in 1618 to teach at the new university at Groningen. A final example points not only to the peripatetic careers of many Reformed intellectuals, but also to ongoing significant links between Scotland and continental Calvinists. John Cameron was born in Glasgow in 1579, and moved to serve as minister at Bordeaux and then at Sedan in 1602. After a brief interlude in Paris, Cameron moved on to Geneva in 1606 and to Heidelberg in 1608. He then returned to serve as minister to the community of Bordeaux in 1608 until 1618. Cameron then taught theology at Groningen, Saumur, and at Glasgow in 1621. He returned to France to become a professor at the Montauban academy in 1624 and was killed in a riot there in 1625.[41]

The international profile of teachers in Reformed universities and academies was matched by the diverse student body at many institutions. One in five of the students who matriculated at the university of Basel between 1532 and 1600 was a non-German speaker, including 500 students from France and 250 students from the Netherlands. Towards the end of the sixteenth century the numbers of central European students at Basel increased, and students came to the city in substantial numbers from Poland and Bohemia.[42] Students from across the Empire travelled to study at Heidelberg, and around one in three of the university's students came from outside the Empire before the outbreak of the Thirty Years' War. The largest number of foreigners at Heidelberg was from France. Between 1560 and 1610 some 500 French students registered for study in the Palatinate, but this number declined as alternative universities and academies were founded in France. By that stage there were growing numbers of central European students at Heidelberg, and after 1610 one-third of the university's international students came from Poland, Bohemia, Moravia, Hungary or Transylvania.[43]

The importance of these universities in building relations between Calvinists from the 1560s, and the significant changes over time in the Reformed intellectual environment, are both highlighted by the pattern of academic peregrination undertaken by student ministers from the Reformed churches in Hungary and Transylvania. Transylvania's princes and Protestant nobles in Hungary developed their own academies and schools at home. However, the region lacked a Reformed university and, alongside the opportunity to study under the Continent's leading theologians, this encouraged hundreds of students to make often perilous journeys to western European universities. From the 1560s Hungarian students had visited both Zurich and Geneva, but during the second half of the sixteenth century most students attended universities in the Empire. Initially Reformed students joined Hungarian Lutherans in a college at Wittenberg university. However, by the 1580s Hungarian Calvinist students began to attend Heidelberg university and Herborn academy in Nassau. By the turn of the century over 100 Hungarian Calvinist clergy had been educated at Heidelberg university alone.[44]

The security of academic centres in Reformed Germany was threatened after the outbreak of war in 1618. When Heidelberg fell to Spanish forces in 1622, Hungarian students turned instead to the new university at Frankfurt-an-der-Oder in Brandenburg, to the college at Bremen, and to the universities of Franeker, Leiden, Groningen and Utrecht in the Dutch Republic. Leading academics from Germany also sought safety in the Dutch Republic, while in 1629 Johann Heinrich Alsted and Johann Heinrich Bisterfeld moved from Herborn academy to teach at the college at Gyulafehérvár (Alba Iulia) in the Transylvanian principality. During the early seventeenth century the universities of the Dutch Republic attracted increasing numbers of foreign students. Around half of the students at the university of Franeker in Friesland during the second quarter of the seventeenth century came from outside the Dutch

Republic. Leiden had more foreign than Dutch students during the same period, with Hungarians accounting for one in twenty of some 5500 foreign students attending the university during that period.[45] Over one hundred Hungarian Reformed students also travelled as far as England in the early decades of the seventeenth century. Most met with more success than Márton Szepsi Csombor, who sadly recalled in 1620 that he had failed to find anyone who could resolve his confusion on not finding any university colleges in Canterbury (he was looking for *Cantabrigia*).[46]

The impact on the Hungarian church of these decades of close interaction with western European academic centres was considerable. Generations of university-educated students went on to become superintendents and senior clergy in the Hungarian church. They profited from the competent training which they had received in Reformed dogmatic and polemic theology, and many western teachers were particularly keen to ensure that their Hungarian co-religionists were well trained in how to refute anti-Trinitarianism before returning home. Many students also brought copies of the latest western theological texts back to Hungary, others translated western devotional works into Hungarian, and the most capable students produced their own works. One outstanding figure was Albert Szenczi Molnár, who produced a Hungarian version of the Genevan *Psalter* in 1607, in 1612 translated the Heidelberg *Catechism* and published a revised edition of the Bible in Hungarian, and in 1624 published a translation of Calvin's *Institutes of the Christian Religion*.[47]

Various strands of Reformed thought and spirituality also affected different groups of Hungarian students. David Pareus, the Silesian who was professor of New Testament theology at Heidelberg university taught many Hungarian students, and corresponded with the Reformed prince of Transylvania, Gábor Bethlen. Pareus' irenic plans for Protestant union were taken up in Hungary by some of his former students. Meanwhile, the moralistic piety of both English Puritans and advocates of further reform in the Dutch church also impacted on a number of student ministers, later themselves dubbed as Puritans in Hungary. However, it would be unfair to conclude that the key intellectual centres of the international Reformed community simply shaped the outlook of visiting students from the movement's eastern periphery. Hungarian student ministers who travelled to the west for periods of study, who were taught about irenicism in Heidelberg, or who worshipped with Puritans in London, were taking part in a complex pattern of intellectual and social relationships. Hungarians did not have their spiritual attitudes altered by whichever strand of western Reformed religion they first came into contact with. The characterisation of eastern Europeans as being simply moulded by encounters with western religious life is related to long-standing prejudices about western intellectual superiority over the east. Thus, rather than discovering intense moralism in the Dutch Republic and England, Hungarian students encountered a way of articulating their own desire for further reform in Hungarian society, and used their experiences to promote changes which they wanted to encourage in the Hungarian Reformed church, in domestic schools and in parish life.[48]

Authority and Advice

Contact with the leading figures of intellectual and moral authority in the international Reformed community was eagerly sought out by many students and visitors to Geneva, Zurich, Heidelberg and other centres. Correspondents also engaged Calvin, Beza, Bullinger, Bucer, Martyr and others to offer advice on doctrine, ceremonies and church government. One feature of Calvin's correspondence was his efforts to encourage leading noblewomen in France to support the Reformed cause. Correspondents in receipt of Calvin's advice on political and spiritual matters included such high-born figures as Marguerite d'Angoulême and Jeanne d'Albret, queens of Navarre, and Renée de France, duchess of Ferrara.[49] While France remained the prime focus of Calvin's attention, leading clergy from churches in Germany, Poland, Hungary and England often sought advice from Bullinger at Zurich. When Jan Utenhove accompanied Johannes à Lasco to the Polish court in 1557, Utenhove encouraged Bullinger to assist in their attempts to persuade Sigismond Augustus to support reform. Utenhove claimed that Bullinger's influence was 'great in all quarters, and even with the king himself'. Beza also corresponded with leaders of the churches in Poland and Hungary, especially during the crucial years of the 1560s when the churches were settling on confessions of faith and battling against the challenge posed by anti-Trinitarianism. Reformers in Hungary also looked to Bullinger for advice, and already in 1567 a synod of ministers at Debrecen had adopted his 1566 *Second Helvetic Confession*. The same synod recognised the 1562 *Confessio Catholica* compiled by locals Péter Méliusz Juhász and Gergely Szegedi from the insights of a range of western reformers.[50]

A complex network of correspondence linked leading Reformed clergy across the Continent from the early years of reform, which supports a view of the international Reformed community as an alliance of

churches which did not by any means rely on the leadership and guidance
of Calvin alone. The role played by Bullinger and his colleagues in
Zurich, for example, emerges very clearly from their correspondence
with leaders of the English church. Bullinger closely followed the
progress of the church under Edward through a range of correspondents. Many leaders from England who later sought refuge on the
Continent turned for help to Zurich, including Thomas Lever who
looked on Bullinger as 'a good shepherd' for his flock of refugees at
Aarau.[51]

In 1554 some of the English exile community at Frankfurt led by John
Knox turned rather to Calvin to intervene in disputes within their congregation over forms of worship and ceremony. Calvin encouraged them
to permit 'tolerable foolish things' in the Edwardian Prayer Book and
avoid unnecessary disputes. Divisions emerged again within the
Frankfurt church in 1555 over the conduct of services, and Knox was forbidden to preach. Reformers including Knox, Anthony Gilby and
William Whittingham then abandoned Frankfurt for Geneva and Basel in
the autumn of 1555. In a letter of April 1555 the conservative leadership
of the Frankfurt church had acknowledged that Calvin's authority 'is, and
ought to be, most highly esteemed and regarded, not only by ourselves
but by the world at large'. However, when Knox and the reformers were
warmly received in Geneva, Frankfurt's conservatives complained that 'it
is quite evident, that you [Calvin] are entirely ignorant of almost all the
circumstances of our case'.[52] Although Calvin had encouraged the two
parties of English exiles at Frankfurt to resolve their dispute peaceably,
he was drawn into their argument and his relationship with one wing of
the English exile community was badly damaged as a result. Worse was to
follow after the publication at Geneva in 1558 of works on rights of resistance to royal authority by Christopher Goodman and on the limits of the
authority of queens by John Knox.[53] Calvin found himself associated with
troublemaking reformers and political radicals in the eyes of the new
English queen, and he wrote in vain to William Cecil in 1559 of his grief
at Elizabeth's reaction to the 'thoughtless arrogance' of Knox's 'ravings'.[54]

The practices followed by foreign Reformed churches became a significant benchmark in debates between conservatives, moderates and
reformers over the direction of the Elizabethan church from the 1560s.
This was partly because many of the Marian exiles who had found refuge
in Germany and in Swiss cities returned after 1558 to positions of authority in the English church including Edmund Grindal, Edwin Sandys,
Robert Horne, John Jewel and John Parkhurst among the ranks of

the episcopate. From their return to England, bishops and other clergy maintained a correspondence with Bullinger, Martyr, Rudolph Gwalther and others. The subjects covered in their letters ranged from exchanging news and gossip to discussion of the extent of appropriate episcopal authority, the importance of parish presbyteries and the need for reforms to church ceremonies. English letter-writers were certainly sincere when they sought advice, as when Thomas Sampson wrote to his 'father' Martyr. However, Sampson also wrote in the hope of gaining Martyr's support for further reform of the church in England. Engaging the help of foreign divines could also pose dangers in England, and in a postscript to a letter of 1560 Sampson warned Martyr that if he or Bullinger 'should think of writing to the queen's majesty, you are well aware that it must not seem as if you had been urged by any one to do so'.[55]

Foreign figures of authority could also be useful to opponents of reform within the Elizabethan church. When Edwin Sandys, the bishop of London, wrote to Bullinger in 1573 on the challenge posed to the church by Presbyterians, he suggested that 'if the whole matter in controversy was left to your arbitration, it would doubtless much contribute to the peace of the church'. Sandys knew well that Bullinger would not support a Genevan pattern of church government, and sought to use support from Zurich as a counterweight to the claims of English Presbyterians, who 'are crying out that they have all the Reformed churches on their side'.[56] Many English clergy developed this sort of instrumental attitude towards contacts with foreign divines, trying to gain the backing of authoritative advocates for their own opinions and thereby drawing Continental leaders into their domestic disputes.

Diplomacy and Alliances

Reformed clergy across the Continent shared a belief in a Catholic conspiracy to eliminate Calvinist rulers and states. The general assembly of the church in Scotland wrote in 1567 that a plot had been hatched to exterminate Protestants at the Council of Trent. As Huguenot propagandists spread news of the massacres in Paris and across France in 1572 it seemed to confirm to the assembly the urgency of the need to defend the church in Scotland and elsewhere against the plans of the 'unhappy, devilish and terrible Council of Trent'. The assembly encouraged the Regent to agree a defensive alliance with England and other countries which professed 'true religion' to join together 'in mutual amity and society' and support one another against their common enemies. In the face of apparent threats from the 'Roman beast' at home and abroad, the Scottish church also turned to prayer and fasting in 1578, 1582 and in 1587. In 1583 representatives from the assembly again appealed to James VI to seek an alliance with England and other Christian princes for the 'defence and protection of the Word of God'. In 1589 the assembly called on all nobles to subscribe to a band to defend true religion and support the king to combat Papists working for the 'antichristian league'. In 1595 the assembly remained certain of a universal Catholic plot against 'our brethren of other Churches, under no less danger than we, through all Europe'.[57]

Alongside fears about a conspiracy forged at the council of Trent, there was widespread suspicion in France and the Netherlands that a secret Catholic alliance had been agreed at a conference held at Bayonne in 1565 between Charles IX, Catherine of Medici and the duke of Alva. Much of the correspondence of the late 1560s and 1570s between the Huguenot leadership, Dutch rebels and German princes contained expressions of the need to unite to defend their common cause against this Catholic threat. However, the policies adopted by Reformed courts often did not match this rhetoric with concerted diplomatic and military action. Even when decisions were taken to form alliances with other Reformed states, to commit resources to aid co-religionists under attack, or to send troops into conflict, they were clearly not only made on the basis of what was best for the international Reformed cause. Delays in offers of help, arguments over finances, demands for repayment of loans, territorial claims, and rivalry for prestige between rulers all limited and frustrated united action. Activists who lobbied for princes to defend foreign religious brethren were often disappointed, since interests of state remained absolutely central to foreign-policy decision making in Reformed Europe. However, where rulers could take action which combined their own dynastic interests and the interests of the international Reformed cause, they frequently did so during the French Wars of Religion, the Dutch Revolt and the Thirty Years' War. The religious commitment of princes and interests of national security could not be divorced from each other. Domestic political considerations were also influential, and rulers who allowed a gap to grow too wide between their verbal commitment to the cause of religion and their actual policy risked provoking opposition from their estates.

The record of the English court's commitment to the Reformed cause was certainly a very mixed one. Elizabeth articulated a powerful rhetoric about the need for urgent action against Catholic powers. In 1583 Elizabeth wrote to the cities of Zurich, Bern, Basel and Schaffhausen encouraging them to defend Geneva against Savoyard aggression. Elizabeth saw a conspiracy among enemies of the 'reformed religion which we profess' to 'overwhelm us separately' and 'separate us from each other'. Elizabeth argued that the cities should intervene to protect their neighbour, 'lest the contagion which by our fault has once begun to attack one member, may by an unavoidable fatality be extended over the whole body'.[58]

Fear of Spanish power, concern about the threat posed by Mary Stuart and her Guise relatives, and considerations of strategic interests all weighed heavily in deciding policy in England. Nevertheless, assessment of all these factors and concern for the fate of foreign co-religionists, pointed the English court towards judicious activism in the Dutch revolt and French wars. Despite prevarication and a legendary unwillingness to spend money, Elizabeth committed vast sums and large armies to both theatres of conflict. Around 13 000 English soldiers were sent to northern France in interventions in 1562, 1589 and 1591, and an English army of around 7000 men was sent to the Netherlands in 1585. On top of the expense of maintaining these armies, grants and loans were also made available to raise mercenary armies and to fund Huguenot forces. For example, money was given by Elizabeth to support the 1569 army of 17 000 mercenaries led into France by Wolfgang of Zweibrücken, and in 1591 to raise forces to defend the Dutch Republic against the duke of Parma's army. Elizabeth was also engaged in long negotiations for an alliance with German princes, which resulted in 1577 in an ill-timed plan for a Protestant league in the Empire.[59]

However, some of the details of English intervention in France take the gloss off this apparent generosity in support of the Reformed cause. Money was only offered to support Zweibrücken's army after lengthy delays, and Jeanne d'Albret had to offer the crown jewels of Navarre as security to gain a loan from Elizabeth in 1569. Elizabeth had offered financial and military assistance in 1562 to the Huguenot leadership by the terms of the treaty of Hampton court. However, this intervention ended up remarkably by managing to unite Huguenots and the French crown in a joint attack on English forces at Le Havre in 1564, when Elizabeth held on to the port in the hope of exchanging it for control of Calais.[60]

Huguenot nobles and Dutch rebels also tried to co-ordinate their resistance to their Catholic monarchs. In 1568 William of Orange allied with Louis, prince of Condé, and admiral Gaspard de Coligny. In 1571 and 1572 Coligny pressed for the French crown to take up arms against Spanish forces in the Netherlands. In 1572 Louis of Nassau attacked Flanders, William of Orange moved into Brabant, and ports in Zeeland were seized by the rebels. However, the expected involvement of French royal arms never materialised as the court hesitated from joining an anti-Spanish coalition.[61]

A great deal of assistance was offered to French and Dutch Calvinists by Reformed German princes, and in particular by Frederick III of the Palatinate. Frederick had many international Reformed activists and clergy among his close advisors and diplomatic agents, including his Flemish court chaplain Peter Dathenus, Christoph Ehem, Wenzel Zuleger, François du Jon, Daniel Toussain and Girolamo Zanchi. Agents for the Huguenot leadership such as François Hotman were also visitors to the Heidelberg court to press the case for offering assistance to Calvinists in France. Reformed activists were influential in pushing for Frederick's 1569 marriage to the widow of Hendrik van Brederode, a leading follower of William of Orange and cousin of the prince of Condé, which was seen as evidence of Frederick's dedication to the international Reformed cause. Frederick indeed attempted to get agreement among German Calvinist and Lutheran princes for an active policy during the late 1560s. While Calvinists were willing to seek alliances with Lutherans to defend the 'Protestant cause' when it suited their interests, Lutherans proved reticent about being drawn into Calvinist battles. At a meeting at Erfurt in 1569 the major Lutheran princes of Saxony and Brandenburg remained cautious about disturbing the peace of the Empire, or of making any commitment to support foreign Calvinist rebels.[62]

Frederick nevertheless pressed ahead with military action in France. In 1567 Frederick had told the Emperor that it was his sacred duty to defend religious freedom in France, and sent his son Johann Casimir to France with an army of 11 000 men in alliance with Coligny and Condé, who pledged financial backing for the enterprise. This force saw little action before peace was agreed with the crown in 1568. In 1575 another treaty with the Huguenot leadership saw Johann Casimir return to France. This intervention was on condition of guarantees that the debts owed to Frederick from the 1567 campaign would be repaid, and that Johann Casimir would be given the governorship of Metz, Toul and Verdun. In December 1575 Johann Casimir led an army of 19 000 towards Paris, in a campaign which was significant in winning major concessions for the Huguenots by the peace of Beaulieu in 1576. Johann Casimir was then persuaded to drop his territorial claims, but the pension and rewards he was offered disappointed his expectations. Despite these uncomfortable realities of co-operation with the Huguenot nobility, the Palatinate court in 1576 declared that

> Our good Lord God, in order to help his Church, afflicted and oppressed by the tyranny of our day, has roused our lord the Prince-Elector Palatine to declare himself father and true sustainer of the Church, and our lord his son the duke Johann Casimir, twice to serve as another Joshua to those of the Reformed faith in France.[63]

From 1576 the Palatinate was ruled by Frederick's Lutheran son Ludwig, and new Calvinist alliances were only considered when Johann Casimir took over as regent for the minor Frederick IV in 1583. In 1587 Fabien von Dohna led an army of 35 000 men into France, but this huge force performed badly against Catholic League armies. During the late 1580s Christian I of Saxony also proved sympathetic to the cause of Calvinists outside the Empire, and in 1591 Saxony, the Palatinate and Hesse formed a new German Protestant alliance. With English financial support, a further force of 18 000 men was sent to France under Christian of Anhalt. This army again made little impact on the battlefield, and Henri of Navarre failed to repay his allies for their expenses. By the turn of the century the Palatine Electorate still claimed that it was owed between 750 000 and 850 000 livres by Henri IV for the costs of supporting armies which had come to his aid.[64]

The international outlook of Reformed courts was perhaps most strongly felt in the Empire. The ties between Reformed princes were strengthened by marriage alliances during the 1590s which linked the ruling house in the Palatinate, Johann VI of Nassau, and the duke of Bouillon. Some German princes converted from Lutheranism to Calvinism at least partly with the expectation of gaining diplomatic advantages by joining these allies. Heidelberg remained one central point in this network of princes. Kassel was another, where Maurice of Hesse encouraged foreign Calvinist students to come to his college from 1598, and then to remain in his service as envoys and diplomatic agents. The crisis over the succession of the Cleves-Jülich territories in the northern Rhineland became the focus of diplomacy in the Empire in the 1600s. Fearing that a Catholic succession would threaten co-operation between the Dutch Republic and Palatinate, an alliance was forged in 1604 to try to secure Jülich for the elector of Brandenburg. In 1608

Christian of Anhalt, governor of the Upper Palatinate, led a formal
Evangelical Union to defend Protestant interests against Bavarian and
Catholic power in the Empire. During the early 1610s this Union agreed
alliances with the Dutch Republic and Britain, and James I's daughter
Elizabeth was married to Frederick V of the Palatinate in 1613. While this
diplomatic activity was at least partly effective in the Rhineland, there
were also complaints about Christian of Anhalt's leadership of the
Evangelical Union, and disunity as princes pursued their own particular
interests.[65]

German Reformed princes not only looked north and west for allies
but were also active in the east, where after 1600 Habsburg and Catholic
power in central Europe was challenged by a loose coalition of Protestant
nobles and estates. The Calvinist István Bocskai led the Hungarian nobility in a successful revolt against Rudolf II in 1604. Bocskai's revolt gained
him the title of Transylvanian prince, and the Hungarian estates won
guarantees of religious freedoms for Calvinists and Lutherans.[66]
Protestant nobles in Bohemia, Moravia, Austria and Silesia also used the
battle for power between Rudolf and Matthias to gain statements which
permitted religious freedoms for Protestants in 1608 and 1609. There was
some degree of co-ordination across the region, and Christian of Anhalt
sent representatives to the Austrian and Bohemian estates. Leading
Protestant nobles across the Habsburg monarchy were also in contact
with one another, linked together by activists such as Karel von Žerotín
and the Austrian Calvinist Georg Tschernembl. By the 1610s, Protestants
feared that their hard-won legal liberties were being eroded by the
Habsburg court. The destruction of Protestant churches on crown lands
in Bohemia brought these fears to a point of crisis in 1618, and the
estates deposed Ferdinand. Protestant nobles in Lower Austria, Silesia
and Moravia joined the Bohemian estates' resistance and refused to
accept Ferdinand's rule.[67]

Frederick V of the Palatinate's acceptance of the Bohemian estates'
offer of the crown in August 1619 reflected his dynastic ambition as well
as his concern for Bohemian Protestantism. During the same month the
Transylvanian Reformed prince Gábor Bethlen advanced his army
against Habsburg forces in Hungary. Bethlen claimed to act in defence
of Protestant freedoms, but he also held ambitions for power in Hungary.
Bethlen's army swept across Royal Hungary in October 1619, and by the
end of the month Bohemian, Moravian, Hungarian and Transylvanian
forces were fighting a Habsburg army to the north of Vienna. A formal
alliance was agreed between Frederick, Bethlen, and the Bohemian and

Hungarian estates in April 1620. Gábor Bethlen sent 8000 troops to aid the Bohemian rebel forces, but the disaster at the White Mountain in November 1620 dramatically revealed the limited strength of the Protestant cause in the Habsburg monarchy. Frederick then hoped for help from western Europe to save the Palatinate from Spanish invasion, and his father-in-law James I was pledged to go to war should the Spanish army not withdraw. However, James reassured the Spanish court that he wanted to reach a peaceful settlement, and in April 1621 the Evangelical Union also abandoned Frederick. Frederick's only remaining allies were the dukes of Saxe-Weimar, Christian of Brunswick and Gábor Bethlen, and in December 1621 Bethlen also agreed to terms with Ferdinand.[68]

The record of diplomatic and military co-operation between Reformed courts is therefore a very mixed one, and interests of state usually prevailed over the religious ideals of princes. Attempts to form alliances during the 1610s ended with a series of terminal disasters for Calvinists in central Europe. Meanwhile the Dutch Republic faced renewed conflict against the Spanish from 1621. In France the early 1620s were marked by critical defeats and failed efforts to get meaningful external assistance. In 1620 Louis XIII's armies imposed Catholicism on Béarn, and citadels of the Protestant south at Montauban and La Rochelle later fell to royal sieges. In the midst of these disasters, James I responded to appeals for help only by promising to mediate on behalf of the Huguenots at the French court. British policy in the 1620s was a mixture of attempts to forge a marriage alliance with Spain, passivity, and injudicious activity at La Rochelle, none of which measured up to memories of past Elizabethan glories as political opponents of the court were swift to point out.[69]

Chapter 3: Politics and Rebellion

Calvinist reformers announced their desire to free individuals and communities from the tyranny of Rome so that they could live under the authority of Christ. Free Christians would be dependent only upon God, the true Church and God's appointed magistrates on earth. Reformers looked to those magistrates to help bring about necessary reforms in the Church, and to challenge the false claims to spiritual and secular power of the Pope and Catholic hierarchy. Calvinists' search for godly rulers who would lead societies to embrace true religion found some heroes including Jeanne d'Albret in Béarn, Frederick III in the Palatinate, Edward VI and Elizabeth I in England, James VI in Scotland and Johann Sigismund in Brandenburg. Jeanne d'Albret was repeatedly encouraged during the 1560s to establish Reformed religion in Béarn. Calvin wrote to the queen in 1563 warning of

> arguments advanced to prove that princes should not force their subjects to lead a Christian life ... but, all kingdoms which do not serve that of Jesus Christ are ruined, so judge for yourself.

Hopes about Jeanne's commitment to the Reformed cause were satisfied in 1570 when Catholic clergy were banished from Béarn. New church ordinances in Béarn of 1571 declared that 'there is no monarch alive who is not obligated to use his full powers to place his subjects under the rule of Jesus Christ'.[1]

Where Reformed churches received such active support from princes and magistrates, clergy responded by developing a cult of the godly ruler. Reformed magistrates were frequently showered by ministers with glowing comparisons to the faithful kings of Biblical Israel. However,

Calvinists were often faced with the problem of how to react when their lawful magistrate failed to act as a new David, Solomon, Hezekiah, Josiah or even Deborah.[2] Calvinists then turned to others in society with positions of public authority to promote reform and to offer protection against the Catholic church and hostile rulers. Godly nobles and magistrates were found in France, the Netherlands, in Scotland and in Hungary willing to play that role. However, the question arose as to what degree of resistance to royal authority could be justified even in the cause of defending true religion? Also, could ministers preach without legal permission, could individual believers break idols, form underground churches, release friends and neighbours from prisons, or ought Calvinists only passively to resist Catholic rulers and embrace martyrdom if necessary?

Although opponents made much of allegations about the seditious nature of Calvinism, political militancy and challenges to lawful authority were by no means intrinsic to Reformed thought. Reformed writers shared a clear understanding of the Bible which stressed the need for ordinary people to show absolute obedience to all established rulers. Where Reformed churches faced persecution from Catholic magistrates, they struggled to decide on how to respond appropriately to God's appointed lieutenants on earth. This chapter will focus on the development of Reformed political ideas about the powers of magistrates and about rights of resistance against lawful authorities. It will consider how Calvinist writers identified limits to royal power, and found a role for godly nobles, and, according to some, even for godly individuals, to act against tyrants and to punish idolaters. It will also suggest that the development of Calvinist theories of rights of political resistance highlights international connections between Reformed intellectuals. Activists exchanged ideas about rights of resistance and adapted existing arguments to provide answers to the different political problems which churches faced across the Continent.

Obedience to Princes

Leading reformers agreed that the Bible was clear about the need for Christians to obey their lawful rulers. Calvin wrote in the *Institutes of the Christian Religion* about the high authority granted by God to princes and about the requirement on ordinary people to obey them. Calvin argued that 'civil authority is not merely a holy and legitimate vocation, but by far the most sacred and honourable of all human vocations.' According to Calvin, magistrates were endowed with divine authority, and were responsible for protecting the true Church and pure doctrine.[3] The lectures given by Peter Martyr Vermigli at Strassburg, Zurich and Oxford, which were published after Martyr's death in 1576, contained his influential ideas about magisterial authority. For Martyr, when believers obeyed princes they obeyed God, and even evil regimes were instituted by God to punish the wickedness of the people and could not be challenged in any way. Martyr also stated that godly kings and magistrates ought to have 'the chief place in the church', able to correct any faults in the practice of religion in their territory.[4]

Martin Bucer shared this broad vision of the rights and powers of kings. At the invitation of archbishop Thomas Cranmer, Bucer moved to England in 1549, and in 1550 completed De Regno Christi which outlined a plan of reform for the young Edward VI to follow. Bucer advised Edward that bishops could not be trusted to reform the church in England. Rather the king should follow the worthy examples of David and Josiah who undertook the renewal of religion in Israel 'as a matter of royal right and duty'. Bucer advised Edward to set up a supreme council to implement reforms in the church and to oversee religious instruction across his kingdom. Once the Gospel had been preached, Bucer advised Edward to then pass 'holy' laws on education, morality and the practice of religion.[5] Bucer's vision of Edward as a model Christian governor concluded that the king should

> renew, institute, and establish the administration not only of religion but also of all other parts of the common life according to the purpose of Christ our Saviour and supreme King.[6]

Although reformers supported princely power in both secular and ecclesiastical affairs, Calvin also commented on the dangers to kings 'lest the height to which they are elevated should dazzle their eyes'. Calvin suggested to Edward VI in 1552 that 'it is a great thing to be a king, especially of such a country; yet I have no doubt but that you esteem it incomparably better to be a Christian'.[7] Calvin also wrote in the Institutes that because of the dangers of tyrannical rule by kings and of anarchy through popular rule, a mixed aristocratic form of government was probably the best of all. However, he stressed that whichever form of government had been appointed by God to each territory should not be challenged. Calvin warned, 'make no mistake: it is impossible to resist the magistrate without also resisting God'. Obedience was owed to rulers, 'even if the very last thing they do is to act like princes'. Calvin argued that when rulers gave in to the temptation to exert power without justice, their actions punished the iniquity of the people and 'all that has been assigned to us is to obey and suffer'.[8] This was a message which Calvin repeated in other tracts and sermons, on one occasion arguing that even if 'we were under Turks, under tyrants, and under the deadly enemies of the Gospel, yet is it commanded us to submit ourselves unto them. Why so? Even because it pleaseth God'.[9]

The last sections of Calvin's consideration of civil government in the *Institutes*, however, offered some limits to the obedience owed by local magistrates to princes. Calvin recalled that in ancient Sparta, ephors had been established to restrain the king. He suggested that 'perhaps' the estates of contemporary kingdoms might have a similar role in resisting the 'frenzy of kings'. Calvin also restricted the absolute obedience which was normally owed by ordinary people to their rulers by arguing that if a king commanded anything against God's will 'it must be as nothing to us'.[10] Martyr also looked to Spartan ephors as a precedent for the role of lesser magistrates in contemporary states. He too suggested that

> if the superior prince command the inferior magistrate to receive the Mass in their cities, undoubtedly they ought not to obey. If a man will say: he is the superior power, and therefore ought to be obeyed: I will answer, in things that be civil and human let him obey, as much as behoveth, but in no wise against God.[11]

Martyr's discussion of the powers of local magistrates was grounded in the political situation in the Empire after the 1548 Interim. Martyr was certain that private citizens could not take any action against this injustice, but allowed for territorial princes and urban magistrates to resist the Emperor's attempt to impose Catholicism.[12] He argued that since councillors were appointed to defend their cities, they could not permit idolatry to flourish as it would bring plague and famine to their communities. Martyr therefore argued that lesser magistrates could be empowered to act against a prince

> there be others in the commonweal, which in place and dignity are inferior unto princes, and yet in very deed do elect the superior power, and by certain laws do govern the commonweal: as at this day we see done by the Electors of the Empire: and perhaps the same is done in

other kingdoms. To these undoubtedly if the prince perform not his covenants and promises, it is lawful to constrain and bring him into order, and by force to compel him to perform conditions and covenants which he had promised, and that by war when it cannot be otherwise done.[13]

Calvin, Bucer and Martyr agreed about the complete obedience which was normally due to princes as God's appointed lieutenants on earth. However, ancient historical precedent and the constitutions of contemporary states were used to suggest that lesser magistrates could act against princes who broke their promises or who supported false religion. This right of resistance was most obvious in states where the ruler was elected and had agreed to certain conditions for his rule, but was also thought possibly to extend to kingdoms where coronation oaths expressed the duties of princes towards the estates of the realm. These arguments had first been deployed by Lutherans in the Empire. Philip Melanchthon had been clear about the obedience due to magistrates as ministers of God, even if they abused their power, ignored laws and became tyrants. However, when the city of Magdeburg led defiance of the Interim in 1548, the city's preachers declared in a 1550 *Confession* that it was the duty of lower authorities in the Empire to resist elected higher powers if they turned from godly rule to idolatry and the devil.[14]

Such arguments about the rights of lesser magistrates in the Empire were deployed by Martyr at Strassburg, by Calvin at Geneva and by Theodore Beza at Lausanne. In 1554 Beza suggested that if the Church was opposed by a cruel prince, believers should first take refuge in 'prayers and tears'. The faithful should depend on God, but inferior magistrates could act autonomously of princely power to defend pure religion. Beza suggested that 'a signal example of this has been shown in our times by Magdeburg'.[15] He added that when

several princes abuse their office, whoever still feels it necessary to refuse to use the Christian magistrates offered by God against external violence whether of the unfaithful or of heretics, I charge deprives the Church of God of a most useful, and (as often as it pleases the Lord) necessary defence.[16]

Beza's 1558 *Confession of Faith* again argued that if a ruler ignored the country's laws and ruled as a cruel tyrant, then individuals ought to respond by repenting for their own sins and praying for deliverance. Beza maintained, however, that those in positions of public authority, such as the seven Electors of the Empire or the estates of monarchies, were duty-bound to combat the outrages of tyrants.[17]

England and Scotland

Exiles from the Marian regime at Strassburg and Geneva were influenced by these arguments about the rights of lesser magistrates and applied them to the situation in England. John Ponet, formerly bishop of Winchester, arrived in Strassburg in 1554, where he wrote *A Short Treatise of Politike Power*. Ponet discussed how public officers in a kingdom should act as modern versions of Spartan ephors and ensure that kings did not oppress their people. Ponet suggested that

> kings, princes and other governors, albeit they are heads of a politic body, yet they are not the whole body. And though they be the chief members, yet they are but members: neither are the people ordained for them, but they are ordained for the people.[18]

Ponet believed that kings in England had at first been elected to rule and that, although the royal title later became hereditary, obedience to the crown remained conditional on royal commands being in accordance with God's will. Otherwise kings revealed themselves to be agents of the devil and nobles had a duty to act against their rule. Ponet also reflected on the implications of tyrannical rule for private individuals, leaving it as a matter of conscience for each person to decide whether God's glory would be served more by fleeing abroad or remaining at home and being persecuted and martyred. However, where nobles conspired with the prince, as they had apparently done in England, then Ponet suggested that private individuals might have just occasion to take up arms if they had some 'special inward commandment or surely proved motion of God'.[19]

Another exile from Marian England, Christopher Goodman, spent time at Strassburg, Frankfurt and Geneva, before later becoming the minister at Ayr in 1559. While at Geneva in 1558, Goodman published *How Superior powers ought to be obeyed of their subjects*. This tract again applied the logic of political ideas circulating in the Empire to the situation in England. Goodman argued that royal commands against God's will must not be obeyed, since kings were elected to rule according to

God's laws. Goodman questioned whether 'any man [is] naturally born a king, or hath he it of God?' The electors or estates in a kingdom were responsible for choosing a ruler who would promote God's laws, and they must avoid 'that monster in nature, and disorder among men, which is the Empire and government of a woman'.[20] Goodman therefore concluded that in England Mary Tudor's rule could not be seen as 'lawful by the word of God, but an express sign of God's wrath, and notable plague for the sins of the people'. Since the English estates had connived in the false authority of an idolatrous queen, Goodman decided that although

> it appear at the first sight a great disorder, that the people should take unto them the punishment of transgression, yet, when the magistrates and other officers cease to do their duty, they are is it were, without officers, yea, worse than if they had none at all, and then God giveth the sword into the people's hands, and he himself is become immediately their head.[21]

Another exile, John Knox, added his particular rhetorical ferocity to these arguments about the rights of nobles and ordinary people to resist tyrannical and idolatrous queens. Knox sought refuge at Frankfurt in 1554, before moving to Geneva in 1555, and then travelling to Scotland to appeal to Mary of Guise to support reform. After retreating from Scotland to France, Knox then returned again to Geneva in 1558.[22] Knox followed other Reformed writers in offering an idealised view of how godly princes ought to introduce religious reform and establish a covenant between God and their nation. Knox believed that Mary Tudor had broken England's covenant with God which Edward VI had established, and his rage against her government poured out in his 1558 *First Blast of the trumpet against the monstrous regiment of women*. Drawing arguments from nature, history and from scripture, Knox argued that to promote any woman to rule over men was 'repugnant to nature and a thing most contrarious to that order which God had approved in that commonwealth which He did institute and rule by His word'.[23]

Knox denounced both Mary of Guise's rejection of reform in Scotland and Mary Tudor's rebellion against reform in England. Knox wondered why the English were so blind that they could not see that 'where a woman reigneth, and papists bear authority, that there must needs Satan be president of the council'.[24] Knox acknowledged that in the history of Biblical Israel, Deborah had been granted exemption from the 'common malediction given to women'. However, he argued that

> when the males of the kingly stock failed, as oft as it chanced in Israel and sometimes in Judah, it never entered into the hearts of the people to choose and promote to honours any of the king's daughters..., but knowing God's vengeance to be poured forth upon the father by the away-taking of his sons, they had no further respect to his stock, but elected one man or other as they judged most apt for that honour and authority.[25]

Knox had no doubt that Mary, 'that horrible monster Jezebel', would face divine vengeance for her cruel and unjust hold on authority. For assuredly, he concluded, 'her empire and reign is a wall without foundation. I mean the same of the authority of all women.'[26] Knox's attack on the authority of women was a spectacular piece of bad timing in the year of Elizabeth's accession to power. Knox's subsequent failure to offer a full endorsement of Elizabeth's authority ensured his exclusion from any role in the English church. While Knox had completely failed to win endorsement for his views from either Calvin or Bullinger, and Beza explicitly opposed those who argued that women could never be given authority by God as magistrates, his work also badly compromised Elizabeth's relations with the Genevan church.[27]

Some returning exiles tried to undo some of the damage done by Knox to relations with Elizabeth. In 1559 John Aylmer, a former resident at Strassburg and later bishop of London, argued that God could ordain for some 'secret purpose' that a king might have no male heir, and that women could succeed in hereditary monarchies such as England. He also tried to play down the significance of Knox's views

> And though it be the property of northern blasts to coole and freeze: yet in the heart of good Christians, faithful subjects, and true Englishmen, well warmed with natural love, and defended with the walls of wisdom, obedience, and duty: it can do nothing.[28]

The *Geneva Bible* which was completed in 1560 was also loyally dedicated to Elizabeth. However, explanatory annotations on texts in the Bible suggested that rulers could not command people to oppose the word of God, and only stated that no 'private man' could oppose any government which God had appointed. These marginal notes only attracted more bitter criticism from archbishop Matthew Parker.[29]

In 1586 Thomas Bilson, who was later bishop of Winchester, tried to distinguish between Calvinist and Catholic political ideas in *The true difference between Christian subjection and unchristian rebellion.* Bilson defended Calvin's opinion that princes had no power to command their subjects in opposition to God's commands, and pointed out that Calvin had never argued in favour of popular armed resistance against rulers. Bilson suggested that discussions about rights of resistance in the Empire and Scotland only related to elected magistrates, and did not apply to England. Bilson also defended the actions of Henri of Navarre as a sovereign prince who did not owe 'simple subjection' to the Valois monarchy, and argued that Calvinists in the Netherlands had taken up defensive arms against the Pope's Inquisition and not against the laws of country. Bilson concluded by conceding, however, that no matter how terrible the provocation, where ordinary nobles had no legal right to take up arms to depose a prince, their actions could not be excused.[30] These attempts to break the association in England between Calvinism and immoderate politics largely failed. Richard Hooker was able to use ideas about politics as another reason to assert that the church in England should stand between the extremes of Rome and Geneva. Hooker dismissed suggestions that ancient practices of elective kingship were still evident in coronation ceremonies which alone granted sovereignty to England's kings. Hooker thought of these ideas as

> strange, untrue and unnatural conceits, set abroad by seedsmen of rebellion, only to animate unquiet spirits, and to feed them with a possibility of aspiring unto thrones and sceptres if they can win the hearts of the people ...[31]

In 1558 John Knox had turned his attention back to Scotland. Knox did not call on the nobility to remove Mary of Guise from power, but rather appealed to them to take on the responsibility to reform religion. Knox encouraged Scotland's nobles to be inspired by the examples of Josiah and Hezekiah to cleanse their country of idolatry. Knox warned the nobility that they were deceived if they thought that 'the reformation of religion and defence of the afflicted doth not appertain to you because you are no kings but nobles and estates of the realm'. Since Mary of Guise was failing in her responsibilities and giving commands contrary to God's laws, Knox argued that the nobility must act as 'bridles' to check her power.[32] In 1558 Knox also addressed the ordinary people of Scotland, instructing them that the 'reformation and care of religion' was also a matter for them:

> For albeit God hath put and ordained distinction and difference betwixt the king and subjects, betwixt the rulers and the common people, in

the regiment and administration of civil policies, yet in the hope of the life to come He hath made all equal.[33]

These radical calls for action in Scotland were only of limited significance in the unfolding rebellion against Mary of Guise. In 1559 the Lords of the Congregation justified their armed defiance of the regent by claiming they were 'compelled to take the sword of just defence against all that shall pursue us for the matter of religion'. The triumph of reform was secured when the assistance of English troops secured the withdrawal of the French army in June 1560, and in August 1560 the Scottish parliament outlawed the Mass. The Reformed church proclaimed in its 1560 *Confession* that anyone who conspired to overthrow the civil powers were 'not merely enemies to humanity but rebels against God's will'.[34] Reformers hoped that when Mary Stuart returned to Scotland she would prove willing to live up to her assigned role to maintain true religion and suppress idolatry. In 1561 Mary faced several lectures from Knox demanding that she abide by this image of godly rule. Knox told Mary that princes were often the 'most ignorant of all others in God's true religion', and that princes who attacked the children of God should be locked up until 'they be brought to a more sober mind'. While Knox did not repeat the assertions he had made in the *First Blast*, he contented himself by declaring that

if the realm find no inconvenience from the regiment of a woman, that which they approve shall I not further disallow than within my own breast, but shall be as well content to live under your Grace as Paul was to live under Nero.[35]

In June 1564 the general assembly in Scotland debated how to approach their relationship with Mary. Many ministers and nobles questioned the wisdom of Knox's prayer that God would 'purge the heart of the Queen's Majesty from the venom of idolatry, and deliver her from the bondage and thraldom of Satan'. However, Knox continued to defend the right to resist an idolatrous ruler, and backed up his claims by presenting the assembly with a copy of the 1550 Magdeburg *Confession*. In a proposal for a 'Second Blast', Knox had also returned to the lessons learned in the Empire, when he explained that an election and not 'birth only or propinquity of blood' made a king. Knox suggested that if an elected king broke the conditions of his election and persecuted the true church, then the estates had the right to depose him.[36]

Knox was not the only writer to set out ideas about a contractual relationship between the kings and nobles of Scotland. John Mair's *History of Greater Britain* had asserted in the 1520s that Scottish nobles could act on behalf of the people to remove a king whom they had appointed. One of Mair's students, George Buchanan, developed these ideas in *The Right of the Kingdom in Scotland*. Buchanan's work was written before Mary Stuart's deposition in favour of James VI, although Mary's conduct rather than Buchanan's arguments determined her fate. Buchanan, who tutored James VI in the 1570s, argued that the powers of Scotland's kings were derived from the community and were limited by the country's laws. Buchanan suggested that Scotland's monarchs had at first been elected from among the relatives of the reigning king, until Kenneth III introduced a law of succession by primogeniture during the tenth century. Although Scotland's kings thereafter gained power by hereditary right, Buchanan argued that the principle of mutual consent between ruler and ruled remained in place and was symbolised by the promises made by Scotland's kings at their coronations. A monarch could therefore be held to account by the nobility for any failure to abide by these promises.[37]

Rather than develop such theories of the limits of elective royal power in Scotland, or continue to battle against their monarch, more than anything the general assembly wanted Scotland to be granted a godly monarch who would advance true religion. In 1579 they appealed to James to purge the church of all corruption as a 'singular instrument' of God. When at times James seemed to be living up to the kirk's image of godly kingship, he received enthusiastic support. In 1590 James told the assembly that he praised God 'that he was born in such a time, as in the time of the light of the Gospel, to such a place as to be King, in such a Kirk, the sincerest Kirk in the world'. The assembly so rejoiced at hearing this, 'that there was nothing but loud praising of God, and praying for the King, for a quarter of an hour'.[38] However, when James was seen to be too lenient towards Catholic nobles, Andrew Melville voiced the harsh line taken earlier by Knox, announcing to James in 1586 that he was but 'God's sillie vassall', and a subject of Christ who truly reigned over Scotland's spiritual realm. James proved extremely reluctant to take lectures from any ministers on the extent of his powers. In 1598 James absolutely refuted claims that royal sovereignty was derived from elections, coronation oaths or contracts between the king and the people, and maintained that God alone was the judge of how well kings discharged their offices. James also warned his son about pests who taught that kings and princes were natural enemies of the liberty of the church.[39] James also proved to have a long memory, and in 1606 Andrew Melville was called to London to explain his opposition to episcopacy, was first imprisoned and then forced into exile at Sedan until his death.[40]

France

In 1559 the French *Confession* committed the Reformed church to respect public magistrates as God's lieutenants, 'whom he has commissioned to exercise a legitimate and holy authority' over civil and religious matters.[41] This outlook on politics in the Reformed church in France was heavily influenced by the works of Calvin and Beza. Another important figure was Pierre Viret, who stressed the obligation on Christians to obey their king so long as this did 'not affect adversely or infringe in any way upon one's salvation or the glory of God'.[42] The Reformed church in France also responded to the practical problems of life under a Catholic monarch. In 1560 the national synod debated the limits of obedience to the lawful authorities, and whether ministers could preach without any sanction to do so from local magistrates. The synod concluded that while this was permissible, ministers should ensure that public order was maintained, and prevent any disturbances from breaking out as a result of their preaching.[43]

When the Huguenot noble party took up arms in 1562, their leaders claimed to be fighting not against the twelve-year-old Charles IX but rather against his regency council under Catherine de Medici. This same justification for action had been used by the conspirators of Amboise after their failed bid in 1560 to seize the sixteen-year-old François II from the control of François de Guise. However, arguments that the Huguenot nobility were not actually rebelling against their monarch became more difficult to sustain when the civil wars started again in 1567 and in 1568. Huguenot writers then began to consider theories which offered justifications for resisting the direct commands of their king. Towards the end of the 1560s Jean de Coras, chancellor to Jeanne d'Albret, suggested that the French estates did not owe blind obedience to their kings. Coras argued that kings gained authority over public administration and national defence only on condition that they governed according to the laws of the country. Coras suggested that this obligation was established by the coronation oaths which kings swore, which he believed symbolised their election to office.[44]

In the aftermath of the massacres of 1572, the organisation of Huguenot resistance to the crown developed with regular meetings of an assembly in southern France to co-ordinate political and military plans. Huguenot political writing reflected increasingly bitter responses to the violent persecution which Calvinists were suffering. Propagandists appealed for foreign intervention by Protestant princes to aid the Huguenot cause.[45] Some writers still primarily blamed the king's advisors, and particularly the Guises, for inspiring the massacres of Huguenots. In 1576 Innocent Gentillet, a refugee in Geneva, argued that it was Catherine de Medici who was the source of a Machiavellian and Italian infection of French politics.[46] Other writers faced the need to produce credible justifications for noble resistance against their apparently tyrannical king. François Hotman had begun to investigate the origins and extent of royal power in France before the events of 1572. In 1573 his *Francogallia* was published in Geneva, dedicated by Hotman to Frederick III of the Palatinate. Hotman had left France during the late 1540s for Lausanne and Geneva. He then lived in Strassburg during the mid-1550s, at the same time when Peter Martyr Vermigli and John Ponet were resident in the city. Hotman returned to France in 1562, joining Beza at Orléans in the camp of Louis, prince of Condé. Hotman was then caught up in the civil wars, surviving the siege of Sancerre before fleeing again to Geneva in 1572.[47]

Although Hotman was a long-standing political activist and agent for the Huguenot cause, the Genevan authorities mistook his text for a dry history of the French constitution. In fact, Hotman attempted to demonstrate in *Francogallia* that sovereignty in France was shared between the king and the estates. Hotman based this conclusion on his rather dubious discovery that the laws of the early French kingdom were based upon the elective traditions of Germanic tribes. Hotman suggested that France's kings had at first been elected on condition that they maintained the liberties of the people, and that a public council held the right to force kings to abdicate if they broke the conditions of their rule.[48]

While Hotman did not suggest that France should return to these early practices of electing kings, he believed that the coronation oaths which French kings swore provided a continuing public demonstration of the mutual obligations which existed between kings and the nobility. According to Hotman, obedience to royal authority in France therefore remained conditional on whether a king abided by the promises which he had made at his coronation.[49] Hotman's discussion of royal sovereignty in France also dealt with the right of women to rule. Hotman suggested that France's history showed that 'whenever women got into their hands the procuration of the kingdom, they have been always the occasion of wonderful tragedies'. Hotman argued that when any power was held by royal widows, regents or queen mothers it led to disastrous consequences for France. His message to Catherine de Medici could hardly have been made more clearly; 'she, who cannot be queen in her own right, can never have any power of governing in another's right.'[50]

Theodore Beza returned to the subject of monarchical power in 1574, and his book *On the right of magistrates over their subjects* had already been published in ten editions by 1581. Beza offered examples of how figures such as Spartan ephors and imperial electors could remove rulers from office if they broke the conditions of their authority. These conditions were established through coronation oaths or through promises which kings gave on their election. According to Beza, this was also the case in the history of Israel, in which 'although the crown, by God's ordinance was hereditary in the house of David, the people, as long as they were free, chose as they pleased among the children of a deceased king'.[51] Beza also claimed that the kings of France did not only reign by right of succession, since no king could gain power without a meeting of the estates to gain the consent of the people. He therefore concluded that if

> the king, hereditary, or elective, clearly goes back on the conditions without which he would not have been recognised and acknowledged, can there be any doubt that the lesser magistrates of the kingdom, of the cities, and of the provinces, the administration of which they have received from the sovereignty itself, are free of their oath, at least to the extent that they are entitled to resist flagrant oppression of the realm which they swore to defend and protect.[52]

Therefore, according to Beza, armed rebellion could be organised by public authorities in France against a king who was judged to have abandoned the fundamental laws of the kingdom. While private individuals who were persecuted for their faith still had no defence against royal power, Beza pointed out that once the king issued edicts offering rights to Huguenots to exercise their religion, then he was bound to respect those laws or would be judged a tyrant.[53]

In 1574 Nicolas Barnaud from Dauphiné called for true patriots to liberate France from tyranny. He followed the established line of argument already developed among Calvinists that the authority of kings was limited by laws and conditions which reflected mutual obligations between the king and his subjects. Barnaud asserted the right of the French estates not only to appoint kings but also to dismiss tyrants. Barnaud argued that if the king issued evil edicts, obedience was no longer required, since

> people have never been so stupid or ill-advised as to give anyone sovereign power ... without keeping a good strong bridle, for fear that royalty may fall, as on a slippery road, into tyranny.

Barnaud recommended that the best means to avoid tyrannical rule would be for France to elect its kings from candidates within the ruling house. Barnaud highlighted the advantages of elective monarchy by citing the example of Poland. Barnaud suggested that although Poland faced dangers under the rule of Henri, duke of Anjou, the Polish estates had at least been able to impose the condition on Anjou to investigate the causes of the massacres in France and to punish those responsible.[54]

Another Huguenot tract which advocated elective monarchy was completed in 1574 or 1575. When it was published in 1579 *A Vindication of Liberty against Tyrants* was attributed to Philippe Duplessis-Mornay, one of Henri of Navarre's advisors and later governor of Saumur. This tract joined other Huguenot works in asserting that true royal power was derived from elections:

> The sons and relatives of kings sometimes seem to have rendered a kingdom hereditary, and in certain regions the right of free elections almost seems no longer to exist. And yet in all properly constituted kingdoms, the practice still remains inviolate.[55]

The purpose of elections 'was less to give the people a choice than to remind rulers of their obligation' to rule justly and according to the laws of the country. Mornay suggested that the remnant of the early practice of electing kings in France could still be seen in an oath sworn by kings before they were anointed or crowned. The coronation of kings was for Mornay the moment at which a covenant was established between God and the king, and between the king and his people. Kings who later broke their covenant with the people were tyrants, and officers of the kingdom were obliged to resist their authority. While Mornay argued that private citizens must remain passive until called to act by a public magistrate, he judged that it was possible for individuals to be called by God to initiate resistance against tyrants.[56]

Ideas about the elective character of kingship and the conditional nature of royal sovereignty were not only promoted by some Huguenot writers. Supporters of the Catholic League such as Jean Boucher also suggested that kings could be held to account if they broke their promise to defend the Catholic church.[57] However, the notion that the authority of French kings was derived from the consent of the people was challenged by a number of writers, and most notably by Jean Bodin. For Bodin, the principal mark of royal sovereignty was the right to impose laws on all subjects regardless of whether they consented to the laws or not. No royal subject could ever be justified in taking any action against their ruler, even when a prince's commands opposed the laws of God. Bodin advised flight or being killed rather than rebellion against a prince. Bodin also directly challenged the grounds upon which Reformed writers had allowed for the right of magistrates to resist kings. He denied any historic basis for the elective character of the French monarchy, and asserted that stable government only came from hereditary succession in the male line of a ruling family.[58]

Most Huguenot writers on politics restricted the option of active resistance to a tyrant to the estates and nobility. François Hotman advised that private subjects could only offer passive submission to the commands of the Valois authorities. He gave an example from Lyon of what was expected of ordinary Huguenots:

There was in that same Archbishop's prison an aged man called François Collut, a merchant of caps, and two young men his sons, whom he had ever caused diligently to be taught and instructed in religion. When he saw the butchers come toward him with their axes, he began to exhort his children not to refuse the death offered by God. For (said he) it is the perpetual destiny of religion, and that often such sacrifices do betide in Christian churches, and Christians in all ages have ever been and for ever to the world's end so shall be as sheep among wolves, doves among hawks, and sacrifices among priests. Then the old father embraced his two young sons, and lying flat on the ground with them, crying aloud upon the mercy of God, was with many wounds both he and his sons slaughtered by those butchers, and long time afterward their three bodies had knit together and yielded a piteous spectacle to many that beheld them.[59]

The fate of those who passively resisted Catholic persecution was also the focus of the renowned martyrologies compiled by Jean Crespin in

France, by Adriaan van Haemstede in the Netherlands and by John Foxe in England. These martyrologists identified recent victims of Catholic regimes as following those who had died for true faith from the time of the Apostles. The blood of contemporary martyrs was therefore used as proof of the historic authenticity of Reformed religion.[60] The first editions of Jean Crespin's work dwelt on early Calvinist casualties, including five students from Lausanne executed at Lyon in 1553 and five ministers executed at Chambéry in 1555. The details which Crespin provided about the confrontations between Calvinists and Catholic official interrogators at heresy trials were intended to reveal not only the physical courage and spiritual assurance of Reformed martyrs but also the intellectual superiority of Reformed beliefs. For example, François Richardot, the bishop of Arras, apparently responded to Guy de Brès' explanation of Reformed sacramental theology by saying that while he personally agreed with the Reformed understanding of scripture, it did not matter because he must believe what the Roman authorities told him to believe.[61]

By the 1570s there was no shortage of victims in France for Crespin to choose from, as he claimed that the events of St Bartholomew's day in 1572 led to the deaths of 30 000 people. The powerful impact of Crespin's text did not rely alone on his enumeration of a catalogue of Catholic violence. His narratives depicted heart-rending scenes of the idealised deaths of individual martyrs. The unimaginable cruelty of Catholic mobs in Orléans was juxtaposed by Crespin with the behaviour of their innocent victims, who sang Psalms before they were murdered. In Paris, Crespin described how Pierre de la Place prepared his household for death by gathering them together to hear a chapter of Job read from the Bible and to listen to Calvin's commentary on the passage about the justice and mercy of God.[62] Crespin's martyrology included many such stories of the courageous deaths of both contemporary Reformed leaders and of ordinary men and women. The popularity of his work was such that Beza felt the need to point out that not only passive victims of Catholic cruelty deserved to be remembered

> we must honour as martyrs not only those who have conquered without resistance, and by patience only, against tyrants who have persecuted the truth, but those also who, authorised by law and by competent authorities, devoted their strength to the defence of the true religion.[63]

While Crespin's martyrology provided exemplary models to 'instruct and console the faithful' in France, Beza was anxious to ensure that nobles who took up arms against tyranny were also recognised as equally faithful servants of the Reformed cause.

The Netherlands

The rebellion of nobles and towns in the Netherlands faced many comparable problems to the struggle of Huguenot nobles in France. There were also close links between clergy and activists from the two churches. However, of all the Reformed churches which faced persecution from Catholic rulers, the Dutch proved the most reticent to produce theories which justified the actions of rebellious nobles. Dutch synods refrained from comment on rights of resistance against the Spanish authorities, and the 1561 Belgic *Confession* of Guy de Brès instructed the faithful to submit to the authorities in 'all things which are not repugnant to the Word of God'.[64] Discussion of what actions public magistrates and individuals could take in response to the religious and political repression of the Spanish regime at first focused on immediate and practical problems. During the 1560s Reformed ministers debated whether they were justified in arranging illegal church gatherings or in breaking images and statues in churches. In 1562 the consistory of the exile church in London was posed questions by Calvinists in Antwerp as to whether they could carry arms for self-defence or to inspire fear among their enemies, and whether they could organise prison-breaks. The reply from the London ministers permitted their brethren in Antwerp to carry arms as long as they did not attack their persecutors. However, they advised against using violence to free prisoners, suggesting instead using false keys or other peaceful means to rescue fellow believers.[65]

Philip Marnix, who advised William of Orange during the late 1560s, was also cautious in his 1567 *True narrative and apology of the events taken place in the Netherlands concerning the issue of religion.* Marnix argued that the dramatic violence and iconoclasm of 1566 was certainly not the fault of the Reformed church. He also encouraged Reformed clergy to preach to their congregations about the need for obedience to the lawful authorities. By 1568 the violent attempts made by the Spanish authorities to suppress noble dissent and heresy, however, brought Marnix to agree that William had the right to act based on the traditional privileges of the provinces of the Netherlands. Above all the rebel party could point to the 1356 *Joyeuse Entrée,* an agreement made with the dukes of Brabant that their sovereignty was conditional on ruling according to set conditions. William of Orange saw this as a historic contract between the nobility and their ruler which Philip II had broken, and which permitted armed resistance to defend noble freedoms, urban privileges and the laws of the country.[66]

The violence of Alva's repression through the Council of Troubles after 1567 stiffened the resistance of many rebels in their fight for survival up to the Pacification of Ghent in 1576. When the peace agreed between the States General and Philip broke down in 1577, Marnix again argued that the customary laws of the Netherlands meant that if a prince abused his power and broke the conditions of his rule, then the people could choose a new governor to rule until the prince's mistakes were corrected.[67] Some of the ideas articulated by Reformed writers elsewhere about rights of resistance and the conditional sovereignty of elected monarchs then finally emerged in the Netherlands from the late 1570s. Philippe Duplessis-Mornay was among those who composed a 1581 *Apology* as a response to Philip's edict banishing William of Orange in 1580. This *Apology* supported William's right as a sovereign prince to take up arms against the Spanish king. It also defended the right of nobles in the Netherlands to act as 'ephors of Sparta', and to protect their country from tyranny and injustice.[68] In July 1581 the States General of the northern provinces announced that the king of Spain had forfeited sovereignty because of his tyrannical rule. This Act of Abjuration insisted that Philip had broken the conditions of his authority, and so 'in his stead another must be elected to be an overlord'.[69]

In 1581 the Brabant Calvinist Gerard Prouninck advised the northern provinces to adopt an elective monarchy, so that 'if the most recent ruler committed faults or were deceitful, this can be redressed by a new election'.[70] Prouninck expressed this concern about the need to limit the powers of princes in the context of Spanish rule, but by 1586 he had become an enthusiastic supporter of the earl of Leicester as Elizabeth's governor-general in the northern provinces. Prouninck then warned Leicester's critics that:

> Naval experience teaches us that in a storm a ship at sea must be navigated by a single helmsman of high rank. We would wish to be too wise and clever were we to presume, without regard to God's ordinances, to provide against all the faults of princes and kings.[71]

Military necessity had forced the States General to turn to François, duke of Alençon in 1581 and then to Elizabeth in 1585 with offers of sovereignty over the northern provinces. Calvinists supported Leicester's regime in an effort to counterbalance the power of the States of Holland, which blocked efforts to expand the role of the Reformed church in the new state. Gerard Prouninck's earlier concern to limit the powers of any sovereign over the northern provinces was certainly long forgotten by 1586. Prouninck was installed by Leicester as the new head of Utrecht's council, after a violent purge of regents who had opposed consistorial discipline and supported a tolerant policy towards Catholics in the town. Reformed politics in the Netherlands, as elsewhere, was driven primarily by the perceived interests of the church, and arguments about rights of resistance to monarchs were only advanced until Calvinists found a godly ruler to support.

The Empire and Central Europe

Reformed churches in the Empire were often established by princely courts, and so German Reformed clergy and writers had little reason to ponder the potential limits of the power of their territorial rulers. Ideas about the rights of inferior magistrates to resist the tyranny of higher authorities were rather deployed by Calvinists in favour of the autonomy of Reformed territorial rulers against their Catholic Emperor.[72] However, in some circumstances, Reformed churches in the Empire were threatened by territorial rulers, and appeals were then made to a familiar mixture of ideas about local community rights and the conditional nature of sovereign power. In 1603 Johannes Althusius published his *Politics methodically set forth*, which served the cause of the Emden council in its battle to protect Reformed church liberties from encroachment by the counts of East Friesland. Althusius had taught at the Herborn academy before accepting an invitation to move to Emden. He drew on the historic rights of the town to set out the theory that kings could only exercise the rights of sovereignty conceded to them by a commonwealth. He argued that 'kings are constituted by the people for the sake of the people', and that the public estates of the realm had a duty to resist tyranny. Kings were therefore chosen by election, although according to Althusius in some commonwealths this had become restricted to a certain family and considered as held by right of succession. Althusius, however, thought that the best form of government was where the estates chose from among the children and family of a deceased magistrate.[73]

The resistance of nobles in Hungary to their Habsburg king Rudolf provided a further echo of Reformed theories of rights of resistance.

Rudolf's attempt to suppress Protestant worship in Royal Hungary and to gain control over the Transylvanian principality was challenged in 1604 when the Reformed noble István Bocskai led armed resistance in eastern Hungary. Bocskai declared in an *Apology* that his aims in the revolt were 'the maintenance of ourselves, our nation's life and, further, of our religion, liberty, and property'. He appealed to the historic right of Hungarian nobles to resist any ruler who ignored their privileges.[74] Leading Reformed clergy such as Péter Alvinczi supported Bocskai's challenge to the Habsburg court. When Bocskai was elected as ruling prince of Hungary in April 1605 and as prince of Transylvania in September 1605, Bocskai was depicted by clergy as a divinely appointed liberator of Hungary from tyranny, and acclaimed as 'Moses of the Hungarians'. Bocskai himself sent word to Rudolf that;

> God has been with me in this; account for my position through my acting on God's secret counsel; like Moses from his shepherding, David from the sheep-pen, like the fleeing Jehoshaphat, whom God made prince and king over His people.[75]

Calvinists across the Continent supported the right of monarchs to reform the Church. Magistrates were charged to uphold the laws of their territories with justice and to promote the practice of true religion. Where Calvinists lived under princes who, more or less, discharged these responsibilities, they responded with idealised visions of the benefits of godly monarchy. However, many Reformed churches faced persecution from Catholic kings. Most Reformed writers responded by advising ordinary people to respond only with passive resistance or to flee into exile. However, ideas first articulated in the Empire about the conditional loyalty required of lesser magistrates in the face of elected rulers who had become tyrants also circulated among Reformed writers. Taken together with local traditions in many territories about the reciprocal responsibilities between princes and estates, this formed a potent brew of ideas about rights of resistance. Calvinists in Scotland and France in particular discovered elective traditions in their own history, and appealed to nobles to act for the community to ensure that monarchs lived by the conditions of their offices. Calvinists offered a broad latitude to nobles and estates to take part in armed resistance against monarchs who broke God's laws and the customary laws of the country. If noble action failed, then some writers were even prepared to consider a role for popular action in politics to depose a tyrant.

The practical impact of this Reformed literature on political resistance was mostly limited to offering theoretical cover for the planned or current activities of nobles in France, the Netherlands, Scotland and Hungary. However, expressing ideas on rights of resistance led to antagonism between churches and Reformed rulers such as James VI and Elizabeth. Most Huguenots also found the texts published on politics during the 1570s an embarrassment by the early seventeenth century when it was in their interest to support royal power and cling to the provisions of the 1598 edict of Nantes. However, when occasion demanded, ideas about rights of resistance against monarchs who broke the conditions of their rule returned to prominence, as in France during the 1620s or in Britain during the 1640s. In 1644 Samuel Rutherford returned to ideas long familiar among Calvinists across Europe when he wrote in favour of monarchy, but a monarchy where royal power was limited by obligations to law and the community. For Rutherford, 'he who is made king by suffrages of the people, must be more principally king, than he who hath no title, but the womb of his mother'.[76]

Chapter 4: Moral Discipline

All churches during the sixteenth century promoted their understanding of the fundamentals of Christian faith and demanded high standards of moral behaviour from their adherents. Where possible, clergy sought the support of civil authorities to assist in their efforts to enforce religious uniformity and moral discipline on ordinary people. Many of the alliances forged between clergy and princes or urban magistrates not only defended the orthodoxy of one church but also outlawed the practice of minority religions. Church institutions and state bureaucracies used schools, printed propaganda, censorship laws, and a regime of spiritual and secular sanctions in efforts to regulate church life, suppress alternative opinions and traditional forms of religiosity, and to introduce a more standard form of religious experience.[1]

All of this activity benefited not only official churches but also could bolster the position of territorial rulers, as churches lost their autonomy and clergy supported magistrates' claims to power. Some historians have indeed written of this emerging relationship between territorial rulers and Catholic, Lutheran and Reformed churches as a parallel pattern of confessionalization which was essential to the growth of early modern state power.[2] However, there were also risks for both parties in these confessional alliances between churches and states. Ordinary people were not merely passive victims of princely authority, religious indoctrination and the spiritual sanctions of churches. Communities were capable of taking the initiative for themselves in programmes of self-regulation and discipline, largely or entirely autonomous of state power. Minority religions survived in many territories, and state action against their followers risked provoking radical political opposition to rulers.

Although all three of the major confessions of western Europe promoted orthodox beliefs and enforced moral standards of behaviour, Reformed churches remained distinctive in the level of attention and effort which they gave to monitoring popular opinions and punishing lapses in personal conduct. Calvinists' efforts to tighten standards of moral discipline were based on the work of parish bodies, variously called consistories, presbyteries and kirk sessions, which were set up in many parts of the Continent. Local ministers and appointed elders sat in weekly meetings to decide on the appropriate punishment of a wide variety of offences committed by members of congregations. Where possible, Reformed churches exercised moral and social discipline in co-operation with territorial rulers and urban councils. However, Calvin insisted on a wide degree of autonomy for parish disciplinary institutions, and in particular argued for their right to exclude offenders from membership of the church. In territories where Calvinists were allied to sympathetic princes, such claims for independent powers for the church led to suspicions at courts about the potential challenge of consistories and synods to secular authority. On the other hand, where Reformed churches were opposed by Catholic rulers, the system of consistories allowed the beliefs and behaviour of Reformed congregations to be regulated without relying on state support.[3]

This chapter will set out the form of church government which Calvin introduced to Geneva. Many territorial churches adopted Calvin's pattern of church offices, and set up local consistories under the authority of district classes, provincial synods and national synods. However, these ideas about church government and about the role of parish elders in punishing moral offences were not adopted by all Reformed churches. Some churches retained clergy hierarchies, while others left punishment of offences to civil magistrates, and the powers of elders and rights of synods were debated and contested in many churches. The impact of these efforts by Reformed churches to enforce high standards of personal morality will also be discussed in this chapter, and the problems of assessing the effectiveness of the disciplinary campaigns waged by elders and consistories will be considered.

Consistories

Moral discipline was at the heart of Reformed religion and the enforcement of morality was a key objective of Reformed church institutions and officials. This may seem contradictory since the performance of good works played no role in the Reformed scheme of salvation. While Christians were not believed to rely on living well to gain salvation, avoiding sinful behaviour was, for Theodore Beza, a sure testimony to conscience that Christ reigned in the believer.[4] According to the *Heidelberg Catechism*, believers were drawn to moral behaviour out of gratitude of being redeemed from sin, and 'reverent behaviour' also acted as a witness to 'win our neighbours to Christ'.[5] Reformers believed that true Christians lived moral lives, and that the government of the Church ought to be structured in accordance with Biblical principles to assist believers in their personal battle against sin and to protect congregations from immoral and heretical influences.

At Geneva, the power of the prince-bishop had been overthrown before Calvin's arrival in the city. While there was agreement between the council and reformers on rejecting episcopal authority in Geneva, gaining consensus on how the church should be governed proved much less easy to achieve. In 1538 the council decided to adopt the same church order as that of Bern, which placed the regulation of morality firmly under the authority of magistrates. Calvin was banished from Geneva, and moved to Strassburg where he worked in the French refugee church until 1541. Calvin's ideas about church government were heavily influenced during this period by Martin Bucer, who was trying to persuade the Strassburg council to allow clergy to reprimand parishioners about their conduct before they could participate in Communion.[6] While Calvin also supported the right of clergy to admonish offenders and to exclude unrepentant sinners from membership of the church, he did not aim to form perfect gathered communities. Calvin indeed attacked those who behaved as if they were some sort of spiritual and moral elite, and in 1544 argued that

> when under the colour of a zeal of perfection we can bear no imperfection, either in the body or in the members of the church, it is the devil which puffeth us up in pride and seduceth us with hypocrisy.[7]

On Calvin's return to Geneva in 1541 he insisted that he could not properly fulfil his ministry, unless, 'along with Christian doctrine, a regular presbytery with full ecclesiastical authority was established'. This demand for a consistory to be set up was accepted by the city council in the 1541 *Ecclesiastical Ordinances*. These ordinances set out four church offices of a doctor, minister, elder and deacon. Doctors were to study and teach church doctrine, ministers to preach the word of God and administer the sacraments, elders to 'supervise every person's conduct' and warn 'backsliders and those of disorderly life' in a 'friendly fashion', while deacons were responsible for the administration of relief to the poor. The ministers of the Company of Pastors and 12 elders met as a consistory, with the elders chosen from among the city's councillors each February.[8] Elders were selected after consultations between the clergy and the city's executive Small Council, and could remain in their posts for several years. Elders were required to deal with those who offended against norms of moral conduct first by issuing private warnings, then by giving public rebukes in front of the consistory and finally by excluding those who showed no sign of repentance from membership of the church. The objective at each point in this system of spiritual discipline was for the offender to express sincere repentance of their wrongdoing and to dedicate themselves not to repeat their offence.[9]

The leaders of the early exile churches in London and Emden also appointed elders and established consistories to uphold standards of discipline in their congregations. A consistory was established by Johannes à Lasco in the church at Emden in 1544, and selected elders were given responsibility for moral discipline in the London congregation during the 1550s.[10] The church in France adopted the consistorial system, and consistories began to be set up from the mid-1550s. The 1571 Emden synod of the Dutch church also accepted that each congregation should form a council of the minister, elders and deacons to preserve true religion, propagate true doctrine, agree spiritual punishments for moral offences, and to relieve the distress of the poor. Elders were instructed first to give private warnings to offenders about their behaviour before any formal warnings were issued in front of the consistory. The Dutch church also claimed the right to exclude serious offenders from access to Holy Communion, and district classes were given the responsibility to pronounce sentences of excommunication.[11]

In territories governed by Reformed rulers, churches looked to cooperate with local magistrates to enforce moral discipline on congregations. The church in Scotland adopted a system of parish kirk sessions, and the 1560 *First Book of Discipline* envisaged elders as being 'men of best knowledge in Gods word and cleanest life', who punished faults which the 'civil sword either doth neglect or not punish'.[12] In the kingdom of Béarn, the ecclesiastical ordinances approved by Jeanne d'Albret in 1571 gave power to the church to enforce its disciplinary standards. However, members of consistories took their oaths of office before local magistrates and the church's powers remained under the ultimate authority of their sovereign.[13] In Calvinist states in the Empire, Reformed clergy inherited Lutheran patterns of church government through superintendents and state councils. Congregational presbyteries were set up in the Palatinate and in Nassau, but these bodies remained under the overall control of state councils made up of clergy and civil officials. In Bremen a new church order in 1595 offered greater autonomy to the city's morals' court but, as elsewhere in the Empire, the punishment of offences remained under the close supervision of secular magistrates.[14]

The ultimate spiritual sanction at the disposal of Reformed churches was to suspend or excommunicate church members. People were prevented from participating in Communion services if they did not accept the discipline of the church or were deemed not to understand the meaning of the sacrament. The right of the consistory in Geneva to exercise this power without reference to the city council was contested by a Perrinist party of some of the city's leading families. Opposition to the consistory mounted during the 1540s and early 1550s as elders turned their attention to a series of moral campaigns in the city. While Perrinists attacked the pretensions of foreign clergy and the influence of French refugees in Geneva, Calvin preached against 'Libertines' who, he claimed, wished to evade proper moral discipline. On one occasion Calvin declared that he would rather 'die sooner than this hand shall stretch forth the sacred things of the Lord to those who have been judged despisers'. Beza recalled that after Calvin had spoken, Holy Communion 'was celebrated with extraordinary silence, not without some degree of trembling, as if the Deity himself were actually present'.[15] In December 1554 Calvin again spoke of his shame at the perceived immorality of Genevans, declaring that 'if it were left to my own wishes, I would desire God to take me out of the world, that I might not have to live for three days in the disorder that is here'.[16] In the end the Perrinist faction on the council was defeated in January 1555 when Calvin's supporters gained power in the Small Council. Thereafter, the exercise of moral discipline tightened in the city with a rising tide of excommunications, and the terminal defeat of Calvin's opponents in Geneva also allowed him to turn more of his attention to affairs outside the city.

The importance of the right of consistories to establish controls over who had access to Communion was accepted across most of the Reformed world. According to the 1563 *Heidelberg Catechism*, if unbelievers were admitted to Communion God's covenant would be profaned and his wrath provoked against the whole congregation. Thus, only those who are 'displeased with themselves for their sins', and who 'desire more and more to strengthen their faith and improve their life' ought to come to the Lord's table.[17] The 1560 Scots *Confession* agreed that only those inspired by the Holy Spirit to fight against sin could participate in Communion. Before Communion services, ministers and elders in Scotland were instructed to examine the faith and conduct of church members. All those who did not understand the purpose of the sacrament, who had no faith or who did not show 'peace and goodwill to their brethren' were to be excluded from taking part.[18]

Churches took practical measures to ensure that only those who were supposed to participate actually gained access to Communion services. In various churches across the Continent tokens were distributed by clergy and elders to those permitted to attend. At St Andrews, the minister gave the names of those allowed to receive Communion to the clerk of the kirk session, who wrote out named tickets for each person. Elders distributed the tickets which were then collected at the church door, and anyone found with a forged ticket faced punishment. Occasionally the elders noticed fake tickets, as in July 1583 when John Huniman confessed that he had received a forged ticket, and Andrew Brown admitted he had brought his master's ticket to church. In 1590 the session tried to combat fraud and paid Patrick Guthrie to make 2000 iron tokens. In 1599 the session also decided not to give tickets to anyone who had not paid their contribution to the poor. By 1600, the system used at St Andrews had been refined still further, and tickets were distributed which had the name of the communicant, their elder, and a mark to indicate which service each person was supposed to attend to receive Communion.[19]

Alternative Systems of Discipline

While consistorial discipline became integral to Reformed community life in many parts of the Continent, this was not true of all churches. The church at Zurich maintained an alternative approach to discipline, under church ordinances which were redrafted after the disaster of Kappel in 1531. Under the leadership of Heinrich Bullinger, Zurich's clergy were charged to preach the Gospel and to look after the pastoral needs of their congregations. Meanwhile the civil authorities retained supervision over the operation of discipline, and moral offences were punished by a court which remained under the control of the city council.[20] The magistrates of Basel and Bern followed the example set by

Zurich, and Bernese influence was decisive in the pattern of church government adopted in the Pays de Vaud in 1537. Ministers in the Pays de Vaud only had limited powers to chide offenders, but from the late 1540s this position was challenged by many clergy led by Pierre Viret at Lausanne. In 1558 Viret refused to hold any more Communion services until the Lausanne consistory was able to control access to Communion. When Viret's appeal to the Bernese magistrates to allow the Lausanne consistory to excommunicate offenders was rejected, Viret, Beza and around 30 other ministers resigned their posts and left Lausanne.[21]

In his 1566 *Second Helvetic Confession* Heinrich Bullinger warned against rash judgements to exclude people from membership of the church, and opposition to the use of such powers by consistories was also raised in the Palatinate.[22] Under 1564 ordinances the Palatinate Reformed church came under the control of a state council made up of three ministers and three princely officials. Frederick III was encouraged by Caspar Olevian and other Reformed clergy and advisors that the church should have the autonomous right to punish moral offenders and to excommunicate its members when appropriate. However, another voice within Frederick's court argued that the enforcement of moral discipline was in fact a matter for magistrates alone. In 1568 Thomas Erastus suggested that churches which were supported by Christian rulers had no need of any 'new kind of tribunal' to punish the people. Erastus also argued that there was no scriptural basis for forbidding someone to participate in Communion. However, in 1570 under new church ordinances Frederick approved the formation of parish consistories with the right to warn offenders, and of a synod with the right to decide on sentences of excommunication. However, the synod's activities and the government of the Palatinate church remained under the overall control of the state council of clergy and secular officials.[23]

In the Reformed churches of the Polish–Lithuanian Commonwealth and the former Hungarian kingdom there were no appointed lay officials to regulate discipline in congregations. Ministers alone were responsible for enforcing standards of morality, under the supervision of provincial synods and superintendents who conducted visitations of local parishes.[24] Clergy in Hungary worked together with noble patrons to respond to wrongdoing with a mixed pattern of spiritual sanctions, fines and physical punishments. By the early seventeenth century some Hungarian ministers, including many who had travelled to study in the Dutch Republic and England, began to agitate for parish presbyteries to be set up to provide tighter controls over the moral life of congregations. Presbyteries

were introduced in a Reformed church province of Habsburg Hungary
in the 1610s, but when a Presbyterian clergy party pressed for action in
the Transylvanian principality they were opposed by the Reformed
prince, György I Rákóczi. Leading advocates of parish presbyteries such
as János Tolnai Dali and Pál Medgyesi set out their understanding of the
Biblical basis for the offices of elders and deacons, and presented the
practical advantages which they perceived presbyteries could bring to
Reformed communities. However, the Transylvanian prince's concerns
about the political implications of such communal bodies could not be
assuaged, and a national synod called in 1646 to discuss the issue decided
against changing the government of the church.[25]

Similar arguments had been played out in England during the late sixteenth century, when a minority clergy party and their lay supporters
pressed for an end to episcopal government and for presbyteries to be
introduced. Leading English Presbyterians, Thomas Cartwright and
Walter Travers, had both spent time in Geneva during the early 1570s,
and external influences were clear from the arguments which they
advanced. In 1573 Cartwright inquired of those bishops who had spent
time abroad during Mary's reign, 'in which of the reformed churches saw
they a Lord bishop allowed?'[26] Walter Travers meanwhile claimed scriptural backing for parish presbyteries, and argued that the appointment of
elders with the right to excommunicate offenders would provide tighter
controls over moral behaviour than was possible through the old church
courts.[27] The challenge posed by Presbyterians to the episcopal order in
England reached its peak during the 1580s. In 1583 articles were introduced which upheld the established form of church government, and
any ministers who refused to accept them were suspended from their
posts. Despite this attempt to suppress Presbyterian initiatives, some
parish bodies and regional classes were established during the 1580s. For
example, at Northampton the mayor, councillors, clergy and appointed
elders met on Thursdays to discuss any disciplinary cases in the town.
Elders were also given the responsibility to visit church members before
they were permitted to gain access to Communion. Ministers attended
regular meetings of a local classis to confer over church business, and
supporters claimed that the beneficial results of this project were visible
in the piety and morality of the people of Northampton.[28]

Although the challenge mounted by the Presbyterian party in England
was defeated after a crackdown in 1590 against its leaders, advocates of
episcopal government remained strident in their defence of the established order. In 1590 Matthew Sutcliffe, the dean of Exeter, denounced

any prospect of lay involvement in decision-making in the church, and denied that Geneva's four church offices had any Biblical basis. For Sutcliffe, parish presbyteries also savoured too much of popular government and were incompatible with royal power. Sutcliffe was particularly dismissive of the potential role of parish elders, claiming that excommunications would 'fly out upon every light grudge'. He ridiculed the prospect that

> the common sort abandoning their trades, intrude into the government, and from the butchers stall or tailors shop-board ascend to the highest tribunal in the church: and from the tribunal of excommunication, return to the mattock, the spade, or their thatching ladder.[29]

Something of an English parochial mentality, if not admiration for parochial discipline, was also betrayed by Richard Bancroft's 1593 assertion that the English church had nothing to learn from the disciplinary practices of foreign churches. The later bishop of London and archbishop of Canterbury, prayed

> unto almighty God with all my very soul, for the long and happy continuance of this blessed example, which this Church and realm of England hath shewed in this last age of the world, unto all the kingdoms and countries in the earth, that profess the Gospel with any sincerity: and that also of his infinite mercy, not only the kingdoms of France and Scotland: but all other Christian kingdoms and countries may taste so plentifully of his heavenly graces. ...[30]

Bancroft tried to undermine the case for presbyteries by highlighting variations between the forms of government used in different Reformed churches, and quoted Calvin's support for episcopacy in a letter to the Polish king. Bancroft blamed Beza, not Calvin's equal in 'learning or virtue', and the Scots, for stirring up some in England to attack the role of bishops in the church.[31] Bancroft's attack on the 'pretended holy discipline' of Geneva defended English episcopacy as 'more Apostolical than any other form of government, that I know in any other reformed Church in the world'. Here, Bancroft still accepted England's place within the Reformed world, although he argued elsewhere that the English church was under attack from both Rome and Geneva, which was a 'new Papacie' for 'consistorians'. Richard Hooker went even further in trying to recast the English church as separate from the rest of the

Reformed world. While conceding that most 'daughter churches do speak the mother's dialect', Hooker denied that the English church was obliged to follow Geneva on questions of discipline. Hooker wanted diversity between

> both kinds of reformation, as well this moderate kind, which the church of England hath taken, as that other more extreme and rigorous which certain churches elsewhere have better liked.[32]

By the early decades of the seventeenth century such assertions of English distinctiveness, and arguments that episcopacy was the only form of church government which had divine authority had gained ground in England. They were noisily promoted in particular by a rising party of clergy who also defended the English church's ceremonial practices and advanced Arminian criticisms of Reformed orthodoxy.[33]

Synods and Magistrates

Territorial Reformed churches which introduced consistories also had to establish a structure of government above the level of the parish. All of Geneva's city churches and surrounding rural parishes came under the authority of a single consistory. However, after taking Calvin's advice, the church in France established a consistory in each parish, which sent representatives to local classes. The French church *Discipline* envisaged these local meetings being held four times a year as a forum for discussion between ministers, mutual support between parishes, and mediation of any disputes between pastors and their congregations. Parishes also sent their minister and an elder to one of around sixteen provincial synods which were supposed to meet twice a year. These synods in turn sent delegates to the French national synod, which held the power to make definitive judgements over all church affairs.[34]

This hierarchy of synods was criticised by those who supported more autonomy for individual pastors and their consistories. Jean Morély argued that only loose links were needed between parishes, and suggested only limited powers for district classes and provincial synods. Morély proposed, for example, that local communities should retain the right to select their own minister, rather than having that power rest with synods and classes.[35] Morély's ideas were quickly labelled as 'wicked doctrine' by the 1562 French national synod, which concluded that they would lead to confusion and disorder in the church. In 1563 Morély was excommunicated by the consistory in Geneva, and forced to retract his opinions by his own provincial synod in France. The 1563 national synod also confirmed that provincial synods should continue to approve the appointment of parish clergy. However, Morély's stand for the rights of local communities against synodal power won support from some Reformed nobles. In 1565 the national synod was compelled to consider his ideas again, but concluded that 'delivering up the government of the church unto the people' would lead to confusion and endanger the church.[36]

The 1571 Emden synod also adopted a system of district classes, provincial synods and a national synod for the Dutch church. Classes were supposed to meet at least four times a year to discuss any business relating to the work of local clergy, and to hear any disciplinary cases referred to it by parish consistories. However, this assertion by the Reformed church of the powers of its synods was contested by magistrates in the northern Dutch provinces. The Reformed church became the acknowledged public church of the northern provinces, and the Mass was banned in Holland in 1573 and in Utrecht in 1580. However, magistrates in many northern towns argued strongly that they had not rebelled against Catholic ecclesiastical power simply to hand authority over to Reformed clergy. Not only magisterial backing but also popular support for life under Reformed discipline was limited in the northern provinces. A minority of the population of northern towns attended Reformed churches, and an even smaller proportion accepted consistorial discipline and were considered as members of the Reformed church. Between the 1570s and 1610s the proportion of Reformed church members in the Dutch Republic did grow, aided by the arrival of committed Reformed refugees from the southern provinces, but still only ranged between one fifth and one quarter of the population of many towns in Holland, Utrecht and Friesland.[37]

The 1581 Middelburg national synod was forced to acknowledge that since the civil authorities of the northern provinces supported the Reformed church they must be allowed a say in the appointment of clergy. However, the synod defended the autonomous powers of parish consistories and the authority of district classes and synods.[38] The magistrates of Leiden complained about the presumption of the delegates at the Middelburg synod, inquiring 'tell us, gentlemen of the synod, by what authority you pretend to introduce your decrees?' The Leiden magistrates pointed to the synod's new list of prohibited books as a sign that they were usurping magisterial power and restoring a form of Papal authority. The ministers and elders of Holland responded that the Middelburg synod's decrees were not imposed upon anyone but had been submitted to the States for examination. They also demanded that magistrates, and especially those who were not Calvinists, should not be allowed to exercise unreasonable authority over the Reformed church.[39]

While some town governments worked well alongside the consistories and classes of the Reformed church, magistrates in Leiden and Utrecht in particular fought against a church structure which they believed limited local religious liberty. At Utrecht, magistrates supported the alternative vision of an inclusive and autonomous local church under Hubert Duifhuis during the 1570s. There was no provision at Utrecht for regulating access to Communion, and consistorian Calvinists attacked this as Libertinism.[40] Calvinists looked for central political support against local regents who defied orthodoxy and discipline, and who showed too much tolerance towards Catholics. They received support from Leicester's regime after 1585, which purged Utrecht's council and dissolved Duifhuis' former congregation. However, Reformed assertions of synodal authority continued to be stoutly resisted by many urban magistrates, and the church was not sanctioned by the States General to hold a national synod between 1586 and 1618.

The pattern of church organisation in Scotland was also uncertain and contested. After 1567, the Reformed church was supported by both crown and parliament. However, the ministers, nobles and urban officials who met in general assemblies still struggled to secure access to the land and wealth of the old church which was needed to support a new preaching ministry. A compromise scheme of the early 1570s allowed surviving bishops to remain in their posts alongside some district superintendents. However, there was opposition to this role for bishops in the church, and Beza wrote to John Knox in 1572 encouraging action to subdue the 'pestilence' of bishops.[41] From the late 1570s a clergy party led by Andrew Melville, who had returned to Scotland from Geneva in 1574, pushed for district presbyteries and provincial synods to replace the surviving clergy hierarchy. Melville's party proposed a new order of church government through the 1578 *Second Book of Discipline*, which rejected episcopacy outright, advocated the introduction of governing district presbyteries, and sought to limit attendance at general assemblies of the church to clergy and elders.[42]

In 1580 the general assembly agreed that the order of bishops had no Biblical warrant and demanded that bishops abandon their 'pretended offices'. In 1581 the assembly adopted the *Second Book of Discipline* and implemented a pilot scheme of 13 presbyteries to co-ordinate the work of parish kirk sessions.[43] The work of presbyteries was then disrupted by the 1584 Black Acts, which confirmed the place of bishops in the church. Then, in 1586, both bishops and presbyteries were endorsed in a compromise agreement. Despite this confusion, more presbyteries were organised across the country, their authority over parish clergy slowly increased during the 1580s and 1590s, and the powers of presbyteries were finally given legal recognition by the so-called Golden Acts of 1592.[44] While the work of parish kirk sessions received strong support from magistrates, there was, however, continuing tension between the court and the church's presbyteries and synods. Presbyterians demanded autonomy for the church's institutions over spiritual affairs, but James VI perceived that growing clerical power formed a challenge to royal authority. James encouraged the gradual revival of episcopacy in Scotland from the late 1590s as a means of exerting control over the activities of presbyteries and the general assembly. Assemblies were packed with supporters of the king and episcopacy from 1606 to ensure that bishops gained the right to decide on excommunications, controlled the appointment of clergy and acted as moderators of their local presbyteries. Once James had got his way, the general assembly was itself sidelined, and no assemblies were held between 1618 and 1638.[45]

Life under Discipline

The kirk session at St Andrews in Scotland met on Wednesdays to decide on the appropriate punishment for a range of offences committed by members of their congregation. They dealt with cases relating to fornication, adultery, slander, swearing, violent behaviour and public disputes. The elders also punished those who failed to attend church on Sundays, and paid increasing attention to the problems of illicit work and recreation on Sundays, which included playing golf on the local links.[46] The kirk session handed serious cases over to the town's magistrates, who imposed fines and periods of imprisonment on offenders. The elders punished other offences themselves according to the guidance laid down by the 1564 *Book of Common Order.*[47]

The St Andrews kirk session first gave private warnings to people to amend their conduct. If this failed to have an impact, offenders were then called to appear before the kirk session. If this still failed to produce any sign of repentance and a change in lifestyle, or if the session deemed the offence serious enough to merit further punishment, individuals were then called to be admonished before the whole congregation from the stool of repentance, and had to offer public repentance for their sins.[48] For example, in December 1564 John Richardson's challenge to church discipline was punished by his having to stand in front of the pulpit for an hour before the Sunday service while wearing a paper sign on his head describing his offence. Such symbolic punishments were supported by the general assembly in Scotland, which in 1569 ordered that those doing public penance for serious sins should appear bareheaded or wearing sackcloth.[49] In the most serious cases, and very exceptionally, the session at St Andrews excommunicated unrepentant offenders who persistently held the church's discipline in contempt, excluding them from access to Communion and cutting them off from contact with the rest of the community.[50]

In May 1587 the kirk session appointed two bell-men, Andrew Sellar and Alan Robertson. The bell-men were instructed to keep the church clean, look after the clock and to ring the church bell every day at five in the morning, and at five and eight in the evening, and to alert the congregation when a sermon was about to start. Sellar and Robertson were also asked to make sure that church services were not disturbed by any noise, especially by children inside the church or by dogs left outside. They were also charged to distribute bread to the poor of the parish at the direction of the church deacons. Andrew Sellar proved good at his job, for which he received annual payment, and worked for the kirk session for seven years.[51] During these years the kirk session undertook a rigorous campaign to tighten moral discipline in their town of around 2500 people. The dozen or so serving elders often used Andrew Sellar to help them in their work. When the session wanted to issue private warnings to members of the congregation about their conduct, they dispatched Sellar to pass on their decisions. The session also regularly sent Sellar to inform offenders that they must perform public repentance before the whole congregation. Sellar's word was critical to the operation of the session's disciplinary work. If Sellar verified that someone had received a first private warning about their conduct, and the elders saw no subsequent improvement in that individual's behaviour, then the session moved to the next stage of disciplinary action, a public warning. Sellar's name frequently appears in the session's records, and his word condemned recalcitrant offenders to further punishment at the hands of the session. For example, in 1590 Sellar confirmed that he had personally

charged Alan Lentron and Elspeth Bicarton to appear wearing sackcloth
at the stool of penitence in the church, but they had failed to turn up.
Sellar was dispatched by the elders to tell the offenders to appear the following Sunday or face public denunciation.[52]

The first hint of any tension between Sellar and the elders came in
1593. Sellar was asked to agree that if anyone was found in the church-
yard drying wool or corn, or sawing trees, then he would have to pay a
fine to the poor box.[53] Perhaps this incentive scheme had the desired
effect on Sellar's effectiveness, and he continued to work for the session
until the early months of 1594, when his name disappears from the session records. Then, in April 1595 the elders noted that Andrew Sellar was
convicted for ungodly and irreverent behaviour at a meeting of the session. He was required to sit on the stool of repentance in front of the pulpit while wearing sackcloth, and to ask God, the session, and the
congregation for their forgiveness.[54] Whatever Sellar's original offence
had been, his defiance before the session led to this public humiliation.
Had Sellar's years of service encouraged him to speak too boldly before
the elders? These were in any case turbulent years for the St Andrews
church, and within a year the serving ministers David Black and Robert
Wallace, and some of the elders were themselves discharged from their
offices. The reaction of the wider community to Sellar's appearance at
the stool of repentance can also only be guessed at. Sellar, who had for
years scolded noisy children in church and reprimanded their parents,
and who had brought shame to homes when he knocked on doors bringing news of the session's orders, now felt the humiliation of public repentance. Perhaps there were many in the congregation who made sure they
turned up that Sunday to see Sellar on the stool of repentance, but other
friends who hoped that he would soon be restored to a place of respect
within the Christian community.

Public rituals of repentance were feared weapons in the church's disciplinary arsenal, as Sellar above all knew from confronting many people
who tried to avoid such punishments. They were intended to act as a
deterrent to immorality, but also to be occasions which inspired genuine
repentance and the reconciliation of disputes. Sellar may have walked
back into church the Sunday following his appearance on the stool of
repentance a chastened man or a bitter man. At any rate, the relentless
operation of discipline in St Andrews caught up with Sellar again in June
1596. Sellar's final appearance in the session records suggests that in
place of being respected by the town's leading men in the session, Sellar
found comfort and sociability with his old friend Alan Robertson. Both

men were charged with drunkenness, and required to 'make public humiliation'.[55]

The *Discipline* of the church in France explained that for a local church to be properly ordered, the minister and congregation must choose elders and deacons. Once a consistory was established, its existing members could co-opt new elders. Elders were instructed to watch over their neighbourhood, to report any scandals to the consistory, and deal with any matters relating to the good order and government of the parish church. The *Discipline* also set out a process of graded responses to offences from informal warnings to a formal appearance before the consistory, to temporary suspension from the sacraments, and ultimately to excommunication. Elders were instructed carefully to examine the faults of offenders and the circumstances of offences before deciding whether or not to suspend a church member. They were not to publicise the reasons for any suspensions, except in the most extreme cases. When suspended members gave clear proof to the consistory of their repentance, they were then to be publicly reconciled with the church and readmitted to Communion. Only the obstinate and unrepentant were to be completely excommunicated from the church after three Sundays of public warnings.[56]

Evidence from surviving records of consistory meetings in France shows the level of attention which elders gave to the task of disciplining individual church members. For example, the elders of the small consistory in the village of Coutras near Bordeaux spent a considerable amount of time and effort trying to get the Maupille family to behave themselves. The business of the Coutras consistory was dominated during the early 1580s by problems caused by contact between their community and local Catholics, and by cases relating to sexual misconduct, violence, arguments, drinking, blasphemy and banned forms of recreation.[57] The Maupille family were regular attenders on Wednesday meetings of the consistory. In October 1581 the draper Jean Maupille appeared before the consistory for having quarrelled with one of his neighbours. On 18 November 1582 Maupille was one of four people called to the consistory and charged with the offence of dancing. At the same meeting an elder received a complaint from the chambermaid of Maupille's son, Jean, about his behaviour but no action was recorded. The elders were perhaps not entirely convinced by the story, and chose to use discretion in their minutes. On 9 December 1582 Jean Maupille's son was again one of three men called to the consistory following a public dispute between them, and they were reconciled with one another in front of the elders. On 26 December 1582 Jean Maupille senior and his wife, 'despite all warnings', were called for a second time to account for their dancing. Evidently Jean Maupille did not give the elders a satisfactory response, and when he got into further trouble the consistory suspended him from Communion on 19 January 1583 for his disobedience and scandalous life.[58]

Dancing was viewed as a serious social problem by the French Reformed church. The 1560 national synod had first proscribed dancing, and allowed for offenders to be excommunicated if they refused to abide by warnings from consistories not to dance. Dancing was specifically prohibited by the church *Discipline*, and in 1581 the national synod repeated its concern about the prevalence of dancing within Reformed congregations. Consistories were ordered to punish anyone who was discovered dancing, which was associated both with sexual scandal and with traditional Catholic festivities. According to a 1580 tract by the French-born, Genevan minister Lambert Daneau, dancing was a completely inappropriate form of recreation for Christians because it led to both vanity and sexual temptation both for participants and observers.[59]

The Coutras elders did not meet Jean Maupille again until 18 May 1583, and were unimpressed that it had taken Maupille so long to appear before them to repent. They also alleged that despite many warnings he had continued to dance. Although Maupille acknowledged his faults, the consistory judged that he had not shown himself to be 'sharply touched by repentance' and told him to come back the next week to give a more satisfactory response to his sins. On 25 May 1583 Maupille turned up again at the consistory to confess his faults, but the consistory clearly remained unconvinced by Maupille's performance. They decided that he should make a public confession of his faults the next Sunday in church. Maupille duly publicly confessed to his offences, but on 8 June Maupille was back before the consistory. Just after his confession of sin before God and the church, and his declaration that he would no longer commit such faults, he had been spotted dancing. The elders were frustrated and angry with Maupille, but their patience had not yet been completely worn out. They gave Maupille a 'grave warning', and told him that although he merited being excommunicated from the church they were only going to suspend him from Communion, on condition that if he ever fell back into his old ways he would be thrown out of the church for certain. Then, Maupille suddenly drops out of the Coutras records, perhaps, finally a reformed character.[60]

The elders of the French exile church at Threadneedle street in London were equally diligent in their efforts to ensure that the changing membership of their congregation lived within the bounds of Reformed discipline. During the reign of Edward VI, the church order of Johannes à Lasco had provided for elders and deacons to be appointed in the London church.[61] The role of elders in maintaining discipline among existing church members and in screening new members was also laid out by Nicolas des Gallars in his 1561 order for the London church.[62] The clergy and elders issued frequent warnings about problems relating to marriage and sexual conduct, drinking, disputes and public scandals. The London consistory could respond to serious offences by suspending any of its 300 to 400 members during the early 1560s, but only infrequently needed to turn to the bishop of London to pass sentences of excommunication.[63]

The elders of the French-speaking church insisted that new members of their congregation must provide written evidence of their standing in their previous church in France before they could take part in Communion services. Some tried to evade this system. In February 1564 the consistory accused Lezim Lambert of having presented them with a forged testimony from his previous church at Caen. Lambert confessed to having counterfeited the signature of the Caen minister, saying that he did not think he would receive a recommendation from Caen because of past problems with his wife. The consistory was relentless in protecting the reputation of their church and the purity of its sacraments. By the summer of 1565 correspondence with France had revealed that Lambert had also falsified a letter of testimony from Orléans when he moved to Caen, and that he was a bigamist. In September 1565 Lambert was brought before the consistory and ordered to return to Caen.[64] During the early 1570s the size of the French congregation in London grew rapidly to around 1700 members. The consistory maintained the need to check on all new arrivals, and many were reprimanded for having attended Catholic Mass before fleeing to England and were required to acknowledge their fault before gaining access to Communion.[65]

The London elders also spent a great deal of time and effort trying to resolve difficult individual cases. Nicolas Bizeau was called before the consistory in July 1564 and asked why he had not attended Communion for some time. The elders distributed tokens to those allowed to participate in the sacrament, which meant not only that they prevented offenders and outsiders from taking part but also allowed for checks on church members who avoided Communion services. Bizeau answered that he had not felt prepared to participate in the sacrament. When pressed by the elders for his reasons, Bizeau only replied that he did not know.[66] In September 1564 Bizeau came back to the consistory to ask for his child to be baptised. The consistory first required him to confirm that he was a member of the Reformed church. Bizeau responded that he belonged to the church of Jesus Christ, and approved of the doctrine of the Reformed church. He was told to prepare to take Communion the following Sunday and then his child would be baptised. However, Bizeau instead took his child for baptism at his local London parish church.

In March 1565 the consistory returned to Bizeau's case and demanded that he recognise the authority of the French church and make public repentance for his lack of obedience to the consistory. Martin de Ligne, Jean Caulier and other church members intervened on Bizeau's behalf with minister Jean Cousin. They asked Cousin to treat Bizeau gently, hoping thereby to win him over. Antoine de Ponchel, the consistory clerk, noted darkly that Bizeau had been dealt with 'too gently' already. However, when the consistory next met with Bizeau, they gave him a further week to consider his need for repentance and obedience. Bizeau returned to the consistory with Caulier, de Ligne, Pierre Doucet and Thomas des Camps. Bizeau repented of his faults before the consistory and asked for forgiveness from those whom he had offended, apparently including des Camps with whom he had some dispute. The elders, however, demanded that Bizeau make a full and public repentance of all his faults. Bizeau agreed to repent of his offences before the congregation the following Sunday. However, when the minister pressed Bizeau during the Sunday service to acknowledge that he would in future follow the discipline of the church, he replied 'only that he would do his best'. Bizeau's case shows the perseverance of the elders to resolve all the cases which appeared before them, but also points to the limits of what consistories could achieve. The consistory succeeded in gaining a public statement of repentance from Nicolas Bizeau, but their records do not reveal whether the elders really understood what had prevented Bizeau from receiving Communion. Was he merely another backslider, or did Bizeau's friends know something of his troubled conscience which meant he felt he could only say he would try to obey the church's discipline and did not feel worthy to take Communion?[67]

The Impact of Discipline

The disciplinary cases of Andrew Sellar in St Andrews, Jean Maupille in Coutras and Nicolas Bizeau in London are only three individual examples of the operation of Reformed church discipline from parishes with good surviving records. These cases reveal a lot about how church officers went about their work, and give a strong sense of the ideals and processes of Reformed discipline. Despite the relatively detailed records of the experiences of these three men, many questions remain. Did public humiliation prove too much for Sellar to take, and drive him to drink? Did Jean Maupille really stop dancing? Did Nicolas Bizeau continue to doubt his place within the Christian community? These three men drop out of their local church records, but should this be taken to mean that they thereafter lived exemplary lives, and had internalised the need to accept the moral standards of the Reformed church as enforced by local clergy and elders? Some answers to these questions would be required to assess whether the exercise of church discipline across a large part of Reformed Europe affected the behaviour at least, and perhaps even the beliefs, of ordinary parishioners such as Sellar, Maupille and Bizeau.

In efforts to understand the impact of Reformed discipline, historians have subjected the records of many consistories across the Continent to close analysis. Disciplinary cases have been counted and classified to reveal the proportion of different offences committed by congregations, and to view the long-term impact of Reformed discipline on local communities. This work has highlighted key questions about the operation of consistorial discipline: to what extent were all Reformed communities subjected to the same level of moral discipline?; how often was the sentence of excommunication used?; what differences emerge between the application of moral discipline against men and women, people who lived in towns and the countryside, the social elite and ordinary people?; were Reformed discipliners more interested in controlling how people behaved rather than what they believed?; what was the proportion of offences relating to marriage, sexual conduct, violence, swearing and other moral offences?; and how effective was consistorial discipline in altering the beliefs and behaviour of Reformed congregations over time?

The effective exercise of consistorial discipline depended first upon the presence and ability of the local minister. Most Reformed churches struggled to provide enough qualified clergy for their parishes, especially in the countryside. In France, many rural churches only moved slowly towards having a resident minister and working consistory. The Dutch church experienced similar problems with a lack of trained clergy, and vacancies were gradually filled by graduates from the new universities and colleges in the Republic. For example, the classis of Dordrecht included 30 towns and villages, but by 1580 only 5 churches had working consistories, and by 1590 this total had still only risen to 15. Across Scotland, and not only in the Highlands, there was also a considerable shortage of qualified ministers, and in 1596 the general assembly claimed that over 400 Scottish parishes still lacked a resident minister.[68]

Even where parishes had resident clergy, the ability of some ministers to perform their difficult role as agents of moral discipline within their communities must be doubted. If ministers were to be effective disci-pliners of their congregations, then they needed to maintain a certain distance from the rest of their community even if that led to some popu-lar expressions of hostility and resentment towards them. Some sense of the distinct social position required of Reformed clergy was expressed by John Cameron, the exiled Scottish minister at Bordeaux. Cameron wrote in 1610 that he had no intimacy with members of his church and pre-ferred to be thought of as a shepherd of sheep than as a brother among brethren. It seemed to Cameron

> that propriety requires that he [the minister] should not mix up with them, except in the exercise of his ministerial duties, either when preaching in public, or when censuring before the consistory, or when exhorting and catechising from house to house …. I like the pastor to be revered.[69]

The emergence of a class of Reformed ministers able to behave in this way, and to perform their functions effectively in parishes took time. Ministers were certainly becoming more distinct from the rest of the community by virtue of their level of education. Calvinist clergy were also often set apart from their neighbours by their social origins, and in the Rhineland, Hungary and elsewhere a strong pattern developed of Reformed ministers being drawn from clergy families. Regular meetings of classes and synods acted to reinforce a sense among clergy of belong-ing to a professional body with a shared role in society. The isolated position of Reformed clergy within their communities remained most acute in churches which did not set up consistories. In Hungary, ministers were repeatedly instructed by superintendents and synods to act as exam-ples to the rest of the parish in their everyday conduct and use of language. Church articles agreed by an eastern Hungarian synod in 1577 forbade ministers from going into taverns, since they were supposed to provide a example of sobriety to their community. These articles also permitted min-isters to attend decent wedding celebrations, but if dancing began they were to get up and leave the room immediately. With such demands made upon them to remain distinct from local social life, clergy were heavily reliant on their archdeacons and superintendents for support, particularly during any disputes with their congregations.[70]

Variations in the provision of trained clergy able to enforce moral discipline, and the variety of social and political environments of Reformed churches, meant that some communities came under much closer moral supervision and were subject to more frequent punishment of offences than others. At Geneva during the 1560s elders called one in every fifteen adult church members to appear before them each year. While two-thirds of those called before the Genevan consistory received only a reprimand, in a city of over 20 000 people, over 2000 people were excommunicated from the church between 1564 and 1569. During this period the consistory was issuing about five excommunications a week for a wide range of offences including quarrelling, blasphemy and sexual misconduct. This rate of exclusions was much higher than during previous decades in Geneva when the powers of the consistory were contested by Perrinists. The number of excommunications in Geneva was also much higher than elsewhere on the Continent. While one in every 25 Genevans was excommunicated each year during the mid-1560s, at Montauban during the 1590s the consistory excommunicated only 1 in every 140–150 church members each year. In rural French communities in the Midi the rate of appearances by church members in front of village consistories and of excommunications was also substantially lower than in Geneva. At the village of St Gervais only three people were excommunicated between 1564 and 1568. Elsewhere the sanction of excommunication was also only infrequently carried out by consistories. At Delft there were less than ten cases of final excommunication between 1572 and 1640, and at Amsterdam only 33 people were excommunicated between 1578 and 1700. So while it became almost routine for people to be excluded, even if only temporarily, from church membership in Geneva, across the Continent excommunication mostly remained a rare and exemplary punishment reserved for serious offences.[71]

The speed with which consistories and presbyteries were established and the effectiveness of their operation also depended on the degree of support offered by magistrates. The uncertain role of district presbyteries in the Scottish church resulted in problems in getting offenders to obey their instructions. One-third of offenders called to appear before Stirling district presbytery failed to turn up during the early 1580s.[72] The active support of the local social elite for the work of consistories was also vital in order to ensure widespread acceptance of their demands. Elders in towns were commonly drawn from the better educated and more

wealthy residents, and councillors, merchants, lawyers and doctors came
to dominate kirk sessions and consistories from Edinburgh to Nîmes.
The co-option of new elders meant that many consistories had a stable
membership, and in rural areas ministers were also keen to retain competent and dedicated members of consistories where the pool of potential elders was more restricted.[73]

Where the civil authorities and local social elite co-operated with the
church in running consistories, it was very difficult for ordinary people
to escape punishment. Some Calvinists were able to ignore the dictates of
elders, and in some territories had the option of leaving the Reformed
church altogether. However, the poor and lowly in society were the least
able to resist the power of consistories. In Scotland there is some evidence to suggest that both kirk sessions and presbyteries found it easier
to impose their will on ordinary people than on nobles.[74] Consistories
could try to use the distribution of charitable relief as an additional pressure to gain compliance from the poor with their standards of behaviour.
Attempts by deacons in Dutch towns to offer poor relief only to church
members who adhered to the disciplinary demands of consistories were,
however, resisted by some councils.[75]

Reformed disciplinary campaigns often began by paying close attention to the religious beliefs of local congregations in the first years of a
new church. Women were often called before consistories and charged
with continuing to observe traditional religious practices. At Geneva, for
example, twice as many women as men were charged by the consistory
with the adoration of the Virgin Mary.[76] The numbers of religious
offences brought before consistories was also affected by the degree to
which church members continued to come into close contact with those
of other religions. In France and the Netherlands, consistories faced
problems relating to mixed marriages and attendance at Catholic services and festivals. Attempts to enforce attendance at church services also
remained a major problem for many Reformed authorities. In the
Palatinate the state supported the introduction of roll-calls in churches
which revealed widespread absenteeism, particularly from weekday and
Sunday evening services.[77]

The moral agenda of Reformed churches concentrated on promoting
the harmony of local communities and on combating individual vices.
Elders tried to resolve disputes between family members and neighbours,
and acted against sexual misconduct, problems relating to marriage, violence, drunkenness, blasphemy and swearing. There were variations
between the attention given to different offences across the Continent.

In southern France during the latter decades of the sixteenth century, consistories were particularly busy in hearing cases relating to public arguments and fighting, and launched a campaign against dancing and traditional forms of recreation. In the Palatinate the state authorities introduced a law in 1592 against blasphemous oaths which led to an attack by consistories against cursing and swearing. At Emden there was a concerted campaign against drunkenness, while in neighbouring Groningen this issue was not at all prominent in the work of the city's consistory.[78] In Scotland, the early years of kirk sessions' activities were dominated by sexual offences, and only slowly did church discipliners spread their attention to a wider range of social and moral ills. About half of all session cases heard in a range of Lowland parishes between 1560 and 1610 have been found to involve some sort of sexual offence.[79] The church in Scotland was also particularly concerned to defend the Sabbath, expressing repeated concern that Sunday markets drew people away from attending church services.[80] In England much of the attention of church courts during the late sixteenth century was also taken up with cases of fornication and bridal pregnancy, which failed to satisfy Puritan critics who wanted more comprehensive action against a broad range of perceived moral offences.[81]

While the statistics generated by analysis of the formal decisions of consistories and presbyteries provide many points of comparison in the impact of Reformed moral discipline, there are great difficulties in offering rigid interpretations about the work of elders based on consistorial records. Much activity left no written record, since an elder's first response to an offence was to issue a private warning about an individual's conduct. Although many consistories assiduously recorded cases brought to meetings, there are few records of discussions held among elders about how to proceed. Many consistories were also reticent about making permanent written records of details of individuals' misdemeanours, perhaps particularly in cases involving local notables. Also, many cases may not have been entered into the records at all. At Utrecht, the official records of the consistory during the 1620s only contained about one third of the cases mentioned in the private notes made by one of the elders, Arnoldus Buchelius.[82]

Using church disciplinary records to look for changes in the behaviour of communities over time is equally problematic. For example, one of the key disciplinary objectives of Reformed clergy in north-eastern Hungary during the early seventeenth century was to end the use of oaths and curses which were seen to challenge divine authority and which expressed violence and aggression between neighbours and family members. The records of the archdeacons of Zemplén county from the 1620s reveal consistent efforts to get local clergy to enforce discipline on offenders, often women, who blasphemed and swore, and to get local magistrates to deal with the issue seriously. After decades of effort to combat the prevalence of swearing in the Reformed community of Zemplén, the issue begins to crop up much less frequently in the sources. The proportion of swearing as against other offences noted in the Reformed church's disciplinary records had certainly fallen by the mid-seventeenth century. What, though, should our conclusion be? Did the Reformed community of Zemplén stop swearing, and was the Reformed disciplinary campaign effective? Or, did the clergy give up on bringing cases of swearing in the face of community resistance to their campaign and stop reporting incidents of blasphemous oaths? Or, did ordinary people find new, and as yet unregulated, ways of expressing hostility towards one another without uttering blood-curdling curses, and if so, was this a success or a failure of the Reformed disciplinary campaign?[83]

While a comparable institutional framework and process of applying moral discipline was introduced across much of the Reformed world, there were wide variations between the practices of different churches. Despite such differences, and the problems of establishing effective consistories and battles to get their authority accepted by civil magistrates and ordinary people, moral discipline was rigorously enforced in many Reformed communities. Ministers and elders across the Continent tried to persuade people to repent of their sins, promoted community harmony and punished wrongdoing. Reformed discipliners also attempted to spread true religious knowledge and to limit the infection of Catholic and other disorderly and superstitious beliefs within their communities. They promoted an ideal of marriage, and acted severely against sexual licence and forms of behaviour likely to undermine sexual morality. They supported good relations between neighbours, and were intolerant of violence, swearing and drunkenness. However, it remains very difficult to assess accurately how far these ideals and the activity of elders affected the lives of individuals, let alone Reformed communities. Consistories could not abolish human nature, which experienced elders must have understood better than anyone else. Reformed discipliners worked in close co-operation with civil magistrates where possible, and turned to legal regulations to bolster the impact of their spiritual punishments. It would nevertheless be mistaken to think of Reformed discipline only as a form of social control which was ultimately imposed from above and which most ordinary people must have resisted as far as was possible. The work of elders and the sanction of rituals of repentance relied to a large degree on popular acceptance of Reformed moral norms. The system of consistorial discipline simply cannot be seen as merely an instrument of elite social power or as a paradise for nosy neighbours and vindictive gossips. The cases of Andrew Sellar, Jean Maupille and Nicolas Bizeau certainly reveal that elders could be persistent, inflexible and unsympathetic, but also show that the operation of consistorial discipline could be marked by sensitivity and concern for the lives of ordinary Reformed church members.

Chapter 5: Religious Life and Culture

The daily experience of Reformed religious life varied according to the political environment, social setting and pattern of organisation of local churches, and changed over time as Reformed orthodoxy evolved and disciplinary and educational institutions became established. Despite such variations, enough remained held in common between different churches and generations to form an identifiable Reformed religious culture during the sixteenth and early seventeenth centuries. This chapter will build up a portrait of the religious life and culture of Calvinists, including the names given to infants, and the ways in which both children and adults were taught about the fundamentals of their faith. Various aspects of religious life in Reformed churches will then be compared, including the appearance of church buildings, the clothing worn by ministers, and the role of sermons, public prayers, fasts, the Bible and Psalters in church services. Reformed religious culture was significantly informed by the Old Testament, and Calvinists often came to identify their communities with God's first chosen people. The metaphor of Israel became an important means through which Reformed identity was constructed and expressed, and a prism through which many Calvinists, and especially exiles, refugees and migrants, understood both the history and the future of the Church and their communities.

Children and Education

Life as a Calvinist began with reception into the Christian community through the sacrament of baptism. Children were named by parents, and some Reformed churches limited their choices to a range of acceptable options. At Geneva, the Company of Pastors drew up a list of banned names in 1546, which explained that saints' names were inappropriate for Christian families. In 1547 and 1548 some parents continued to present their children to be baptised with some of the names of local saints traditionally used by many Genevan families. However, ministers refused to oblige, and some children were instead given names from the Bible which clergy deemed suitable. Despite these early challenges to the authority of ministers over this issue, by the 1560s previously popular names such as Claude had virtually disappeared from Genevan society. During the 1560s only 3 per cent of boys were baptised with saints' names, with roughly two thirds of boys given names from the New Testament and one third from the Old Testament. This imprint of Reformed ideas in Genevan society continued to be evident during the early seventeenth century, although the popularity of Old Testament names declined somewhat after 1600 and saints' names began to be used more frequently.[1]

The national synod in France also proscribed the use of any names within the Huguenot community which might give rise to superstition or scandal. In 1562 and 1579 the synod banned any names associated with God or angels and pagan names, and the French church *Discipline* encouraged parents only to choose names which appeared in the Bible.[2] Reformed parents in Rouen certainly changed the pattern of naming children in their community, and children's names became a means of easily identifying local Calvinists from their Catholic neighbours. Although both communities used names from the New Testament, Catholics also commonly named their children after saints while over half of Huguenot children during the mid-1560s were baptised with Old Testament names. So in Rouen, someone called Abraham, Daniel, Rachel or Sarah was very likely to be a Huguenot. However, during the 1570s and 1580s the proportion of Calvinist children given Old Testament names in Rouen had fallen back to around a third. This was perhaps a result of the weakening position of Calvinism in Normandy, and a sign that some Huguenot parents had become understandably anxious that their children could be so quickly identified as Calvinists in the wake of Catholic violence against their community.[3]

A meeting of Reformed clergy at Antwerp in 1564 and the Dordrecht synod in 1578 also both forbade the use of names deemed inappropriate or superstitious such as Emmanuel, Salvator, Enghel and Baptista. Parents in the Netherlands were also encouraged only to give their children names which were found in the Bible. Previously rarely heard Old

Testament names certainly became more common among Dutch Calvinists, especially in communities forced into exile.[4] In 1584 the French-speaking churches in England also proscribed the use of any names of pagan origin. Parents were instead advised to think carefully about choosing the name of a character from the Bible which would give their child an example of piety or virtue to follow.[5] A small minority of English Calvinists used naming their children as an opportunity to express even more intense spiritual commitment. Old Testament names became more popular in England from the 1560s, but some Puritan preachers in southern England inspired the use of striking pious names towards the end of the sixteenth century. Richard Bancroft noted that some parents had taken to calling their children names such as 'The-Lord-is-neare, More Tryall, Reformation, Discipline, Joy Againe and Sufficient'.[6]

All the major churches during this period were committed, with varying degrees of enthusiasm, to instructing children in the basic tenets of their religion. The favoured means of teaching children and adults about the fundamentals of their faith was through printed catechisms. Reformed children, as well as other members of congregations deemed in need of instruction, were among the most likely to be required to attend weekly catechism classes. Calvin wrote in the dedication to the 1545 edition of the *Genevan Catechism* that instruction through catechisms was a 'holy custom'.[7] Catechism classes were held on Sunday afternoons in Geneva, and children were tested on their knowledge of the catechism before they were able to receive Communion for the first time. Calvin later suggested that he would never have returned to Geneva in 1541 if the council 'had not pledged me these two things; namely, to keep the catechism and the discipline'.[8] The *Genevan Catechism* which Calvin revised in 1541, and the 1563 *Heidelberg Catechism* which was compiled by Caspar Olevian and Zacharius Ursinus for use in schools in the Palatinate, both became widely used across the Continent. Calvinists from all corners of Europe were taught to recite answers from these manuals about God, salvation and the sacraments, and to learn the Apostles' Creed, the Ten Commandments and the Lord's Prayer.[9]

Congregational catechism classes for children were normally held on Sunday afternoons in Scotland, where Calvin's *Genevan Catechism*, John Craig's *Form of Examination* and the *Heidelberg Catechism* were in common use. In French congregations, ministers, elders or deacons also led classes through the *Genevan Catechism* on Sunday afternoons. In some churches in France only children were compelled to attend as a prerequisite for their first Communion. However, elsewhere adults could also be asked to provide satisfactory answers about their faith before they were given a token which allowed them to gain access to Communion.[10] A number of different catechisms were used in the Hungarian church. Vernacular schools in Hungary and Transylvania often adopted one of the catechisms compiled by local reformers, including the popular text compiled by János Siderius. Congregational catechism classes became more common in Hungarian congregations after 1600, as the numbers of copies of catechisms in circulation increased. The *Heidelberg Catechism* also came to be widely used in Hungary. It had been first translated into Hungarian in 1577 by Dávid Huszár, and Albert Szenczi Molnár published another translation in 1607.[11] Catechising was particularly widespread in the English church. Many ministers seemed convinced that using catechisms had led to a noticeable improvement in the understanding shown by congregations about their religion. Vast numbers of a wide variety of official and unofficial catechisms were published in England, with estimates suggesting that by the early seventeenth century over 750 000 catechisms were in circulation in a country of only around four million people.[12]

Catechisms were adapted into a wide variety of different forms, from the most basic questions and answers directed towards small children, to long and complicated texts which included explanations of doctrine and suggested study of further Bible passages. Catechisms were recommended for use by boys and girls, and across the social spectrum. Philip Marnix advised that young princes and nobles in the Netherlands ought to be taught from catechisms. Marnix claimed that nobles would benefit from the frequent repetition of catechism answers and by learning different passages of Scripture off by heart.[13] The enduring commitment of many clergy and parents across the Continent to teaching children from catechisms offers testament to a widespread perception of their value. However, the suspicion remains that many children and adults may have only learned how to repeat in unison words which were barely understood, while others resented having to attend classes at all. Some catechism authors tried to improve the ways in which their texts were used, suggesting that teachers should check on their pupils' understanding of answers with follow-up questions. However, the degree to which teaching people to learn formal catechism answers off by heart was able to improve popular understanding of Christian ideas or to establish habits of moral behaviour remains unclear.[14]

In 1578 the French national synod felt the need to remind ministers to catechise more frequently, 'by short, plain and familiar questions and answers, accommodating themselves to the weakness and capacity of their people'.[15] Some ministers had already responded to the limitations of their communities, especially in the countryside. Charles Perrot, a Parisian born minister who studied at the Genevan Academy from 1564, then worked as a pastor in two villages near Geneva. He wrote that his experiences in these communities had shown that

> there are questions and doctrines in the catechism which one cannot readily teach people, for fear of confusing them. This being so, in order to do as little harm as possible, my practice used to be to take each article word-for-word as it is in the catechism, paraphrase the content in a couple of lines at most, and then to get all the boys and girls, the menservants and the maidservants, one after another, to recite it twice, out loud.[16]

Perrot was also relatively tolerant of inaccurate answers, and permitted all who gave reasonably clear responses to participate in Communion services. The knowledge which these rural congregations were required by Perrot to display about their religion fell way below the ideal standards set by reformers and also beneath the standards of knowledge achieved in some urban centres, but his efforts still undoubtedly advanced understanding of basic Christian doctrine in his parishes.

Worship

The orders of magistrates and sometimes the hands of ordinary people fundamentally altered the character of church buildings which were used for Reformed worship. Services were conducted in a deliberately simple environment in which it was possible to offer pure, spiritual worship to God. While statues, pictures and screens were taken out of churches, seats and pews were brought in for congregations to use. The plain appearance of churches and the provision of seating was intended to help people to concentrate while hearing the word of God being read out and explained in sermons. Although some forms of decoration survived or crept back into Reformed churches, walls and even windows remained mostly devoid of colour and imagery. Calvin explained that creating such an environment for worship adhered to the purpose of public services, which were not to be held as if 'to amuse the world by a spectacle'.[17]

The experience of attending church services in Geneva was dominated by listening to, and saying or singing, words in French. Calvin's *Forms of Prayers*, which first appeared in 1542 set out an order for Sunday morning services which began with prayers of confession, then a Psalm was sung, followed by a prayer and a reading from the Bible, then the minister preached his sermon, the Lord's Prayer and Apostles' Creed were then recited before another Psalm was sung, and the service closed with a prayer of blessing. There were shorter forms of service for week-day services, and 'prophesying' meetings were also held in Geneva when scripture passages were explained in depth and discussed. These forms of worship in Geneva's churches were taken up and adapted in many other Reformed churches. The 1561 church order of Nicolas des Gallars for the French community in London followed the model set in Geneva, including regular 'prophesying' services.[18] The *Book of Common Order*, which was accepted for use in Scotland in 1564, was based on the liturgy and church order used by the English congregation in Geneva. This order of services had been based on the liturgy first drawn up at Frankfurt by John Knox, William Whittingham and Anthony Gilby, but also drew from Calvin's *Forms of Prayers*. In 1567 this *Book of Common Order* was also translated into Gaelic by John Carswell for use in congregations in the Highlands.[19]

Another significant Genevan export for English-speaking churches was the *Geneva Bible*, which was completed in 1560 by Whittingham, with assistance from Gilby and other colleagues in the exile church at Geneva. The Bible contained 'brief annotations upon all the hard places', which aimed to assist readers to understand the meaning of difficult scripture passages. It also offered some memorable translations of Bible stories, not least in Genesis 3 where after Adam and Eve sinned 'the eyes of them both were opened, and they knewe that they were naked, and they sewed figge tree leaves together, and made them selves breeches'. While the English authorities tried to promote the so-called *Bishop's Bible* as the official version for use in the church in 1568, there was a widespread attachment to the *Geneva Bible*. When Edmund Grindal succeeded Matthew Parker as archbishop of Canterbury in 1575, permission was granted for the *Geneva Bible* to be published. Between 1575 and 1593 the *Geneva Bible* was printed 33 times out of a total of 42 editions of the Bible published during that period. A further 60 editions of the *Geneva Bible* were published even after the production of James I's *Authorised Version* in 1611. The *Geneva Bible* also became widely used in Scotland, where the first published edition appeared in 1579, and by law substantial householders were required to purchase a copy.[20]

The major ceremonial ritual of Reformed church life was the administration of Communion. Calvin had initially wanted to distribute Communion every week in Geneva, but in the end Communion services were only celebrated four times a year at Christmas, Easter, Pentecost and on the first Sunday in September. This pattern of four Communion services each year was followed in France and in Scotland's towns, although the lack of clergy meant that Communion services were normally only held twice a year in rural Scottish parishes. Elsewhere Communion services were held six or seven times a year, or even once a month, which was the practice of the French exile churches in England.[21] The conduct of Communion services was laid out in detail by church order-books. In some churches, Communion tables were placed in the middle of the church and communicants sat down on chairs around the table to receive the bread and wine in groups. The Scottish *Book of Common Order* directed clergy to descend from the pulpit and sit at a table with those who were going to participate in the sacrament. After a prayer

> the minister breaketh the bread, and delivereth it to the people, who distribute and divide the same amongst themselves, according to our Saviour Christ's commandment, and likewise giveth the cup.[22]

In many churches the Communion table remained at the front of the church, and the congregation lined up to receive the bread and wine in turn. Men and women commonly received the sacrament separately, and as communicants came forward a Psalm was sung or a passage read from the Bible. In the Dutch church the 1578 Dordrecht synod made clear that communicants were permitted to stand or sit to receive the bread and wine. However, ministers were not to allow people to kneel, in order to avoid any superstition or adoration of the elements of Communion.[23]

There was therefore some variety between Reformed churches over the conduct and frequency of Communion services, and differences between local practices, such as the use of leavened or unleavened bread. The greatest degree of contention over the administration of Communion undoubtedly occurred in England, where reformers repeatedly pressed parliament and the clergy hierarchy to abolish 'the Popish abuses yet remaining in the English church'. Objections were raised to aspects of the ritual set out in the *Book of Common Prayer*, and reformers particularly highlighted that people were permitted to kneel to receive Communion. A 1572 *Admonition to the Parliament* suggested that the church in England was still very far from being 'rightly reformed', since it lacked appropriate ecclesiastical discipline and retained superstitions in the conduct of Communion services as well as in baptisms, marriage and funeral services.[24] Although John Field and Thomas Wilcox were imprisoned as the supposed authors of the *Admonition*, voices continued to be raised that the English authorities needed to follow the examples provided by foreign Reformed churches. Thomas Cartwright was suspected of writing a *Second Admonition* in 1573, which again advised the English to follow the lead provided by the 'best churches beyond the seas'. Cartwright suggested that the *Book of Common Prayer* should be translated out of English so that it could be assessed by the rest of the Reformed world. Cartwright also came up with a litany of complaints about 'deformities' in the conduct of church services in England.[25] However, these demands for reform met with a firm response from Elizabeth in June 1573. A royal proclamation was issued which ordered ministers to stick to the form of services outlined in the *Book of Common Prayer*.[26]

Some traditional forms of worship used in the Catholic church were criticised because of what reformers regarded as invented rules on external behaviour such as set periods of fasting. Martin Bucer commented that 'it is anti-Christian to prescribe fasting for Christians as something necessary for salvation'.[27] Calvin insisted that the daily lives of 'the godly ought to be tempered with frugality and sobriety, so that throughout its course a sort of perpetual fasting may appear'.[28] Nevertheless, public fasts became a regular feature of the religious life of many Reformed communities. Beza argued that public fasts were a way of encouraging believers to pray, to humble themselves before God and to be brought to repentance of their sins. Beza supported calling fasts 'whenever the season requires it and there is some calamity near with which we are justly threatened on account of our sins'. The *Second Helvetic Confession* and *Discipline* of the French church agreed that public prayers and fasts were to be called by ministers during times of adversity and affliction for the church.[29]

During the 1560s the church in Emden regularly called days of fasting and prayer for the rulers of East Friesland, and in 1562 fasted for their brethren living in 'great fear and danger' in France. In 1565 the community at Emden again fasted and prayed for the French church, for the church in the Netherlands, and in response to the advancing armies of the Ottoman Sultan.[30] Exile churches showed a particular commitment to holding fasts and prayers for their co-religionists back home. In 1577, 1590 and 1593 the consistory of the French church in London organised a public fast and prayers for the persecuted churches in France and Flanders.[31] There was also a ready resort in Scotland to hold public fasts. From the mid-1560s the general assembly called for fasts and prayers as a response to sin and in the face of dangers to the church at home and abroad. Local records show that these fasts were often called as periods of particular reflection before Communion services.[32] In May 1566 the general assembly in Scotland appointed two successive Sundays as a period of public fasting across the country. The assembly made clear that the days of fasting were not to be seen as having any particular significance in themselves, but were rather opportunities for everyone to examine their consciences and confess their faults before God. During the week of fasting the assembly asked for daily services to be held in towns, and for people not to wear 'gorgeous apparel'. Total abstinence was only demanded from Saturday evening until the end of the Sunday morning service. During Sunday services, ministers and congregations were instructed to 'prostrate themselves, and remain in private meditation a reasonable space, as the quarter of an hour or more'.[33]

The Psalms

Calvinist reformers also found fault with the traditional use of music during church services. Organs were often destroyed by iconoclasts or were removed from church buildings on the instructions of local magistrates. No music was heard inside Zurich's churches from 1524 until 1598, and at Bern music was banned until 1558 when one unaccompanied Psalm was allowed to be sung before the sermon.[34] Calvin acknowledged that music was a powerful device which swayed the soul and the emotions, but he believed that if the use of music was controlled then it could be used in the worship of God. However, Calvin deemed the use of musical instruments in churches as entirely inappropriate, and only permitted the singing of Psalms in the vernacular by the congregation. The Psalms, as prayers set to music, should replace songs previously sung in churches which were 'in part empty and frivolous, in part stupid and dull, in part obscene and vile, and in consequence evil and harmful'. As with all aspects of public worship, Calvin thought that it was vital that the congregation ought to understand the words being sung.

> For a linnet, a nightingale, a parrot may sing well, but it will be without understanding. Now the peculiar gift of man is to sing knowing what he

is saying. After the intelligence must follow the heart and the affection which is impossible unless we have the hymn imprinted on our memory in order never to cease from singing.[35]

The musical settings for the Psalms therefore had to allow the words to be clearly heard, be 'seemly' and 'carry gravity and majesty appropriate to the subject'. Calvin published a first edition of some Psalms in verses in Strassburg in 1539, and later editions in 1542 and 1545 added more Psalms. The *Genevan Psalter* was completed in 1562 by Beza and Clément Marot, to tunes by Louis Bourgeois and others which were simply structured in order to allow ordinary people to learn the music and to enable the words to be heard clearly.

Many Reformed churches also permitted a wider range of hymns and songs to be used in church services, but the use of Psalms in the Genevan church was widely copied across the Reformed world. Anthony Gilby, who produced an English edition of the Psalter, later recalled his first dramatic experience of hearing a Psalm sung in a Genevan church

... the company did sing this Psalm [91], by the singing whereof as though I had heard God himself calling me particularly, I felt myself so comforted, that I have kept it since that time most dearly graven in my heart, and I may truly witness before God, that I have received marvellous comforts by it, both in sickness and in sorrow ....[36]

The English exile congregation at Geneva used the Psalm verses written by Thomas Sternhold and John Hopkins, and new Psalms were added to the collection by William Kethe and William Whittingham. A Psalter was published in England in 1562, and in 1564 a completed Psalter was included in the Scottish *Book of Common Order*. This was the Psalter which James Melville had learned to sing at school in Montrose, which he thought had ever since been a 'great blessing and comfort to him', and Psalms were sung in Scotland both before and after sermons.[37]

In France, the Psalms quickly became the signature tunes of Huguenot public identity and collective piety. The Psalter was translated into the dialects of the south, including into Gascon in 1565 and into Béarnais in 1583. The Psalms proved popular not only during church services but also on a range of other occasions. According to one observer, in the spring of 1560 the Calvinists of Dieppe gathered in the town's market place every night to sing Psalms. Singing Psalms staked a claim for space in which to worship, and Calvinist mobs often sang Psalms to disrupt

Catholic services and processions or as they destroyed statues and pictures in Catholic churches. Psalms were sung by Huguenot armies going into battle, and Beza wrote that Psalms also brought comfort to French believers suffering under the Valois regime and Psalms were sung by martyrs on their way to execution.[38]

The Catholic authorities in the Netherlands were also unable to prevent the sale of Psalters and spread of Psalm-singing. Psalms were sung to the Genevan tunes in the Walloon congregations of Tournai and Valenciennes by the early 1560s. Psalm verses were composed for Dutch-speaking congregations by Jan Utenhove, the Ghent noble who worked in England and at Emden. Utenhove's verses were first printed in the 1550s, and a complete Psalter was published after Utenhove's death in 1565. However, the verses translated in 1566 by Peter Dathenus to the tunes of the Genevan church soon overtook Utenhove's Psalter in popularity, and Dathenus' translation received official backing from the Dordrecht synod in 1574. Dathenus deliberately aimed to unify the style of worship across the Reformed world, writing that 'as we are united in doctrine and ceremonies with the evangelical churches in France, so have I wished with all my heart that we may be like them too in the singing of psalms'. Indeed, Reformed communities in the Netherlands followed their French brethren in singing Psalms not only during formal services, but also to celebrate triumphs against Spanish armies, to encourage imprisoned believers and to console martyrs before their execution.[39]

The 1567 Debrecen synod of the church in Hungary lambasted Papist 'howling', and congregations were only permitted to sing unaccompanied hymns in Hungarian. These songs were collected into hymnals, the most widely used of which was published by György Gönczi Kovács in 1592.[40] During the early decades of the seventeenth century the Hungarian church became more closely integrated into the international Reformed world with growing links between Hungarian clergy and western churches. One product of these contacts was that the sound of Genevan settings for the Psalms came to be heard during Hungarian church services. In 1607 Albert Szenczi Molnár worked at Frankfurt from the German translation of the Psalter by Ambrosius Lobwasser to compose the verses of his *Hungarian Psalter*. Although there were some initial complaints about how difficult congregations found it to learn the new music, Molnár's Psalter quickly became popular across Hungary and Transylvania. This was despite the best efforts of one Transylvanian superintendent, who tried to restrict use of the Psalter and promoted his own hymnal instead.[41]

Some Psalms proved to be particular favourites among Calvinists. Psalm 124 was sung at Beza's request on 12 December 1602 as Genevans fought the Savoyard army on the walls of their city. The same Psalm had rung out through the streets of Edinburgh in 1582 as a crowd of 2000 welcomed the preacher John Dury back from a period of banishment by the regency regime. The crowd marched in triumph to St Giles church, according to David Calderwood, singing 'with such a great sound and majesty, that it moved both themselves and all the multitude of the beholders'. The same words of Psalm 124 had also greeted Louis, prince of Condé, when he arrived in Orléans in April 1562 to begin the defence of the Huguenot community after the massacre at Vassy.[42] All three crowds sang of God's help in time of trouble:

Had not the Lord been on our side, may Israel now say;
Had not the Lord been on our side, when men rose us to slay;
Alive they had us swallowed then, in rage beyond control;
The waters had us overwhelmed, the stream gone o'er our soul.

While not all Reformed congregations and crowds made a joyful noise as they tried to remember the words of the Psalms, many communities enthusiastically embraced the chance to sing in unison. Singing Psalms could be an opportunity for personal reflection, and Psalms were used in church services as Calvin had intended. However, Psalm-singing to Genevan tunes also became a means by which Reformed communities could demonstrate public commitment to the cause and identify with ancient Israel. The sweet sound of the Psalms to Calvinist ears could, however, also be a noise that brought terror to their opponents.

Clerical Dress

In most Reformed churches ministers wore dark gowns to preach, to conduct the sacraments and to rebuke members of their congregations. Clergy were required to abandon wearing traditional liturgical vestments, which were not found to have any warrant in the New Testament. Vestments were also thought to sustain popular superstition about the powers of the clergy, especially during Communion services. Ministers across the Reformed world instead adopted loose-fitting, full-sleeved gowns which were reminiscent of academic dress. This reflected the view that clergy ought to appear as professionals who were qualified to perform their functions of preaching and teaching. Ministers and their wives were also encouraged by the resolutions of various church synods to dress in everyday life in a way which reflected Reformed values of moderation and sobriety in the consumption of goods.[43] However, in England the clergy under Edward VI and Elizabeth were instructed to continue to wear a white linen surplice during Communion services, and a long clerical gown and black square cap in their everyday dress. This aberration from normal practice within the Reformed community was an issue which advocates of further reform of the Elizabethan church found intolerable. The importance of this campaign to get rid of traditional vestments in England can also be seen through the direct involvement of leading figures from a number of foreign churches.

Divisions in England between conformists and reformers on the issue of clerical dress had first emerged in 1549. John Hooper, who had recently returned to England from Zurich, refused to be consecrated as a bishop because of the vestments he was required to wear. Hooper wrote to Heinrich Bullinger in June 1550 explaining his decision on 'account of those Aaronic habits'.[44] In December 1550 Thomas Cranmer wrote to Martin Bucer asking for his judgement on the issue. In response, Bucer expressed the hope that traditional vestments would quickly be abandoned in the English church, but suggested that ministers could be permitted to wear vestments.[45] In 1551 Peter Martyr reported to Bullinger from Oxford that he too had expressed opposition to the use of vestments, but had also advised reformers to show some patience on the issue. However, only after being imprisoned for a month, was Hooper finally prepared to give way and agreed to be consecrated in traditional vestments as bishop of Gloucester in March 1551.[46]

In 1559 Rudolph Gwalther wrote from Zurich to Elizabeth asking if 'your majesty is aware of the saying of Christ, who declares that the new piece of evangelical doctrine will not suit the old garments of superstition?' While many of Elizabeth's bishops also hoped for a clear break from the Catholic past on the issue of vestments, they soon had to recognise that Elizabeth was determined that the surplice and cap should be retained. John Jewel, bishop of Salisbury, reported to Martyr that since the English church did 'not differ from your doctrine by a nail's breadth', it seemed best to obey over matters of indifference such as vestments.[47] However, during the 1560s Bullinger, Martyr and Gwalther were all repeatedly contacted for their views on clerical dress by a number of former exiles including Jewel, Edmund Grindal, Edwin Sandys, Robert Horne, Lawrence Humphrey and Thomas Sampson. Both reformers and conformists looked to the authority of the leaders of the church in Zurich to influence the outcome of the debate in England. However, the letters transported by merchants down the Rhine to Strassburg and beyond were sent by correspondents who were also seeking support for their own established positions on the issue.

Divisions over clergy vestments flared up into a crisis during the mid-1560s. In 1564 James Pilkington, bishop of Durham, lobbied the earl of Leicester about clergy apparel, asking him to consider why 'we make so precious that, that other reformed places esteem as vile?' Pilkington also wondered why

> all countries, which have reformed religion, have cast away the popish apparel with the pope; and yet we, that would be taken for the best, contend to keep it as a holy relic.[48]

However, archbishop Matthew Parker moved to enforce the regulations on clerical dress through so-called 'Advertisements'. Parker demanded that known opponents of vestments such as Lawrence Humphrey and Thomas Sampson in Oxford adhere to the rules on clerical dress. In March 1566 Parker and Grindal summoned the ministers of London to view a mannequin dressed according to the regulations on vestments, and demanded that they agree to assume the same dress. When 37 ministers declined, they were all suspended from their offices.[49] A number of tracts about the requirement to wear vestments during church services also appeared in 1566. Were surplices, caps and gowns things indifferent, or did they hold back the work of the ministry? Those who decried the 'garments of Babylon', recalled that Bucer and Martyr had agreed that vestments should be removed. They argued that removing vestments would help bring the English church 'to most perfect purity', and into agreement with 'the most excellent reformed churches of France, Germany and Scotland'. Conformists, however, printed correspondence from 1550 in which Bucer and Martyr had urged Hooper to avoid unnecessary divisions in the church, and suggested that vestments could be worn by clergy as things indifferent to salvation.[50]

In 1566 reformers gained the support of the superintendents of the church in Scotland who wrote to the bishops in England in support of reform arguing

> What fellowship is there betwixt light and darkness? If surplice, corner-cap and tippet have been the badges of idolaters in the very act of their

idolatry, what hath the preachers of Christian liberty, and the rebukers of superstition to do with the dregs of that Romish beast.[51]

Sampson and Humphrey wrote on several occasions to Bullinger, asking him to express a clear view on whether distinct clothes for clergy had any Biblical validity, and if it was an indifferent matter to wear the vestments of 'monkery, popery and Judaism'.[52] Bullinger answered that he could not support the use of the surplice and other 'dregs of popery', and that the queen should be persuaded to change her view. Retaining vestments was a stain on the English reformation, which Bullinger wrote gave the impression of disunion between England and 'the neighbouring churches of Scotland and France'. However, a letter of May 1566 from Bullinger and Gwalther to Sampson and Humphrey, which the Zurich leaders also sent to Grindal, Horne and Parkhurst, argued that ministers in England should not resign from their posts on account of an issue which could be treated as a matter of indifference.[53]

This was hardly the response that Humphrey and Sampson had hoped for. They wrote a joint letter in July 1566 asking for Bullinger to think again, claiming that clerical vestments were marks of Antichristian superstition in the English church. Humphrey and Sampson asked

Why should we look for precedents from our enemies, the papists, and not from you, our brethren of the reformation? We have the same confession in our churches, the same rule of doctrine and faith: why should there be so great a dissimilarity and discrepancy in rites and ceremonies?[54]

Grindal also wrote to Bullinger in August 1566 updating him on events over the summer. He reported that some clergy, including Sampson, had been dismissed because of their failure to comply with the regulations on vestments. However, while many ministers had threatened to resign over the issue, Grindal related that few had in fact done so. This was not least, Grindal claimed, because of the impact made by the publication of Bullinger's letter on the subject. Bullinger wrote back to Grindal, surprised to find that his letter had been published, and concerned that it had been used to support what he regarded as ceremonial abuses in the English church. Gwalther also wrote to Parkhurst, expressing his distress that many in England now suspected that the Zurich clergy had 'given our sanction to the abominations of popery'. Bullinger also wrote back to Humphrey and Sampson in September 1566 acknowledging that they were dissatisfied with his position, but saying that he had nothing further to add.[55]

Meanwhile Humphrey, Sampson and Miles Coverdale had also written to Theodore Beza, Guillaume Farel and Pierre Viret seeking their opinion on vestments and on allowing people to kneel to receive Communion.[56] While they had failed to gain advantage out of contact with Zurich, their attempt to win support from Geneva still had some prospect of success. In September 1566 Beza wrote to Bullinger on reports he had received from brethren in England, which led him to think that 'papacy was never abolished in that country, but rather transferred to the sovereign'. Beza suggested that someone from Zurich should go to England or write to the queen and bishops, admitting that while the Zurich church held influence in England, the Genevans were seen as too precise, linked with the works of Goodman and Knox, and were 'hateful to that queen'.[57] However, Gwalther responded that while he had written to the English bishops and would gladly go to England, he would not receive permission to travel from a queen not inclined to 'receive counsel from a foreigner'.[58]

Consultations between Geneva and Zurich confirmed the reputation of many English clergy, first gained during the Marian exile, as argumentative troublemakers. Beza and Gwalther agreed that those who held out against vestments were 'rather hard to please'.[59] Bullinger told Beza in 1567 of his suspicions about the 'troublesome' Sampson, whom he described as a man of 'exceedingly restless disposition'. Bullinger concluded that England 'has many characters of this sort, who cannot be at rest, who can never be satisfied, and who have always something or other to complain about'. When more unnamed Englishmen arrived in Geneva in 1567, full of complaints about their bishops at home, Beza was concerned but advised patience. Meanwhile Bullinger wrote that he was determined to have nothing to do with any new English controversy stirred by 'disorderly young men'.[60] English reformers then turned to a new avenue of potential support in the Palatinate, claiming that their opponents were trying to bring Lutheranism back to England. Grindal tried to explain the stance taken by the bishops on vestments to Girolamo Zanchi, an Italian exile who worked in Strassburg and Chiavenna before moving to Heidelberg in 1568. However, at Frederick III's request, Zanchi wrote to Elizabeth presenting the case for ridding the church of all 'popish ceremonies and trickeries'. Zanchi asserted that retaining vestments, which were symbols of idolatry and superstition, harmed the church in England and set a bad example to churches in Germany.[61]

The level of international engagement over the issue of clergy dress in England was considerable, and church leaders in Zurich, Geneva, the Palatinate and Scotland all expressed the view that traditional vestments should not be worn by Reformed ministers. Despite the consensus which emerged from discussions across the Continent on this issue, the opinion of the English church's governor remained decisive. Elizabeth's insistence on retaining vestments set the English church apart from the rest of the Reformed world. Reformers continued to press for change, and Thomas Cartwright and John Whitgift carried on the debate about the scriptural basis and practical effect of clergy vestments into the 1570s. The retention of vestments became a significant part of growing disaffection among the emerging Puritan party towards the English church's shortcomings, and fired enthusiasm to get rid of bishops who enforced such regulations. Meanwhile, although conformists initially only regarded vestments as a matter of indifference, wearing the surplice later became a badge of pride for conservatives trying to construct a distinct identity for the English church.[62]

Reformed Identity: The Past and the Future

Calvinists drew on the Bible, and in particular on the model of God's relationship with Israel, as a source to help structure a sense of collective identity and to make sense of their history and current circumstances. Some reformers identified themselves with Old Testament prophets. Propagandists also used the faithful kings and leaders of Biblical history to fashion idealised images for godly magistrates to follow. Edward VI was often described as a new young Josiah leading reform in the practice of religion and tearing down idols across his realm. In the Netherlands, William of Orange was depicted as a new Moses leading his people to deliverance from the Catholic church and Spanish king. It was not only the prophets and kings of the Old Testament that seemed to be revived within Reformed societies, but Israel itself. God had made the old covenant with Israel, and then a new covenant through Christ with the true Church. The history of Israel therefore prefigured God's relationship with his Church, and provided a way of describing an international brotherhood of true believers. The ways in which Calvinists drew from the model of Israel were by no means unique or novel, but they were at least distinctive in their intensity and frequency. Indeed, use of the metaphor of Israel became so habitual to many Reformed preachers and writers that it perhaps over time lost some of its rhetorical impact on congregations.[63]

Reformed preachers commonly used examples from the history of Israel to explain the reasons why reform was needed in the Church. In 1563 the Hungarian reformer Gáspár Károlyi explained how disobedience of God's laws had led to Israel's destruction and exile. Károlyi then paralleled ancient Israel's history with the position of the Hungarian kingdom which had suffered disastrous Ottoman invasions. Károlyi argued that 'the Turkish emperor is a servant of God for the punishment of the Hungarian nation' for its idolatry. To avoid further divine punishment, Károlyi urged Hungarians to accept the need for religious reform.[64] The example of Israel was also widely used by preachers to deliver warnings about the importance of moral behaviour. Reformed congregations were called to repent if they wanted to avoid the same divine punishments which the people of Israel had brought on themselves through their sins. For example, in 1580 the Genevan minister Lambert Daneau suggested that God's anger would bring desolation to France as it had done to Israel if people did not repent of the sin of wearing sumptuous clothing.[65]

When Calvinist ministers used the motif of Israel to try to inspire reform in their communities, on occasion their language suggested that God held a particular interest in his relationship with one church or nation. According to John Bale, the church in England had a leading role in bringing a final reformation of the universal Church before the return of Christ.[66] The idea that the people of Scotland had entered into a covenant with God fused ideas about the church and the nation among Scottish Calvinists. In this context, Samuel Rutherford could announce, without abandoning the notion that Israel was a figure of the true Church, that he had discovered Scotland's name and destiny in the Psalms and in Ezekiel:

> Now, O Scotland, God be thanked, thy name is in the Bible. Christ spoke to us long since, ere ever we were born. Christ said, 'Father, give me the ends of the earth, put in Scotland and England, with the isles-men in the great charter also: for I have them among the rest....'[67]

Offering a particular people the sense of being the only new Israel or an elect nation chosen by God was not, however, what most preachers intended. The often troubled relationship between Reformed churches and civil magistrates also limited any possible identification of Israel with any particular territorial state. Dutch Calvinists' unease about the attitudes of many urban magistrates towards the Reformed church certainly prevented the Dutch Republic from being widely seen as a new Israel.[68]

Those who often most closely identified themselves with Israel were rather individuals and communities who were forced into exile or who chose to abandon their homes. The idea of following in Israel's footsteps and being directed by God to a new land held a powerful role in the imagination of many Reformed refugees. When a French minister arrived during the 1570s on the largely uninhabited island of Sark, it was for him a rather unlikely 'new Jerusalem'.[69] When John Dane was uncertain whether or not to emigrate from England to America in the 1630s, he opened the Bible searching for divine direction. The first verse he saw was; 'Come out from among them, touch no unclean thing, and I will be your God and you shall be my people.' John Dane and his parents needed no further encouragement, and 'hastened' to settle in Massachusetts.[70]

Not only Reformed refugees found inspiration in comparisons with Israel. Preaching which drew on vivid stories of Israel's struggles against surrounding nations could receive enthusiastic popular responses in some settler and frontier societies. A group of Scottish Puritan preachers in south Antrim and north Down in Ulster attracted large crowds to sermons and outdoor Communion services in the 1620s. This was something of a surprise, since as one minister commented, the settlers from the Scottish Borders and from England were 'generally the scum of both nations'.[71] Heyduck communities of refugees from Ottoman-occupied Hungary who moved to the eastern Hungarian plain also formed an unlikely bastion of support for Reformed religion. While Heyduck communities had a recent experience of displacement, more broadly Hungarians also recalled the historic migration of Magyar tribes from Asia to Europe. Reformed writers developed a narrative of the history of the Hungarians, which as Albert Szenczi Molnár insisted in 1604, showed direct parallels with the history of God's relationship with Israel. Molnár wrote that as Israel had been directed by God from Egypt across the Sinai desert towards their promised land, so Hungarians had been led out of the Scythian steppe to occupy their promised land in the Danubian basin.[72] These ideas of divine direction of settlers to new lands were important in cementing the Reformed religious identity of migrant communities, and also offered a powerful tool for later attempts to construct national identities. Although Afrikaner nationalism, for example, primarily reflected responses to modern political problems, a heritage of Reformed ideas of being chosen by God and directed to occupy land continued to be frequently invoked.[73]

Reformed ideas about history extended into expectations about the future, although the interest shown by Calvinists in apocalyptic prophecy was far from unique. Lutheran reformers had suggested that their effort to reform the Church was a crucial turning point in world history. Martin Luther identified figures in the prophecy of Daniel of Gog and Magog as the Turk and the Pope. In a crisis where evil powers were overtaking the world, only those who supported a true reform of the Church would escape looming destruction. Both Luther and Philip Melanchthon expected the end of history to come before the close of the sixteenth century. Meanwhile Calvin had very little to say about how long Christians would have to wait before the end of the world, and he did not offer any speculation on exactly when Christ would return to earth. He commented on the prophecies of Daniel about the end times, that in

> numerical calculations I am no conjurer, and those who expound this passage with too much subtlety, only trifle in their own speculations and detract from the authority of prophecy.[74]

The confessions of faith adopted by Reformed churches followed a similarly cautious line. The *Confession* of the Dutch church looked forward 'with a most ardent desire' to the day of Last Judgement when Christ would return to deliver vengeance on the wicked, and the elect 'shall be crowned with glory and honour'. This would occur at a time appointed by God, 'which is unknown to all creatures'.[75]

Belief in the imminence of the end times featured in the thought of many Reformed theologians and intellectuals. Ideas about the apocalypse gained a wider audience especially in circumstances where Reformed communities were under threat of persecution or war, or when writers suggested a particular role for their own country in the eschatological dramas to come. In 1563 Gáspár Károlyi thought that Hungary would soon become an apocalyptic battleground where the faithful would face the power of the twin Antichrists of Constantinople and Rome. According to Károlyi, history had moved into its final sixth age, and there were growing signs that final judgement was at hand in nature and in recent wars against Ottoman armies.[76] Expectations about the imminence of the end times were raised in 1569, when a popular prophet called for a holy army to fight against the Turks. This prophet, György

Karácsony, gathered his forces on the eastern plain around Debrecen.
A frontier commander wrote that his own garrison had to be dissuaded
from joining Karácsony, since

> religion had gripped them as if thunder-struck, they broke no law, did
> not curse or swear, and reprimanded one another for such offences.

In expectation of a miraculous victory Karácsony led a band of 600 men
to face the Turks, only to be crushed by Ottoman frontier forces.[77]

Most Calvinists agreed that the Papacy was at least one manifestation of
Antichrist. In England, John Bale and John Foxe wrote histories of the
persecution of the true Church by the Antichrist from the time of the
first martyrs to events in their own generation. This scheme of history
encouraged conjecture as to when the Antichristian power of Rome
would be broken, and Christ would return to judge the world. English
exiles were suitably encouraged by the prospect of the restoration of true
religion under Elizabeth. The dedication of the *Geneva Bible* claimed that
Elizabeth was 'our Zerubbabel for the erecting of this most excellent temple'. Belief in the imminence of the last times was sustained by some
across the latter decades of the sixteenth century. William Perkins shared
in the belief that the end could not be far off, since he thought that all
the Biblical prophecies which were to precede Christ's return to earth
had already been fulfilled.[78] Writers who discussed the prospect of the
apocalypse mostly stuck to the Biblical requirement not to seek knowledge about the exact timing of Christ's return. However, the temptation
at least to guide readers about the date of the end of history proved too
much for some. In Scotland, John Napier wrote an interpretation of
Revelation in 1593, which explained that history was in the seventh and
last age, and that the reign of the Papal Antichrist was therefore coming
to an end. Napier expected that by 1639 the Papacy would fall, and that
Christ would return to earth before 1700.[79]

Ideas about an imminent apocalypse provided Calvinists with a clear
imperative for urgent moral reform, allowed for confident predictions
about the defeat of their enemies and offered solace to communities facing persecution and war. Apocalyptic expectation particularly resonated
with exiles such as Girolamo Zanchi. Although Zanchi refused to offer
any comments as to when the Last Judgement would come, he looked to
a future time when all the present suffering of believers would be over-
turned. This strong appeal of apocalypticism was also found among later
French Reformed refugees. When Pierre Jurieu was forced into exile in

the Dutch Republic in 1681, he brought comfort to Huguenots at home and in exile with his prediction that the Antichrist would be defeated by 1715.[80]

At the beginning of the seventeenth century, the growing challenge to Habsburg power in the Empire and central Europe had raised hopes of a coming decisive victory of the true Church over the Antichrist. Johann Heinrich Alsted at Herborn academy looked forward to the triumph of the true Church, the conversion of the Jews and the day of judgement. Based on his understanding of scriptural history and prophecy, and on his interpretation of astronomical evidence, Alsted calculated that the world would end in 1694. However, amid the devastation brought to Reformed Germany during the early 1620s, Alsted revised this rosy view and decided that the triumph of the Church might only begin in a glorious millennial age to come.[81] The idea of a golden age on earth before the day of judgement had been condemned outright by the *Second Helvetic Confession*, but was revived amid the stalled expectations of the 1620s.[82] Alsted moved his prediction of Protestant recovery in the Empire back from 1625 to 1642, and suggested that 1694 would mark the beginning of a new golden thousand years. The world would end finally come, Alsted predicted, in 2694 with the return of Christ and the Last Judgement. Ideas about a future millennium also made an impact in England, where Thomas Brightman had looked forward to the triumph of true religion and to the conversion of the Jews to Christianity as signs of a new glorious age. In 1627 Joseph Mede predicted the eventual destruction of all enemies of the Church, after which Christ would reign for a thousand years in a utopian world where a full and final reformation had been achieved.[83]

Reformed apocalypticists and millenarians of the early seventeenth century also looked forward to dramatic improvements in human understanding of God and nature, which initiated enthusiasm for encyclopedias, and for more mystical keys to unlocking knowledge through numerology and Kabbalah. While some of these projects emerged from the fringes of the Reformed intellectual world, they were seriously considered in some courts and academies. This was certainly the case with the plans produced during the 1630s and 1640s by the Bohemian Brethren leader, Jan Amos Comenius, for educational reforms and a new universal language to achieve 'the quick and complete overthrow of the great Babylon of our confusions and the establishment of God's Zion' in the world. Comenius's ideas gained an audience from England to Transylvania for universal restoration before an imminent apocalypse as an escape route from the labyrinth of the world to the paradise of the heart.[84]

Commonly held ideas about how God should be worshipped and close contact between Reformed churches led to comparable patterns of religious life and culture being adopted across the Continent. Being a member of a Reformed church normally involved a life under rigorous moral discipline, learning catechism answers, and worshipping in whitewashed churches under the direction of a minister dressed in black. The practice of Reformed religion was dominated by the Bible, prayers, Psalm-singing, and by simple sacramental rituals. If God's presence could no longer be discerned in bread, wine, water, wood and stone, his written Word was a ready source of direction and guidance. Calvinists were encouraged to consider how their communities should draw lessons from the history of God's relationship with Israel, and to remember that the end times were approaching, perhaps even imminent. While this sharp focus on the approaching return of Christ was not shared by all, apocalyptic expectations were particularly strongly felt among exiles and others on the move, who proved to be so often at the heart of the international Reformed world.

Notes

Introduction

1. For 'International Zwinglianism' see B. Gordon, *The Swiss Reformation* (Manchester: Manchester University Press, 2002), 283–316. D. MacCulloch, *Reformation. Europe's House Divided, 1490–1700* (London: Penguin, 2003), 253.
2. H. Oberman, 'Calvin and Farel: the dynamics of legitimation in early Calvinism', *Journal of Early Modern History* 2 (1998), 35. P. Benedict, *Christ's Churches Purely Reformed. A Social History of Calvinism* (New Haven [CT]: Yale University Press, 2002), xxii–xxiii.
3. '*Approbatae Constitutiones*', in *Magyar Törvénytár. 1500–1848 évi erdélyi törvények* (eds) S. Kolozsvári, K. Óvári, D. Márkus (Budapest, 1900), 'Pars prima', article 1/1/2.

Chapter 1: Reformed Ideas

1. John Calvin, *Institutes of the Christian Religion* (Geneva, 1559) (ed.) H. Beveridge (2 vols), (Edinburgh: Calvin Translation Society, 1845), vol. 1, preface. For Calvin's sermons, see for example *Sermons of Maister John Calvin upon the Booke of Job* (tr.) Arthur Golding (London, 1574). A. Ganoczy, *The Young Calvin* (Edinburgh: T&T Clark, 1988). Q. Breen, *John Calvin: a study in French humanism* (London: Archon, 1968). F. Wendel, *Calvin. The origins and development of his religious thought* (London: Collins, 1963).

2. P. McNair, *Peter Martyr in Italy. An anatomy of apostasy* (Oxford: Clarendon, 1967). F. C. Church, *The Italian Reformers, 1534–1564* (New York: Columbia University Press, 1932).

3. J. P. Donnelly, *Calvinism and Scholasticism in Vermigli's doctrine of man and grace* (Leiden: Brill, 1976). R. A. Muller, *The Unaccommodated Calvin. Studies in the foundation of a theological tradition* (Oxford: Oxford University Press, 2000). D. Steinmetz, *Calvin in Context* (Oxford: Oxford University Press, 1995). J. P. Donnelly, 'Italian influence on the development of Calvinist scholasticism', *SCJ* 7 (1976), 81–101.

4. Calvin, *Institutes* (1559), 4/1/9. W. J. Bouwsma, *John Calvin. A sixteenth-century portrait* (Oxford: Oxford University Press, 1988), 215.

5. Theodore Beza, *Confession de Foi du Chrétien* (Geneva, 1558) (ed.) J. Clarke (Lewes: Focus Christian Ministries Trust, 1992), 73.

6. *Reformed Confessions of the 16th Century* (ed.) A. C. Cochrane (London: SCM Press, 1966), 154, 176–7, 210.

7. John Calvin, *Excuse de Jehan Calvin, a Messieurs les Nicodemites, sur la complaincte qu'ilz sont de sa trop grand rigeur* (Geneva, 1544) in *Jean Calvin. Three French Treatises* (ed.) F. Higman (London: Athlone Press, 1970), 131–53. B. C. Milner, *Calvin's Doctrine of the Church* (Leiden: Brill, 1970).

8. *Reformed Confessions* (ed.) Cochrane (1966), 320.

9. *Reformed Confessions* (ed.) Cochrane (1966), 152–3. The French *Confession* was subject to ongoing revision by the national synod.

10. Philip Marnix van St Aldegonde, *The Bee Hive of the Romishe Churche. Wherein the author a zealous Protestant, under the person of a superstitious Papist, doth so driely repell the grose opinions of Popery, and so divinely defend the articles of Christianitie, that (the sacred Scriptures excepted) there is not a booke to be founde, either more necessarie for thy profite, or sweeter for thy comfort* (London, 1579), 187r–v.

11. Marnix, *The Bee Hive of the Romishe Churche* (1579), 338–44.

12. C. Z. Wiener, 'The beleaguered isle. A study of Elizabethan and early Jacobean anti-Catholicism', *PP* 51 (1971), 49. P. Lake, 'The significance of the Elizabethan idenitification of the Pope as Antichrist', *JEH* 31 (1980), 161–78. P. Lake, 'William Bradshaw, Antichrist, and the community of the godly', *JEH* 36 (1985), 570–89. R. G. Asch, 'Antipopery and ecclesiastical policy in seventeenth-century Ireland', *AFR* 83 (1992), 258–301.

13. *Scots Confession, 1560, and Negative Confession, 1581* (ed.) G. D. Henderson (Edinburgh: Church of Scotland Publications, 1937).

14. C. Garside, *Zwingli and the arts* (New Haven [CT]: Yale University Press), 178.

15. L. P. Wandel, *Always among us. Images of the poor in Zwingli's Zurich* (Cambridge: Cambridge University Press, 1990). R. Scribner, 'Popular piety and modes of visual perception in late medieval and Reformation Germany', *Journal of Religious History* 15 (1989), 448–69. C. C. Christensen, 'Iconoclasm and the preservation of ecclesiastical art in reformation Nuernberg', *AFR* 61 (1970), 205–21.

16. F. Higman, 'The origins of the image of Geneva', in J. B. Roney, M. I. Klauber (eds), *The Identity of Geneva. The Christian Commonwealth, 1564–1864* (Westport [CT]: Greenwood Press, 1998), 27–9.

17. John Calvin, *Advertissement tresutile du grand proffit qui reviendroit à la Chrestienté s'il se faisoit inventoire de tous les corps sainctz, et reliques qui sont tant en Italie, qu'en France, Allemaigne, Hespaigne, et autres Royaumes et pays* (Geneva, 1543) in *Three French Treatises* (ed.) Higman (1970), 47–97.

18. Guillaume Farel, *Du Vray Usage de la Croix de Iesus Christ, et de l'abus et de l'idolatrie commise autour d'icelle, et de l'authorité de la parole de Dieu, et des traditions humaines* (1560).

19. Pierre Viret, *Du Vray Usage de la Salutation faite par l'ange a la vierge Marie, et de la source des chadelets, et de la maniere de prier par conte, et de l'abus qui y est: et du vray moyen par laquel la vierge Marie peut estre honorée* (1556).

20. *Reformed Confessions* (ed.) Cochrane (1966), 325.

21. L. P. Wandel, *Voracious idols and violent hands. Iconoclasm in Reformation Zurich, Strasbourg, and Basel* (Cambridge: Cambridge University Press, 1995). S. Ozment, *The reformation in the cities. The appeal of Protestantism to sixteenth-century Germany and Switzerland* (New Haven [CT]: Yale University Press, 1980). G. R. Potter, *Zwingli* (Cambridge: Cambridge University Press, 1976).

22. C. M. N. Eire, *War Against the Idols. The Reformation of worship from Erasmus to Calvin* (Cambridge: Cambridge University Press, 1986), 111.

23. C. M. N. Eire, 'Prelude to sedition? Calvin's attack on Nicodemism and religious compromise', *AFR* 76 (1985), 137.

24. D. McRoberts, 'Material destruction caused by the Scottish reformation', in McRoberts (ed.), *Essays on the Scottish reformation, 1513–1625* (Glasgow: Burns, 1962), 415–62. J. Dawson, ' "The face of ane perfyt Reformed kyrk": St Andrews and the early Scottish reformation', in J. Kirk (ed.), *Humanism and Reform: The Church in Europe, England, and Scotland, 1400–1643. Essays in Honour of James K. Cameron* (Oxford: Blackwell, 1991), 413–35.

25. P. M. Crew, *Calvinist Preaching and Iconoclasm in the Netherlands, 1544–69* (Cambridge: Cambridge University Press, 1978). P. M. Crew, 'The wonderyear. Reformed preaching and iconoclasm in the Netherlands' in J. Obelkevich (ed.), *Religion and the People, 800–1700* (Chapel Hill [NC]: University of North Carolina Press, 1979), 191–220. G. Marnef, *Antwerp in the age of Reformation. Underground Protestantism in a commercial metropolis, 1550–1577* (Baltimore [PA]: The Johns Hopkins University Press, 1996).

26. Philip Marnix, *A true narrative and apology of what has happened in the Netherlands in the matter of religion in the year 1566* (1567), in E. H. Kossman, A. F. Mellink (eds), *Texts Concerning the Revolt of the Netherlands* (Cambridge: Cambridge University Press, 1974), 80–1.

27. W. Naphy, *Documents on the Continental Reformation* (Basingstoke: Macmillan, 1996), 85.

28. J. P. Meyer, *Reformation in La Rochelle. Tradition and change in early modern Europe, 1500–1568* (Geneva: Droz, 1996). P. Benedict, 'The dynamics of Protestant militancy: France, 1555–1563', in P. Benedict, G. Marnef, H. van Nierop, M. Venard (eds), *Reformation, Revolt and Civil War in France and the Netherlands, 1555–1585* (Amsterdam: Royal Netherlands Academy, 1999), 35–50.

29. B. Diefendorf, *Beneath the Cross: Catholics and Huguenots in sixteenth-century Paris* (New York: Oxford University Press, 1991). P. Benedict, *Rouen during the Wars of Religion* (Cambridge: Cambridge University Press, 1991). P. Roberts, *A City in Conflict: Troyes during the French wars of religion* (Manchester: Manchester University Press, 1996). N. Z. Davis, 'The Rites of Violence: Religious riot in sixteenth-century France', *PP* 59 (1973), 51–91. J. Davies, 'Persecution and Protestantism: Toulouse, 1562–1572', *HJ* 22 (1979), 31–51. J. Farr, 'Popular religious solidarity in sixteenth-century Dijon', *French Historical Studies* 14 (1985), 192–214.

30. 'La Discipline Ecclesiastique des Eglises Reformées de France selon qu'elle a este arrestée aux Synodes nationaux par les deputes des provinces et ratifiée par toutes les Eglises, revue et confermee par le dernier Synode tenu a La Rochelle le 12 Avril 1571 et a Nismes le 7 May 1572' (ed.) G. S. Sunshine, *French History* 4 (1990), 376.

31. P. Benedict, 'The Saint Bartholomew's massacres in the provinces', *HJ* 21 (1978), 205–25. M. Greengrass, 'The anatomy of a religious riot in Toulouse in May 1562', *JEH* 34 (1983), 367–91. D. Nicholls, 'Protestants, Catholics and magistrates in Tours, 1562–1572: The making of a Catholic city during the religious wars', *French History*

8 (1994), 14–33. M. Konnert, 'Urban values versus religious passion: Châlons-sur-Marne during the wars of religion', *SCJ* 20 (1989), 387–405. M. Greengrass, *France in the Age of Henri IV: The struggle for stability* (2nd edn) (London: Longman, 1995).

32. S. Michalski, *The Reformation and the visual arts. The Protestant image question in western and eastern Europe* (London: Routledge, 1993), 76.

33. M. Aston, *England's Iconoclasts* (Oxford: Clarendon, 1988). J. Phillips, *The Reformation of Images: Destruction of Art in England, 1535–1660* (Berkeley [CA]: University of California Press, 1973).

34. H. Cohn, 'The territorial princes in Germany's second reformation, 1559–1622', in M. Prestwich (ed.), *International Calvinism, 1541–1715* (Oxford: Clarendon, 1985), 135–66. B. Nischan, 'The Second Reformation in Brandenburg: aims and goals', *SCJ* 14 (1983), 173–87.

35. *Miscellaneous Writings and Letters of Thomas Cranmer. Parker Society vol. 24* (ed.) J. Cox (Cambridge: Cambridge University Press, 1846), 431–4. *Original Letters Relative to the English Reformation Written During the Reigns of King Henry VIII, King Edward VI, and Queen Mary: Chiefly from the Archives of Zurich. Parker Society vols 23 and 28* (ed.) H. Robinson (2 vols) (Cambridge: Cambridge University Press, 1846–47), vol. 2 (1847), 711–14.

36. David Pareus, *Irenicum, sive de unione et synodo evangelicorum concilianda, votivus paci ecclesiae et desideriis pacificorum dicatus* (Heidelberg, 1614). J. M. Batten, *John Dury: Advocate of Christian reunion* (Chicago [IL]: University of Chicago Press, 1944).

37. *Acts and Proceedings of the General Assemblies of the Kirk of Scotland* (1839), vol. 1, 90. *The Zurich Letters, comprising the correspondence of several English bishops and others, with some of the Helvetian reformers, during the early part of the reign of Queen Elizabeth. The Parker Society, volumes 7 and 18* (ed.) H. Robinson (Cambridge: Cambridge University Press, 1843–45), vol. 18 (1845), 362–5.

38. Beza, *Confession de Foi du Chrétien* (1992), 77.

39. Jean-François Salvard, *An Harmony of the Confessions of the Faith of the Christian and Reformed Churches, which purelie professe the holy doctrine of the Gospell in all the chiefe kingdomes, nations, and provinces of Europe* (first pub. 1581) (Cambridge, 1586).

40. Salvard, *Harmony of the Confessions* (1586), preface.

41. *Actes Ecclesiastiques et civiles de tous les synodes nationaux des eglises reformées de France* (2 vols) (ed.) J. Aymon (The Hague, 1710), vol. 1, 131–3, 145.

42. *Les Actes des Colloques des Églises Françaises et des Synodes des Églises Étrangères Refugiées en Angleterre, 1581–1654 (Publications of the Huguenot Society 2)* (ed.) A. C. Chamier (Lymington: Huguenot Society, 1890), 1, 3–4.

43. *Actes de tous les synodes nationaux de France* (ed.) Aymon, vol. 1 (1710), 157–8, 170.

44. *Actes de tous les synodes nationaux de France* (ed.) Aymon vol. 1 (1710), 201, 227.

45. *Actes de tous les synodes nationaux de France* (ed.) Aymon, vol. 1 (1710), 300.

46. *Actes de tous les synodes nationaux de France* (ed.) Aymon, vol. 2 (1710), 38, 57–9. W. B. Patterson, 'James I and the Huguenot synod of Tonneins of 1614', *Harvard Theological Review* 65 (1972), 241–70.

47. *Actes de tous les synodes nationaux de France* (ed.) Aymon, vol. 2 (1710), 108–9.

48. C. Kooi, *Liberty and Religion. Church and State in Leiden's Reformation, 1572–1620* (Leiden: Brill, 2000), 125–61. B. J. Kaplan, *Calvinists and Libertines. Confession and community in Utrecht, 1578–1620* (Oxford: Clarendon, 1995), 229–60.

49. *Golden Remains of the ever memorable Mr. John Hales* (3rd edn) (London, 1688), 445–7, 454, 575. C. Grayson, 'James I and the religious crisis in the United Provinces, 1613–1619' and J. Platt, 'Eirenical Anglicans at the synod of Dort' in D. Baker (ed.), *Reform and Reformation: England and the Continent, c. 1500–1750. Studies in Church History Subsidia 2* (Oxford: Blackwell, 1979), 195–243.

50. *The Iudgement of the Synode holden at Dort, concerning the five articles: as also their sentence touching Conradus Vorstius* (London, 1619). *Golden Remains of John Hales* (1688), 455, 461. W. B. Patterson, 'The synod of Dort and the early Stuart church', in D. S. Armentrout (ed.), *This Sacred History* (Cambridge [MA]: Cowley Publications, 1990), 199–221.

51. *The Iudgement of the Synode holden at Dort* (1619), 75.

52. *Actes de tous les synodes nationaux de France* (ed.) Aymon, vol. 2 (1710), 182–4, 298–323.

53. *Petit Traicté de la Saincte Cene de nostre Seigneur Jesus Christ. Auquel est demonstrée la vraye institution, profit et utilité d'icelle. Ensemble, la cause pourquoy plusieurs des modernes semblent en avoir escrit diversement* (Geneva, 1542) in *Three French Treatises* (ed.) Higman (1970), 99–130.

54. *Consensus Tigurinus* (1549), in *John Calvin* (eds) G. R. Potter, M. Greengrass (London, Arnold, 1983), 129–30. Theodore Beza,

The Life of John Calvin (Geneva, 1564) in *Tracts and Treatises on the Reformation of the Church* (3 vols) (ed.) T. F. Torrance (Edinburgh: Oliver & Boyd, 1958) vol. 1, xcii. H. Oberman, 'The "extra" dimension in the theology of Calvin', *JEH* 21 (1970), 43–64. P. Rorem, *Calvin and Bullinger on the Lord's Supper* (Nottingham: Grove Books, 1989).

55. Beza, *Confession de Foi du Chrétien* (1992), 57, 64–7. J. Raitt, *The Eucharistic theology of Theodore Beza* (Chambersburg [PA]: American Academy of Religion, 1972).

56. See for example J. Raitt, *The Colloquy of Montbéliard. Religion and politics in the sixteenth century* (Oxford: Oxford University Press, 1993).

57. *The Formula of Concord* (1577) in *The Book of Concord. The Confessions of the Evangelical Lutheran Church* (ed.) T. G. Tappert (Philadelphia [PA]: Fortress Press, 1959), 481–7.

58. *Reformed Confessions* (ed.) Cochrane (1966), 157.

59. *Reformed Confessions* (ed.) Cochrane (1966), 179–80.

60. *Reformed Confessions* (ed.) Cochrane (1966), 216.

61. Péter Méliusz Juhász, *Catekizmus, az egész keresztyéni tudománynak fundamentoma és sommája… Calvinus János írása szerint* (Debrecen, 1562) in *Tanulmányok és szövegek a magyarországi református egyház xvi. századi történetéből. Studia et acta ecclesiastica 3* (ed.) T. Barth (Budapest, 1973), 222–77.

62. Bálint Szikszai, *Az egri keresztyén anyaszentegyháznak… rövid catechismus* (Debrecen, 1574). Bálint Szikszai, *A mi keresztyéni hitünknek és vallásunknak három főarticulusárol… való könyvecske* (Debrecen, 1574).

63. *Reformed Confessions* (ed.) Cochrane (1966), 280–1, 284–7. B. A. Gerrish, 'Sign and reality: the Lord's Supper in the Reformed Confession', in Gerrish, *The Old Protestantism and the New. Essays on the Reformation heritage* (Edinburgh: T&T Clark, 1982), 118–30.

64. L. D. Bierma, *The Doctrine of the sacraments in the Heidelberg Catechism: Melanchthonian, Calvinist or Zwinglian?* (Princeton [NJ]: Princeton Theological Seminary, 1999).

65. *Reformed Confessions* (ed.) Cochrane (1966), 318–19.

66. Calvin, *Institutes* (1559), 3/21–24, 3/21/5. T. H. L. Parker, *Calvin's doctrine of the knowledge of God* (Edinburgh: Oliver Boyd, 1969).

67. Calvin, *Institutes* (1559), 3/24/4.

68. Calvin, *Institutes* (1559), 3/10/6, 1/16/3, 4/14–17.

69. Jerome Bolsec, *Histoire de la vie, moeurs, actes, doctrine, constance et mort de Iean Calvin iadis ministre de Geneve (1577)* (ed.) L–F. Chastel (Lyon: Scheuring, 1875). P. C. Holtrop, *The Bolsec controversy on*

predestination, from 1551 to 1555 (Lewiston [NY]: Edwin Mellen Press, 1993), 290.

70. John Calvin, *De aeterna praedestinatione Dei* (Geneva, 1552) (ed.) J. K. S. Reid, *Concerning the Eternal Predestination of God* (London: James Clarke, 1961), 45–184, especially 69, 162.

71. R. A. Muller, *Christ and the Decree. Christology and Predestination in Reformed theology from Calvin to Perkins* (Durham [NC]: Labyrinth Press, 1986). B. Hall, 'Calvin against the Calvinist', in G. E. Duffield (ed.), *John Calvin* (Abingdon: Sutton Courtenay Press, 1966), 19–37.

72. Beza, *Life of John Calvin* (1958), xcvi.

73. J. S. Bray, *Theodore Beza's doctrine of predestination* (Nieuwkoop: B de Graaf, 1975).

74. *Reformed Confessions* (ed.) Cochrane (1966), 148.

75. *Reformed Confessions* (ed.) Cochrane (1966), 240–2. J. W. Baker, *Heinrich Bullinger and the Covenant: The other Reformed tradition* (Athens [OH]: Ohio University Press, 1980). C. P. Venema, 'Heinrich Bullinger's correspondence on Calvin's doctrine of predestination, 1551–1553', *SCJ* 17 (1986), 435–50.

76. Beza, *Confession de Foi du Chrétien* (1992), 26, 36, 39.

77. L. D. Bierma, *German Calvinism in the confessional age. The covenant theology of Caspar Olvenianus* (Grand Rapids [MI]: Baker Brooks, 1996). L. D. Bierma, 'The role of covenant theology in early Reformed orthodoxy', *SCJ* 21 (1990), 453–62.

78. William Perkins, *A Case of conscience, the greatest that ever was: how a man may know whether he be the child of God or no* (1592). *The work of William Perkins* (ed.) I. Breward (Abingdon: Sutton Courtenay Press, 1970). J. G. Moller, 'The beginnings of Puritan covenant theology', *JEH* 14 (1963), 46–67.

79. P. Collinson, *The Puritan character. Polemics and polarities in early seventeenth-century English culture* (Los Angeles [CA]: University of California, 1987). P. Collinson, *The Elizabethan Puritan movement* (Oxford: Clarendon Press, 1990). P. Lake, 'Calvinism and the English church, 1570–1635', *PP* 114 (1987), 32–76. D. Zaret, 'Ideology and organization in Puritanism', *European Journal of Sociology* 21 (1980) 83–115.

80. *Two Elizabethan Puritan diaries by Richard Rogers and Samuel Ward* (ed.) M. M. Knappen (Chicago: American Society of Church History, 1933), 57, 65. J. Stachniewski, *The Persecutory Imagination. English Puritanism and the literature of religious despair* (Oxford: Clarendon Press, 1991). C. Haigh, 'The taming of Reformation: Preachers, pastors and parishioners in Elizabethan and early Stuart England', *History* 85 (2000), 572–88.

81. P. Seaver, *Wallington's World. A Puritan artisan in seventeenth-century London* (London: Methuen, 1985).

82. A. Walsham, *Providence in early modern England* (Oxford: Oxford University Press, 1999).

83. Arthur Dent, *The plaine mans path-way to heaven* (London, 1601), 319.

84. Dent, *The plaine mans path-way to heaven* (1601), 33–5, 273–4, 320.

85. Max Weber, *The Protestant ethic and the spirit of capitalism* (1930), (London: Harper Collins, 1996). E. Troeltsch, 'Calvin and Calvinism', *Hibbert Journal* 8 (1909), 102–21. P. Seaver, 'The Puritan work ethic revisited', *Journal of British Studies* 19 (1980), 35–53.

86. John Calvin, 'De Luxu' (1546/7) in F. L. Battles, 'Against luxury and licence in Geneva. A forgotten fragment of Calvin', *Interpretation* 19 (1965), 192–5.

87. Weber, *The Protestant ethic and the spirit of capitalism* (1996), 98–128, 155–85. M. H. Lesnoff, *The Spirit of capitalism and the Protestant ethic. An enquiry into the Weber thesis* (Cambridge: Edward Elgar, 1994). D. Little, 'Max Weber revisited. The "Protestant ethic" and the Puritan experience of order', *Harvard Theological Review* 59 (1966), 415–28. G. Marshall, *In Search of the spirit of capitalism. An essay on Max Weber's Protestant ethic thesis* (Aldershot: Gregg Revivals, 1982). M. H. MacKinnon, 'The Longevity of the thesis: a critique of the crisis' in H. Lehmann, G. Roth (eds), *Weber's Protestant ethic. Origins, evidence, contexts* (Cambridge: Cambridge University Press, 1993), 211–44. G. Poggi, *Calvinism and the capitalist spirit. Max Weber's Protestant ethic* (London: Macmillan, 1983).

88. D. G. Mullan, *Scottish Puritanism, 1590–1638* (Oxford: Oxford University Press, 2000). L. Makkai, *A magyar puritánusok harca a feudálizmus ellen* (Budapest: MTA, 1952). G. Murdock, *Calvinism on the Frontier, 1600–1660. International Calvinism and the Reformed Church in Hungary and Transylvania* (Oxford: Clarendon, 2000).

89. J. R. Beeke, *Assurance of Faith. Calvin, English Puritanism, and the Dutch Second Reformation* (New York: Peter Lang, 1991). K. L. Sprunger, *The Learned Doctor William Ames: Dutch backgrounds of English and American Puritanism* (Urbana [IL]: University of Illinois Press, 1972). K. L. Sprunger, *Dutch Puritanism: a history of English and Scottish churches of the Netherlands in the sixteenth and seventeenth centuries* (Leiden: Brill, 1982). K. L. Sprunger, *Trumpets from the tower. English Puritan printing in the Netherlands 1600–1660* (Leiden: Brill, 1994).

90. Gisbert Voetius, *Selectae Disputationes Theologicae* (1648–69) in *Reformed Dogmatics* (ed.) J. W. Beardslee (New York: Oxford University Press, 1965), 263–334, 279. F. A. van Lieburg, 'From Pure church to pious

culture: The Further Reformation in the seventeenth-century Dutch Republic', in W. F. Graham (ed.), *Later Calvinism. International Perspectives. Sixteenth Century Essays and Studies* (Kirksville [MO]: North East Missouri State University, 1994), 409–29.

91. C. Bangs, *Arminius. A Study in the Dutch Reformation* (Nashville [TN]: Abingdon, 1971). W. Nijenhuis, 'Variants within Dutch Calvinism in the sixteenth century', *Acta Historiae Neerlandicae* 12 (1979), 48–64. D. Nobbs, *Theocracy and Toleration. A study of the disputes in Dutch Calvinism from 1600 to 1650* (Cambridge: Cambridge University Press, 1938).

92. P. Lake, *Moderate Puritans and the Elizabethan church* (Cambridge: Cambridge University Press, 1982), 201–42.

93. *Articles of Religion agreed upon by the Archbishops and Bishops, and the rest of the cleargie of Ireland, in the convocation holden at Dublin in... 1615* (Dublin, 1615), 11–17. A. Ford, *The Protestant reformation in Ireland* (Frankfurt: Lang, 1987). A. Ford, 'Dependent or independent? The church of Ireland and its colonial context', *Seventeenth Century* 10 (1995), 163–87.

94. *The Iudgement of the Synode holden at Dort* (1619), 67–73. H. D. Foster, 'Liberal Calvinism: the Remonstrants at the synod of Dort in 1618', *Harvard Theological Review* 16 (1923), 1–37.

95. *Golden Remains of John Hales* (1688), 460, 465, 480. R. Peters, 'John Hales and the synod of Dort' in D. Baker, G. J. Cuming (eds), *Councils and Assemblies. Studies in Church History Volume 7* (Cambridge: Cambridge University Press, 1971), 277–88.

96. *The Iudgement of the Synode holden at Dort* (1619), 7, 1–56.

97. Johannes Wolleb, 'Compendium Theologiae Christianae' (1626) in *Reformed Dogmatics* (ed.) Beardslee (1965), 26–262, 50–3. J. R. Beeke, 'The order of the divine decrees at the Genevan Academy: from Bezan supralapsarianism to Turretinian infralapsarianism', in J. B. Roney, M. I. Klauber (eds), *The Identity of Geneva. The Christian Commonwealth, 1564–1864* (Westport [CT]: Greenwood Press, 1998), 57–75. B. G. Armstrong, *Calvinism and the Amyraut heresy: Protestant scholasticism and humanism in seventeenth-century France* (Madison [WI]: University of Wisconsin Press, 1969).

Chapter 2: International Connections

1. H. A. Oberman, '*Europa afflicta*: The reformation of the refugees', *AFR* 83 (1992), 91–111.

2. Jan Utenhove, *Simplex et fidelis narratio de instituta ac demum dissipata Belgarum, aliorumque peregrinorum in Anglia, ecclesia: et potissimum de susceptis postea illius nomine itineribus, quaeque eis in illis evenerunt* (1560).

3. *The Vocacyon of Johan Bale* (eds) P. Happé, J. King (Binghamton [NY]: Medieval and Renaissance Texts and Studies, 1990), 79.

4. Theodore Beza, *The Life of John Calvin* (Geneva, 1564) in *Tracts and Treatises on the Reformation of the Church* (3 vols) (ed.) T. F. Torrance (Edinburgh: Oliver & Boyd, 1958), vol. 1, lxvi–lxvii.

5. Beza's 1560 letter in D. R. Kelley, *The Beginning of Ideology. Consciousness and society in the French Reformation* (Cambridge: Cambridge University Press, 1981), 53.

6. Beza, *Life of John Calvin* (1958), lxxvii–lxxviii.

7. R. M. Kingdon, *Geneva and the coming of the wars of religion in France, 1555–1563* (Geneva: Droz, 1956), 135–48. R. M. Kingdon, *Geneva and the consolidation of the French Protestant movement, 1564–1572* (Geneva: Droz, 1967), 30.

8. E. W. Monter, 'Historical demography and religious history in sixteenth-century Geneva', *Journal of Interdisciplinary History* 9 (1979), 399–427. P. Denis, *Les Églises d'étrangers en pays Rhénans (1538–1564)* (Liège: L'Université de Liège, 1984). L. J. Abray, *The People's reformation. Magistrates, clergy, and commons in Strasbourg, 1500–1598* (Oxford: Blackwell, 1985), 126–39.

9. E. W. Monter, 'The Italians in Geneva, 1550–1600: A new look' in L. Monnier (ed.), *Genève et L'Italie* (Geneva: Droz, 1969), 53–77.

10. J. E. Olson, *Calvin and Social Welfare. Deacons and the Bourse Française* (Cranbury [NJ]: Associated University Presses, 1989), 145–6.

11. Jerome Bolsec, *Extrait de l'histoire de la vie, moeurs, doctrine, et déportements de Théodore de Bèze* (1582) (ed.) L– F. Chastel (Lyon: Scheuring, 1875), 141.

12. J. Lindeboom, *Austin Friars. History of the Dutch Reformed church in London, 1550–1950* (The Hague: Martinus Nijhoff, 1950), 201. M. Anderson, 'Rhetoric and reality: Peter Martyr and the English reformation', *SCJ* 19 (1988), 451–69.

13. Johannes à Lasco, *Forma ac ratio tota ecclesiastici ministerij, in peregrinorum, potissimum vero Germanorum ecclesia: Institut a Londini in Anglia, per pietissimum principem Angliae etc. regem Eduardum, eius nominis sextum* (1554). B. Hall, *John à Lasco, 1499–1560. A Pole in Reformation London* (London: Dr William's Trust, 1971).

14. *Original Letters Relative to the English Reformation Written During the Reigns of King Henry VIII, King Edward VI, and Queen Mary: Chiefly from*

the Archives of Zurich. Parker Society vols 23 and 28 (ed.) H. Robinson (Cambridge: Cambridge University Press, 1846–47), vol. 28 (1847), 570–3.

15. C. H. Garrett, *The Marian Exiles. A Study in the origins of Elizabethan Puritanism* (Cambridge: Cambridge University Press, 1938). N. M. Sutherland, 'The Marian exiles and the establishment of the Elizabethan regime', *AFR* 78 (1987), 253–86. A. Pettegree, *Marian Protestantism. Six Studies* (Aldershot: Scolar, 1996).

16. Miles Coverdale, *Certain most godly, fruitful, and comfortable letters of such true Saintes and holy Martyrs of God, as in the late bloodye persecution here within this Realme, gave their lyves for the defense of Christes holy gospel: written in the tyme of theyr affliction and cruell imprysonment* (London, 1564), 51–6. D. G. Danner, *Pilgrimage to Puritanism. History and theology of the Marian exiles at Geneva, 1555–1560* (New York: Peter Lang, 1999). H. J. Cowell, 'The sixteenth-century English-speaking refugee churches at Strasbourg, Basle, Zurich, Aarau, Wesel, and Emden', *PHS* 15 (1933–37), 612–55.

17. Nicolas des Gallars, *Forma Politiae Ecclesiasticae, nuper institutae Londini in coetu Gallorum* (London, 1561).

18. A. Pettegree, *Foreign Protestant communities in sixteenth-century London* (Oxford: Clarendon, 1986). P. Collinson, 'Calvinism with an Anglican face: the stranger churches in early Elizabethan London and their superintendent', in D. Baker (ed.), *Reform and Reformation: England and the Continent, c. 1500–1750. Studies in Church History Subsidia 2* (Oxford: Blackwell, 1979), 71–102. A. Spicer, *The French-speaking Reformed community and their church in Southampton, c. 1567–1620* (Stroud: Sutton Publishing, 1999). L. F. Roker, 'The Flemish and Dutch community in Colchester in the sixteenth and seventeenth centuries', *PHS* 21 (1965–70), 15–30.

19. A. Soman (ed.), *The Massacre of St Bartholomew. Reappraisals and documents* (The Hague: Nijhoff, 1974), 66. P. A. Welsby, *George Abbot. The unwanted archbishop, 1562–1633* (London: SPCK, 1962). M. Greengrass, 'Protestant exiles and their assimilation in early modern England', *Immigrants and Minorities* 4 (1985), 68–81.

20. The only similar scale of exile was when at least 150 000 Huguenots left France during the 1680s.

21. F. A. Norwood, *The Reformation refugees as an economic force* (Chicago: The American Society of Church History, 1942), 172.

22. H. Schilling, 'Innovation through migration: The settlements of Calvinistic Netherlanders in sixteenth- and seventeenth-century central and western Europe', *Histoire Sociale-Social History* 16 (1983), 15.

23. A. Pettegree, *Emden and the Dutch Revolt. Exile and the development of Reformed Protestantism* (Oxford: Clarendon, 1992). A. Pettegree, 'The Exile churches and the churches "under the cross": Antwerp and Emden during the Dutch revolt', *JEH* 38 (1987), 187–209. A. Pettegree, 'The exile churches during the Wonderjaar', in J. van den Berg, P. G. Hoftijzer (eds), *Church, change and revolution. Transactions of the Fourth Anglo-Dutch history colloquium* (London: Brill, 1991), 80–99.

24. Pettegree, *Foreign Protestant communities in sixteenth-century London* (1986), 253–5.

25. M. F. Backhouse, *The Flemish and Walloon communities of Sandwich during the reign of Elizabeth I* (Brussels: Koninklijke Academie van België, 1985), 31. M. F. Backhouse, 'The official start of armed resistance in the Low Countries: Boeschepe, 12 July 1562', *AFR* 71 (1980), 198–225. M. F. Backhouse, 'Guerilla war and banditry in the sixteenth century: the Wood Beggars in the Westkwartier of Flanders (1567–1568)', *AFR* 74 (1983), 232–51.

26. W. Steven, *The History of the Scottish church, Rotterdam* (Edinburgh: Waugh and Innes, 1882). A. Carter, *The English Reformed Church in Amsterdam in the seventeenth century* (Amsterdam: Scheltema and Holkema, 1964). C. de Jong, 'John Forbes (c. 1568–1634), Scottish minister and exile in the Netherlands', *Archief voor Kerkgeschiedenis* 69 (1989), 17–53.

27. P. Collinson, 'The Elizabethan puritans and the foreign Reformed churches in London', *PHS* 20 (1962–63), 528–55. O. P. Grell, 'The French and Dutch congregations in London in the early seventeenth century', *PHS* 24 (1987), 362–77. M. Greengrass, 'Samuel Hartlib and International Calvinism', *PHS* 25 (1993), 464–75.

28. B. Cottret, *The Huguenots in London. Immigration and settlement, c. 1550–1700* (Cambridge: Cambridge University Press, 1991). O. P. Grell, *Calvinist Exiles in Tudor and Stuart England* (Aldershot: Scolar 1996), 45–8. O. P. Grell, *Dutch Calvinists in early Stuart London. The Dutch Church in Austin Friars, 1603–1642* (Leiden: Brill, 1989).

29. *The Scottish contributions to the distressed church of France in 1622. Publications of the Scottish History Society. Second series. Volume 19. Miscellany Volume 3* (ed.) D. H. Fleming (Edinburgh: Edinburgh University Press, 1919), 179–202.

30. *Acts and proceedings of the General Assemblies of the Kirk of Scotland from the year MDLX* (2 vols) (Edinburgh: The Maitland Club, 1839–45), vol. 1 (1839), 356.

31. *Register of the minister, elders and deacons of the Christian congregation of St Andrews. Comprising the proceedings of the kirk session and of the court of*

the superintendent of Fife, Fothrik and Strathearn, 1559–1600 (2 vols) (ed.) D. H. Fleming (Edinburgh: Edinburgh University Press, 1889–90), vol. 1 (1889), 610.

32. *Narratives and Extracts from the Records of the Presbytery of Ellon* (ed.) T. Mair (Peterhead: David Scott, 1894), 42.

33. David Calderwood, *The true history of the Church of Scotland* (ed.) T. Thomson (8 vols) (Edinburgh, 1842–49), vol. 7, 543. *Acts of the General Assemblies of the Kirk of Scotland* (1845), vol. 2, 1165–67. A. R. MacDonald, *The Jacobean Kirk, 1567–1625. Sovereignty, polity and liturgy* (Aldershot: Ashgate, 1998), 159.

34. D. J. B. Trim, 'Sir Thomas Bodley and the international Protestant cause', *Bodleian Library Record* 16 (1998), 329.

35. Olson, *Calvin and Social Welfare* (1989). R. M. Kingdon, 'Social welfare in Calvin's Geneva', *AHR* 76 (1971), 50–69.

36. T. G. Fehler, *Poor relief and Protestantism. The Evolution of social welfare in sixteenth-century Emden* (Aldershot: Ashgate, 1999).

37. Lindeboom, *Austin Friars* (1950), 78, 81, 87.

38. O. P. Grell, 'Godly charity or political aid? Irish Protestants and international Calvinism, 1641–1645', *HJ* 39 (1996), 743–53.

39. K. Maag, *Seminary or university? The Genevan academy and Reformed higher education, 1560–1620* (Aldershot: Scolar, 1995). G. Lewis, 'The Genevan Academy', in A. C. Duke, G. Lewis, A. Pettegree (eds), *Calvinism in Europe, 1540–1620* (Cambridge: Cambridge University Press, 1994), 35–63. R. M. Kingdon, 'The Political resistance of the Calvinists in France and the Low Countries', *Church History* 27 (1958), 222.

40. E. K. Hudson, 'The Protestant struggle for survival in early Bourbon France: the case of the Huguenot schools', *AFR* 76 (1985), 271–95. R. Stauffer, 'Calvinism and the Universities', in L. Grane (ed.), *University and Reformation. Lectures from the University of Copenhagen symposium* (Leiden: Brill, 1981), 76–98. G. T. Jensma, F. R. H. Smit, F. Westra (eds), *Universiteit te Franeker 1585–1811* (Leeuwarden: Fryske Akademy, 1985), 222.

41. G. Bonet-Maury, 'John Cameron: A Scottish Protestant theologian in France', *Scottish Historical Review* 7 (1910), 325–45.

42. H. R. Guggisberg, *Basel in the sixteenth century. Aspects of the city republic before, during, and after the Reformation* (St Louis [MO]: Center for Reformation Research, 1982), 44, 48–9.

43. B. Vogler, 'Les contacts culturels entre Huguenots français et protestants palatins au 16e siècle', *BSHPF* 115 (1969), 37.

44. G. Szabó, *Geschichte des Ungarischen Coetus an der Universität Wittenberg, 1555–1613* (Halle, 1941), 105–23.

45. B. Nischan, 'The schools of Brandenburg and the "second Reformation": centers of Calvinist learning and propaganda', in R. V. Schnucker (ed.), *Calviniana. Ideas and influence of Jean Calvin: Sixteenth century essays and studies, volume 10* (Kirksville [MO]: Sixteenth Century Journal Publishers, 1988), 215–33. J. Israel, *The Dutch Republic. Its rise, greatness, and fall, 1477–1806* (Oxford: Oxford University Press, 1995), 565–94, 899–902. Th. H. Lunsingh Scheurleer, G. H. M. Posthumus Meyjes (eds), *Leiden university in the seventeenth century. An exchange of learning* (Leiden: Brill, 1975).

46. Márton Szepsi Csombor, *Europica Varietas* (1620) in *Szepsi Csombor Márton összes művei* (eds) S. Kovács, P. Kulcsár (Budapest: Akadémiai Kiadó, 1968), 183–93.

47. Albert Szenczi Molnár, *Psalterium Ungaricum* (Herborn, 1607). Molnár, *Szent Biblia… az palatinatusi catechismussal* (Oppenheim, 1612). Molnár, *A keresztyéni religióra és igaz hitre való tanítás* (Hanau, 1624).

48. G. Murdock, *Calvinism on the Frontier, 1600–1660. International Calvinism and the Reformed Church in Hungary and Transylvania* (Oxford: Clarendon, 2000).

49. N. L. Roelker, 'The role of noblewomen in the French reformation', *AFR* 63 (1972), 168–95. C. J. Blaisdell, 'Calvin's and Loyola's letters to women: politics and spiritual counsel in the sixteenth century' in Schnucker (ed.), *Calviniana* (1988), 235–53.

50. B. Vogler, 'Europe as seen through the correspondence of Theodore Beza', in E. I. Kouri, T. Scott (eds), *Politics and society in Reformation Europe. Essays for Sir Geoffrey Elton on his sixty-fifth birthday* (Basingstoke: Macmillan, 1987), 252–66. I. Schlégl, 'Die Beziehungen Heinrich Bullingers zu Ungarn', *Zwingliana* 12 (1966), 33–70. C. d'Eszlary, 'Jean Calvin, Théodore de Bèze et leurs amis hongrois', *BSHPF* 110 (1964), 74–99. *Original Letters*, vol. 28 (1847), 596–604, 689–92.

51. *Original Letters*, vol. 23 (1846), 169–70.

52. *A brief discourse of the troubles begun at Frankfort in Germany, anno domini 1554, about the Book of Common Prayer and Ceremonies; and continued by the Englishmen there to the end of Queen Mary's reign* (1575). *Original Letters* (ed.) Robinson vol. 23 (1846), 170–2, vol. 28 (1847), 753–63. D. G. Danner, 'Calvin and Puritanism: the career of William Whittingham', in Schnucker (ed.), *Calviniana* (1988), 151–63.

53. Christopher Goodman, *How superior powers ought to be obeyed of their subjects: and wherein they may lawfully by Gods worde be disobeyed and*

resisted, wherein also is declared the cause of all this present misery in England, and the onely way to remedy the same (Geneva, 1558). John Knox, *The First Blast of the Trumpet against the monstrous regiment of women* (1558) in *John Knox. On Rebellion* (ed.) R. A. Mason (Cambridge: Cambridge University Press, 1994), 3–47.

54. *The Zurich Letters, comprising the correspondence of several English bishops and others, with some of the Helvetian reformers, during the early part of the reign of Queen Elizabeth. The Parker Society, volumes 7 and 18* (ed.) H. Robinson (Cambridge: Cambridge University Press, 1843–45), vol. 18 (1845), 36.

55. *Zurich Letters*, vol. 7 (1843), 64–5.

56. *Zurich Letters*, vol. 7 (1843), 296.

57. *Acts of the General Assemblies of the Kirk of Scotland* vol. 1 (1839), 94, 252–4, 409–10, 569–70, 613, 727, 759–61, 854. R. M. Kingdon, *Myths about the St Bartholomew's day massacres, 1572–1576* (Cambridge [MA]: Harvard University Press, 1988).

58. *Zurich Letters*, vol. 18 (1845), 318–19.

59. N. M. Sutherland, 'The origins of Queen Elizabeth's relations with the Huguenots, 1559–62', *PHS* 20 (1958–64), 626–48. R. B. Wernham, 'Queen Elizabeth and the siege of Rouen, 1591', *Transactions of the Royal Historical Society* 15 (1932), 163–79. D. J. B. Trim, 'The "secret war" of Elizabeth I. England and the Huguenots during the early wars of religion, 1562–1577', *PHS* 27 (1999), 189–99. J. Raitt, 'Elizabeth of England, John Casimir, and the Protestant league', in D. Visser (ed.), *Controversy and conciliation. The reformation and the Palatinate, 1559–1583* (Allison Park [PA]: Pickwick, 1984), 117–45.

60. E. I. Kouri, 'For true faith or national interest? Queen Elizabeth I and the Protestant powers', in Kouri and Scott (eds), *Politics and Society in Reformation Europe* (1987), 411–37.

61. N. M. Sutherland, *The Massacre of St. Bartholomew and the European conflict, 1559–1572* (London: Macmillan, 1973). J. Shimizu, *Conflict of Loyalties. Politics and religion in the career of Gaspard de Coligny Admiral of France, 1519–1572* (Geneva: Droz, 1970).

62. C-P. Clasen, *The Palatinate in European History, 1559–1618* (Oxford: Blackwell, 1966).

63. A. C. Duke, G. Lewis, A. Pettegree (eds), *Calvinism in Europe, 1540–1610. A collection of documents* (Manchester: Manchester University Press, 1992), 230.

64. E. I. Kouri, *England and the attempts to form a Protestant alliance in the late 1560s: a case study in European diplomacy* (Helsinki: Suomalainen Tiedeakatemia, 1981), 97, 137. B. Vogler, 'Le rôle des Électeurs

palatins dans les guerres de religion en France (1559–1592)', *Cahiers d'Histoire* 10 (1965), 51–85. M. Greengrass, 'Financing the cause: Protestant mobilization and accountability in France (1562–1589)', in P. Benedict, G. Marnef, H. van Nierop, M. Venard (eds), *Reformation, Revolt and Civil War in France and the Netherlands, 1555–1585* (Amsterdam: Royal Netherlands Academy, 1999), 233–54.

65. H. T. Gräf, 'The Collegium Mauritianum in Hesse-Kassel and the making of Calvinist diplomacy', *SCJ* 28 (1997), 1167–80.

66. D. Daniel, 'The Fifteen Years' War and the Protestant response to Habsburg absolutism in Hungary', *East Central Europe* 8 (1981), 38–51.

67. K. MacHardy, 'The rise of absolutism and noble rebellion in early modern Habsburg Austria, 1570–1620', *Comparative Studies in Society and History* 34 (1992), 407–38. J. Bahlcke, 'Calvinism and estate liberation movements in Bohemia and Hungary (1570–1620)', in K. Maag (ed.), *The Reformation in Eastern and Central Europe* (Aldershot: Scolar, 1997), 72–91. O. Odlozilík, 'A Church in a hostile state: the unity of Czech Brethren', *Central European History* 6 (1973), 111–27. G. Parker, *The Thirty Years' War* (London: Routledge, 1984), 12–25.

68. R. Zaller, ' "Interest of state": James I and the Palatinate', *Albion* 6 (1974), 144–75.

69. D. Parker, *La Rochelle and the French monarchy: conflict and order in seventeenth-century France* (London: Royal Historical Society, 1980). S. L. Adams, 'The Road to La Rochelle: English foreign policy and the Huguenots, 1610–1629', *PHS* 22 (1975), 414–29. J. A. Clarke, *Huguenot Warriors. The life and times of Henri de Rohan, 1579–1638* (The Hague: Nijhoff, 1966).

Chapter 3: Politics and Rebellion

1. 'Ecclesiastical Ordinances of Jeanne d'Albret, November 1571', in N. L. Roelker, *Queen of Navarre. Jeanne d'Albret, 1528–1572* (Cambridge [MA]: Harvard University Press, 1968), 209, 430.

2. G. Murdock, 'The importance of being Josiah: An image of Calvinist identity', *SCJ* 29 (1998), 1043–59.

3. John Calvin, *Institutes of the Christian Religion* (Geneva, 1559) (2 vols) (ed.) H. Beveridge (Edinburgh: Calvin Translation Society, 1845), 4/20/4. *Luther and Calvin on Secular Authority* (ed.) H. Höpfl (Cambridge: Cambridge University Press, 1982), 52. H. Höpfl, *The Christian polity of John Calvin* (Cambridge: Cambridge University Press, 1982).

4. *The Political Thought of Peter Martyr Vermigli. Selected Texts and Commentary* (ed.) R. M. Kingdon (Geneva: Droz, 1980), 12, 20, 24. See also the call to obey magistrates in the *Second Helvetic Confession* in *Reformed Confessions of the 16th Century* (ed.) A. C. Cochrane (London: SCM Press, 1966), 300.

5. Martin Bucer, *De Regno Christi* (1550) in *Melanchthon and Bucer* (ed.) W. Pauck (London: SCM Press, 1969), 174–394. C. Hopf, *Martin Bucer and the English Reformation* (Oxford: Blackwell, 1946), 99–128.

6. Bucer, *De Regno Christi* (1969), 384.

7. *Original letters relative to the English Reformation written during the reigns of King Henry VIII, King Edward VI, and Queen Mary: Chiefly from the Archives of Zurich. Parker Society vols 23 and 28* (ed.) H. Robinson (2 vols) (Cambridge: Cambridge University Press, 1846–47), vol. 28 (1847), 715.

8. Calvin, *Institutes* (1559), 4/20/8, 4/20/23–25. *Luther and Calvin on Secular Authority* (ed.) Höpfl (1982), 56–7, 75–6.

9. W. Balke, *Calvin and the Anabaptist radicals* (Grand Rapids [MI]: William Eerdmans, 1981), 292.

10. Calvin, *Institutes* (1559), 4/20/31–2. *Luther and Calvin on Secular Authority* (ed.) Höpfl (1982), 82–3.

11. *The Political Thought of Peter Martyr Vermigli* (ed.) Kingdon (1980), 51.

12. R. M. Kingdon, 'The political thought of Peter Martyr Vermigli', in J. C. McLelland (ed.), *Peter Martyr Vermigli and Italian Reform* (Waterloo [ON]: Wilfrid Laurier University Press, 1980), 121–39. M. Anderson, *Peter Martyr. A Reformer in Exile (1542–1562). A Chronology of Biblical writings in England and Europe* (Nieuwkoop: De Graaf, 1975).

13. *The Political Thought of Peter Martyr Vermigli* (ed.) Kingdon (1980), 99–100.

14. *Bekentnis Unterricht und Vermanung der Pfarrhern und Prediger der Christlichen Kirchen zu Magdeburgt* (1550). Philip Melanchthon, *Loci Communes Theologici* (1521) in *Melanchthon and Bucer* (ed.) Pauck (1969), 62, 148–50. E. Hildebrandt, 'The Magdeburg *Bekenntnis* as a possible link between German and English resistance theories in the sixteenth century', *AFR* 71 (1980), 227–53. C. G. Schoenberger, 'The development of the Lutheran theory of resistance, 1523–1530', *SCJ* 8 (1977), 61–76.

15. Theodore Beza, *De haereticis a civili magistratu puniendis* (1554) in *Théodore de Bèze. Du Droit des Magistrats* (ed.) R. M. Kingdon (Geneva: Droz: 1971), 69–70.

16. Beza, *De haereticis a civili magistratu puniendis* (1554), 133. R. M. Kingdon, 'The first expression of Theodore Beza's political ideas', *AFR* 46 (1955), 92.

17. Thedore Beza, *Confession de Foi du Chrétien* (Geneva, 1558) (ed.) J. Clarke (Lewes: Focus Christian Ministries Trust, 1992), 114–17.

18. John Ponet, *A short treatise of politike power, and of the true obedience which subiectes owe to kynges and other civile governours, with an exhortacion to all true naturall Englishe men* (1556), 108.

19. Ponet, *A short treatise of politike power* (1556), 53, 75, 111–12. W. S. Hudson, *John Ponet (1516?–1556). Advocate of limited monarchy* (Chicago [IL]: University of Chicago Press, 1942).

20. Christopher Goodman, *How Superior powers ought to be obeyed of their subjects: and wherein they may lawfully by Gods worde be disobeyed and resisted, wherein also is declared the cause of all this present misery in England, and the onely way to remedy the same* (Geneva, 1558), 42, 49, 60, 96. D. G. Danner, 'Christopher Goodman and the English Protestant tradition of civil disobedience', *SCJ* 8 (1977), 61–73. J. Dawson, 'Resistance and revolution in sixteenth-century thought: the case of Christopher Goodman', in J. van den Berg, P. G. Hoftijzer (eds), *Church, change and revolution. Transactions of the Fourth Anglo-Dutch History Conference* (Leiden: Brill, 1991), 69–79.

21. Goodman, *How Superior powers ought to be obeyed* (1558), 185. D. H. Wollman, 'The Biblical justification for resistance to authority in Ponet's and Goodman's polemics', *SCJ* 13 (1982), 29–41.

22. W. S. Reid, *Trumpeter of God. A Biography of John Knox* (New York: Scribner, 1974).

23. John Knox, *The First Blast of the Trumpet against the monstrous regiment of women* (Geneva, 1558) in *John Knox. On Rebellion* (ed.) R. A. Mason (Cambridge: Cambridge University Press, 1994), 3–47, 4, 8, 30, 35, 46.

24. Knox, *The First Blast of the Trumpet* (1994), 27.

25. Knox, *The First Blast of the Trumpet* (1994), 30.

26. Knox, *The First Blast of the Trumpet* (1994), 47.

27. Beza, *Confession de Foi du Chrétien* (1992), 115. J. M. Richards, ' "To promote a woman to beare rule": Talking of queens in mid-Tudor England', *SCJ* 28 (1997), 115.

28. John Aylmer, *An Harborowe for faithfull and trewe subiectes, agaynst the late blowne Blaste, concerninge the government of women, wherein be confuted all such reasons as a straunger of late made in that behalfe, with a briefe exhortation to obedience* (Strasbourg, 1559).

29. *The Geneva Bible* (ed.) L. E. Berry (Madison [WI]: University of Wisconsin Press, 1969), see for example the notes on Romans 13:5 and Titus 3:1. M. S. Betteridge, 'The Bitter notes: The Geneva Bible and its annotations', *SCJ* 14 (1983), 41–62.

30. Thomas Bilson, *The True difference between Christian subjection and unchristian rebellion: wherein the princes lawful power to command for truth, and indepriveable right to beare the sword, are defended against the Popes censures and the Iesuits sophisme* (London, 1586), 273, 278–9, 281–2.

31. Richard Hooker, *Of the Laws of Ecclesiasticall Politie* (ed.) W. S. Hill (6 vols) (Cambridge [MA]: Harvard University Press, 1977–93), vol. 3 (1977), 337–8.

32. *The Appellation of John Knox from the cruel and most injust sentence pronounced against him by the false bishops and clergy of Scotland, with his application and exhortation to the nobility, estates, and commonalty of the same realm* (Geneva, 1558) in *John Knox* (ed.) Mason (1994), 72–114, 94–5, 102. J. Dawson, 'The two John Knoxes: England, Scotland and the 1558 tracts', *JEH* 42 (1991), 555–76. W. S. Reid, 'John Knox's theology of political government', *SCJ* 19 (1988), 529–40.

33. *Letter… to his beloved brethren the commonalty of Scotland* (1558) in *John Knox* (ed.) Mason (1994), 115–27, 118.

34. *Reformed Confessions* (ed.) Cochrane (1966), 182–3. J. Wormald, *Court, kirk, and community. Scotland, 1470–1625* (Edinburgh: Edinburgh University Press, 1991), 115.

35. R. M. Healey, 'Waiting for Deborah: John Knox and four ruling queens', *SCJ* 25 (1994), 382–3. J. Wormald, 'Godly reformer, godless monarch: John Knox and Mary Queen of Scots', in R. A. Mason (ed.), *John Knox and the British Reformations* (Aldershot: Ashgate, 1998), 220–41.

36. *John Knox* (ed.) Mason (1994), 128–9, 176–9, 185, 195–6.

37. George Buchanan, *De Iure Regni apud Scotos, Dialogus* (Edinburgh, 1579), 61, 66. John Mair, *A History of Greater Britain as well England as Scotland* (1521) (ed.) A. Constable (Edinburgh: Edinburgh University Press, 1892), 213–15. R. A. Mason, '*Rex Stoicus*: George Buchanan, James VI and the Scottish polity', in J. Dwyer, R. A. Mason, A. Murdoch (eds), *New Perspectives on the politics and culture of early modern Scotland* (Edinburgh: John Donald 1986), 9–33. J. H. Burns, *The true law of kingship. Concepts of monarchy in early modern Scotland* (Oxford: Clarendon, 1996).

38. *Acts and Proceedings of the General Assemblies of the Kirk of Scotland, from the year MDLX* (2 vols) (Edinburgh: The Maitland Club, 1839–45), vol. 1 (1839), 441–8, 771.

39. James Stuart, *Basilikon Doron, or his Majesties instructions to his dearest sonne, Henry the Prince* and *The Trew Law of Free Monarchies: Or the reciprock and mutuall duetie betwixt a free king, and his naturall subjects* (1598) in *The Political Works of James I* (ed.) C. H. McIlwain (New York: Russell and Russell, 1965), 23–4, 62, 67–9.

40. *The Historie of the Lyff of James Melvill* (ed.) J. G. Fyfe (Edinburgh: Oliver and Boyd, 1948), 66–7.

41. *Reformed Confessions* (ed.) Cochrane (1966), 158.

42. R. D. Linder, *The Political ideas of Pierre Viret* (Geneva: Droz, 1964), 132.

43. *Actes Ecclesiastiques et civiles de tous les synodes nationaux des eglises reformées de France* (ed.) J. Aymon (2 vols) (The Hague, 1710), vol. 1, 22.

44. Jean de Coras, *Question Politique: s'il est licite aux subjects de capituler avec leur prince* (1570) (ed.) R. M. Kingdon (Geneva: Droz, 1989), 5–6.

45. *Le Tocsin, Contre les Massacreurs et auteurs des confusions en France. Par laquel, la source et origine de tous les maux, qui de long temps travaillent le France, est decouverte* (1579).

46. Innocent Gentillet, *Discours, sur les moyens de bien gouverner et maintenir en bonne paix un Royaume ou autre Principauté… contra Nicolas Machiavel Florentin* (1576) in *Anti-Machiavel* (ed.) C. E. Rathé (Geneva: Droz, 1968). J. R. Smither, 'The St Bartholomew's day massacre and images of kingship in France, 1572–1574', *SCJ* 22 (1991), 27–46.

47. D. R. Kelley, *François Hotman. A Revolutionary's Ordeal* (Princeton [NJ]: Princeton University Press, 1973). R. E. Giesey, 'When and why Hotman wrote the *Francogallia*', *BHR* 29 (1967), 581–611.

48. François Hotman, *Francogallia: or, an account of the ancient free state of France* (London, 1711), 42–5.

49. François Hotman, *De iure successionis regiae in regno Francorum. Leges aliquot ex probatis auctorib. collectae studio et opera Francisci Hotomani Iuris–consulti* (1588), 112. R. E. Giesey, *If not, not. The oath of the Aragonese and the legendary laws of Sobrarbe* (Princeton [NJ]: Princeton University Press, 1968).

50. Hotman, *Francogallia* (1711), 126.

51. Theodore Beza, *Du droit des magistrats sur leurs subjects* (Heidelberg, 1574) in *Constitutionalism and Resistance in the sixteenth century. Three treatises by Hotman, Beza and Mornay* (ed.) J. H. Franklin (New York: Pegasus, 1969), 101–35, 115. R. E. Giesey, 'The monarchomach triumvirs: Hotman, Beza and Mornay', *BHR* 32 (1970), 41–56.

52. Beza, *Du droit des magistrats sur leurs subjects* (1969), 111–12.

53. Beza, *Du droit des magistrats sur leurs subjects* (1969), 134–5.

54. Nicolas Barnaud, *Le Reveille-Matin des François, et de leurs Voisins par Eusebe Philadelphe Cosmopolite* (1574), 76–7, 80, 84–5, 152, 190. Barnaud, *Le Miroir des François, compris en trois livres* (1582), 307, 312. D. R. Kelley, *The Beginning of Ideology. Consciousness and society in the French Reformation* (Cambridge: Cambridge University Press, 1981), 304.

55. Philippe Duplessis-Mornay, *Vindiciae contra tyrannos, sive de principis in populum et populi in principem legitima potestate, Stephano Junio Bruto Celta auctore* (1579) in *Consitutionalism and Resistance in the sixteenth century* (ed.) Franklin (1969), 142–99, 160.

56. Mornay, *Vindiciae contra tyrannos* (1969), 156, 180, 182–3, 185, 190, 196, 198. A. L. Herman, 'Protestant churches in a Catholic kingdom: political assemblies in the thought of Philippe Duplessis-Mornay', *SCJ* 21 (1990), 543–57.

57. K. A. Parrow, *From Defense to Resistance: Justification on violence during the French wars of religion* (Philadelphia [PA]: American Philosophical Society, 1993). R. A. Jackson, 'Elective kingship and *consensus populi* in sixteenth-century France', *JMH* 44 (1972), 155–71.

58. Jean Bodin, *Six Books of the Commonwealth* (1577) (ed.) M. J. Tooley (Oxford: Blackwell, 1955), 32, 68, 114, 201–4. J. H. M. Salmon, 'Bodin and the monarchomachs', in H. Denzer (ed.), *Jean Bodin. Verhandlungen der Internationalen Bodin Tagung in München* (Munich: C. H. Beck, 1973), 359–78.

59. François Hotman, *A patterne of Popish peace, or a peace of Papists with Protestants. Beginning in articles, leagues, oathes, and a marriage. And ending in a bloudy massacre of many thousand Protestants* (London, 1644), 104–5.

60. Adriaan van Haemstede, *Historien oft geschiedenissen der vromer martelaren* (Dordrecht, 1579). Jean Crespin, *Histoire des martyrs persecutez et mis a mort pour la verité de l'Evangile, depuis le temps des Apostres jusques à l'an 1597* (1597). Simon Goulart produced the final edition of Crespin's work in 1619. John Foxe, *Actes and monuments of these latter and perillous dayes: Touching matters of the church, wherein are described the great persecutions ... practised by the Romish prelates* (1583).

61. Crespin, *Histoire des martyrs* (1597), 667–71. E. Braekman, 'La pensée politique de Guy de Brès', *BSHPF* 115 (1969), 1–28. E. W. Monter, *Judging the Reformation. Heresy trials by sixteenth-century parlements* (Cambridge [MA]: Harvard University Press, 1999).

62. Crespin, *Histoire des martyrs* (1597), 705, 713, 724–5.

63. D. R. Kelley, 'Martyrs, myths, and the massacre: The background of St Bartholomew', *AHR* 77 (1972), 1340.

64. *Reformed Confessions* (ed.) Cochrane (1966), 217. A. Jelsma, 'The "weakness of conscience" in the Reformed movement in the Netherlands: the attitude of the Dutch Reformation to the uses of violence between 1562 and 1574', in W. J. Sheils (ed.), *The Church and War. Studies in Church History 20* (Oxford: Blackwell, 1983), 217–29. G. Marnef, 'The dynamics of Reformed religious militancy: the Netherlands, 1566–1585', in P. Benedict, G. Marnef, H. van Nierop, M. Venard (eds), *Reformation, revolt and civil war in France and the Netherlands, 1555–1585* (Amsterdam: Royal Netherlands Academy, 1999), 51–58.

65. *Actes du Consistoire de l'Église Française de Threadneedle Street, Londres* (2 vols) (Publications of the Huguenot Society of London vols 38 and 48); vol. 1 (1560–1565) (ed.) E. Johnston (Frome: Huguenot Society, 1937), 38. N. Mout, 'Armed resistance and Calvinism during the revolt of the Netherlands', in van den Berg, Hoftijzer (eds), *Church, change and revolution* (1991), 57–68. A. C. Duke, *Reformation and revolt in the Low Countries* (London: Hambledon, 1990).

66. *The warning of the Prince of Orange to the inhabitants and subjects of the Netherlands, 1 Sep. 1568* in *Texts concerning the revolt of the Netherlands* (eds) E. H. Kossman, A. F. Mellink (Cambridge: Cambridge University Press, 1974), 86–8, 199. M. van Gelderen, *The Political thought of the Dutch revolt, 1555–1590* (Cambridge: Cambridge University Press, 1992).

67. Philip Marnix, *A short account of the true causes and reasons which have forced the States General of the Netherlands to take measures for their protection against Don John of Austria, 1577* in *Revolt of the Netherlands* (eds) Kossman, Mellink (1974), 140.

68. *The Apologie of Prince William of Orange Against the Proclamation of the King of Spaine* (1581) (ed.) H. Wansink (Leiden: Brill, 1969), 78–9.

69. *Edict of the States General* (1581) in *Revolt of the Netherlands* (eds) Kossman, Mellink (1974), 217.

70. Gerard Prouninck, *Emanuel and Ernest. Dialogue of two persons on the state of the Netherlands* (1581) in *Revolt of the Netherlands* (eds) Kossman, Mellink (1974), 210–11.

71. Gerard Prouninck, *Apology* (1587) in *Revolt of the Netherlands* (eds) Kossman, Mellink (1974), 270–1.

72. David Pareus, *Oratio de quaestione: Utrum leges magistratus obligent in conscientia?* (Heidelberg, 1616). David Owen, *Anti-Paraeus, or a Treatise in the Defence of the Royall Right of Kings: against Paraeus and the rest of the anti-monarchians, whether presbyterians or Jesuits* (1619).

73. *The Politics of Johannes Althusius [Politica methodice digesta, atque exemplis sacris et profanis illustrata]*, (ed.) F. S. Carney (London: Eyre and Spottiswoode, 1964), 66, 100, 117–19, 124, 127, 190. H. Schilling, *Civic Calvinism in northwestern Germany and the Netherlands. Sixteenth to nineteenth centuries* (Kirksville [MO]: Sixteenth Century Journal Publishers, 1991), 69–104.

74. K. Révész, 'Bocskay István apologiája', *Protestáns Szemle* 18 (1906), 304–12.

75. K. Benda, 'A kálvini tanok hatása a magyar rendi ellenállás ideológiájára', *Helikon* 17 (1971), 322–30. L. Makkai, 'Nemesi köztársaság és kálvinista teokrácia a 16. századi Lengyelországban és Magyarországon', *Ráday Gyűjtemény Évkönyve* 3 (1983), 17–29. D. Daniel, 'The Fifteen Years' War and the Protestant response to Habsburg absolutism in Hungary', *East Central Europe* 8 (1981), 38–51.

76. Samuel Rutherford, *Lex, Rex: The law and the prince. A dispute for the just prerogative of king and people. Containing the reasons and causes of the most necessary defensive wars of the kingdom of Scotland, and of their expedition for the ayd and help of their dear brethren of England* (London, 1644), 79–82. John Milton, *The Tenure of Kings and Magistrates: Proving, that is is lawfull, and hath been held so through all ages, for any who have the power, to call to account a tyrant, or wicked king, and after due conviction, to depose and put him to death* (London, 1649).

Chapter 4: Moral Discipline

1. H. Schilling, ' "History of crime" or "history of sin"?: Some reflections on the social history of early modern church discipline', in E. I. Kouri, T. Scott (eds), *Politics and Society in Reformation Europe* (Basingstoke: Macmillan, 1987), 289–306. R. Po-Chia Hsia, *Social Discipline in the Reformation: Central Europe, 1550–1750* (London: Routledge, 1989).

2. W. Reinhard, 'Zwang zur Konfessionalisierung? Prolegomena zu enier Theorie des konfessionellen Zeitalters', *Zeitschrift für Historische Forschung* 10 (1983), 257–77. E. W. Zeeden, *Konfessionsbildung. Studien zur Reformation, Gegenreformation und Katholischen Reform* (Stuttgart: Klett–Cotta, 1985). H. Schilling, 'Die Konfessionalisierung im Reich. Religiöser und gesellschaftlicher Wandel in Deutschland zwischen 1555 und 1620', *Historische Zeitschrift* 246 (1988), 1–45. W. Reinhard, 'Reformation, Counter-Reformation, and the early modern state.

A reassessment', *Catholic Historical Review* 75 (1989), 383–404. J. F. Harrington, H. W. Smith, 'Confessionalization, community, and state building in Germany, 1555–1870', *JMH* 69 (1997), 77–101.

3. H. Schilling (ed.), *Die Reformierte Konfessionalisierung in Deutschland-Das Problem der 'Zweiten Reformation'* (Gütersloh: Mohn, 1985). H. Schilling, 'The Reformation and the rise of the early modern state', in J. D. Tracy (ed.), *Luther and the modern state in Germany* (Kirksville [MO]: Sixteenth Century Journal Publishers, 1986), 21–30. H. R. Schmidt, 'Sozialdisziplinierung? Ein Plädoyer für das Ende des Etatismus in der Konfessionalisierungsforschung', *Historische Zeitschrift* 265 (1997), 639–82.

4. Theodore Beza, *Confession de Foi du Chrétien* (Geneva, 1558) (ed.) J. Clarke (Lewes: Focus Christian Ministries Trust, 1992), 26, 31.

5. *Reformed Confessions of the 16th Century* (ed.) A. C. Cochrane (London: SCM Press, 1966), 322.

6. J. Kittelson, *Toward an established church. Strasbourg from 1500 to the dawn of the seventeenth century* (Mainz: von Zabern, 2000). T. A. Brady, *Ruling class, regime and reformation at Strasbourg, 1520–1555* (Leiden: Brill, 1978).

7. W. Balke, *Calvin and the Anabaptist radicals* (Grand Rapids [MI]: William Eerdmans, 1981), 226–7. W. R. Stevenson, *Sovereign Grace. The place and significance of Christian freedom in John Calvin's political thought* (Oxford: Oxford University Press, 1999).

8. *Ecclesiastical Ordinances* (1541) in *John Calvin* (eds) G. R. Potter, M. Greengrass (London, Arnold, 1983), 71–4. A. N. Burnett, *The Yoke of Christ: Martin Bucer and Christian discipline* (Kirksville [MO]: Sixteenth Century Journal Publishers, 1994).

9. Theodore Beza, *The Life of John Calvin* (Geneva, 1564) in *Tracts and Treatises on the Reformation of the Church* (3 vols) (ed.) T. F. Torrance (Edinburgh: Oliver & Boyd, 1958), vol. 1, lxxvi. E. W. Monter, *Calvin's Geneva* (London: Wiley, 1967). W. G. Naphy, *Calvin and the consolidation of the Genevan Reformation* (Manchester: Manchester University Press, 1994). R. M. Kingdon, 'Calvin and the establishment of consistory discipline in Geneva: the institution and the men who directed it', *Nederlands Archief voor Kerkgeschiedenis* 70 (1990), 158–72. R. White, 'Oil and vinegar: Calvin on church discipline', *Scottish Journal of Theology* 38 (1985), 25–40.

10. Johannes à Lasco, *Forma ac ratio tota ecclesiastici ministerij, in peregrinorum, potissimum vero Germanorum ecclesia: Institut a Londini in Anglia, per pietissimum principem Angliae etc. regem Eduardum, eius nominis sextum*

(1554). A. Pettegree, *Foreign Protestant communities in sixteenth-century London* (Oxford: Clarendon, 1986).

11. *Acta van de Nederlandsche Synoden der Zestiende Eeuw* (ed.) F. L. Rutgers (Utrecht: Kemink and Zoon, 1889), 31, 70. 'Memorie uth Acten Synodael tho Middelborch in Zeelant von den 30 Maii tot den 21 Junii 1581' (ed.) W. van't Spijker in J. P. van Dooren (ed.), *De Nationale Synode te Middelburg in 1581. Calvinisme in Opbouw in de Noordelijke en Zuidelijke Nederlanden* (Middelburg: Koninklijk Zeeuwsch Genootschap der Wetenschappen, 1981), 43, 82, 84, 85. *Reformed Confessions* (ed.) Cochrane (1966), 211.

12. *The First Book of Discipline* (ed.) J. K. Cameron (Edinburgh: Saint Andrews Press, 1972), 165–7, 174.

13. 'Ecclesiastical Ordinances of Jeanne d'Albret, November 1571', in N. L. Roelker, *Queen of Navarre. Jeanne d'Albret, 1528–1572* (Cambridge [MA]: Harvard University Press, 1968), 430–1.

14. J. Moltmann, *Christoph Pezel (1539–1604) und der Calvinismus in Bremen* (Bremen: Forschungen zur Bremischen Kirchengeschichte, 1958), 109–11.

15. Beza, *Life of John Calvin* (1958), c–ci.

16. T. H. L. Parker, *Calvin's Preaching* (Edinburgh: T&T Clark, 1992), 121–2.

17. *Reformed Confessions* (ed.) Cochrane (1966), 320–1.

18. *Reformed Confessions* (ed.) Cochrane (1966), 182.

19. *Register of the minister, elders and deacons of the Christian congregation of St Andrews. Comprising the proceedings of the kirk session and of the court of the superintendent of Fife, Fothrik and Strathearn, 1559–1600* (ed.) D. H. Fleming (2 vols) (Edinburgh: Edinburgh University Press, 1889–90), vol. 1 (1889), 365–6, 379, 505, 677, and vol. 2 (1890), 815, 818, 884, 920. M. Todd, *The Culture of Protestantism in early modern Scotland* (New Haven [CT]: Yale University Press, 2002), 96–7.

20. J. W. Baker, 'Christian discipline and the early Reformed tradition: Bullinger and Calvin', in R. V. Schnucker (ed.), *Calviniana. Ideas and influence of Jean Calvin: Sixteenth century essays and studies, volume 10* (Kirksville [MO]: Sixteenth Century Journal Publishers, 1988), 107–20. J. W. Baker, 'Church, state and dissent: The crisis of the Swiss Reformation, 1531–1536', *Church History* 57 (1988), 135–52. B. Gordon, *Clerical discipline and the rural reformation. The synod in Zurich, 1532–1580* (Bern: Lang, 1992). B. Gordon, *The Swiss Reformation* (Manchester: Manchester University Press, 2002), 249–57.

21. R. D. Linder, *The Political ideas of Pierre Viret* (Geneva: Droz, 1964), 36–7. H. R. Schmidt, 'Moral courts in rural Berne during the early

modern period', in K. Maag (ed.), *The Reformation in eastern and central Europe* (Aldershot: Scolar, 1997), 155–81.

22. *Reformed Confessions* (ed.) Cochrane (1966), 267.

23. Thomas Erastus, *An Examination of that most grave question, whether excommunication, or the debarring from the sacraments of professing Christians, because of their sins, be a divine ordinance or a human invention* (ed.) R. Lee (Edinburgh: MacPhail, 1844). V. Press, *Calvinismus und Territorialstaat. Regierung und Zentralbehörden der Kurpfalz, 1559–1619* (Stuttgart: Klett, 1970), 111–44.

24. M. Kosman, 'Programme of the Reformation in the Grand Duchy of Lithuania and how it was carried through (*c.* 1550–*c.* 1650)', *Acta Poloniae Historica* 35 (1977), 21–50.

25. Pál Medgyesi, *Dialogus Politico-Ecclesiasticus, azaz két keresztyén embereknek eggy mással való beszélgetések:... az egyházi igazgató presbyterekről, avagy vénekről, öregekről és a presbyteriumról, eggyházi tanátsról* (Bártfa, 1650).

26. *Puritan Manifestoes. A study of the origin of the Puritan revolt* (eds) W. H. Frere, C. E. Douglas (2nd edn) (London: SPCK, 1954), 112.

27. Walter Travers, *A full and plaine declaration of Ecclesiasticall Discipline, out of the word of God and of the declininge of the Churche of England from the same* (London, 1574), 158, 164. S. J. Knox, *Walter Travers: Paragon of Elizabeth Puritanism* (London: Methuen, 1962).

28. C. D. Cremeans, *The reception of Calvinistic thought in England* (Urbana [IL]: University of Illinois Press, 1949), 101–2.

29. Matthew Sutcliffe, *A treatise of Ecclesiasticall Discipline: Wherein that confused forme of government, which certeine under false pretence, and title of reformation, and true discipline do strive to bring into the Church of England is examined and confuted* (London, 1590), 120, 182, 187, 201.

30. Richard Bancroft, *A Survay of the pretended Holy Discipline. Contayning the beginninges, successe, parts, proceedings, authority, and doctrine of it: with some of the manifold, and material repugnances, varieties and uncertainties in that behalfe* (1593), 460–1.

31. Richard Bancroft, *Dangerous positions and proceedings, published and practised within this iland of Brytaine, under pretence of Reformation, and for the Presbyteriall discipline* (1593), 3, 18, 21, 41, 44. Bancroft, *A Survay of the Pretended Holy Discipline* (1593), 119–128, 214. J. M. Krumm, 'Continental Protestantism and Elizabethan Anglicanism (1570–1595)', in F. H. Littell (ed.), *Reformation Studies. Essays in honor of Roland H. Bainton* (Richmond [VA]: John Knox Press, 1962), 129–44.

32. Richard Hooker, *Of the laws of Ecclesiasticall politie* (ed.) W. S. Hill (6 vols) (Cambridge [MA]: Harvard University Press, 1977–93), vol. 1 (1977), 25–6, 335, 342–3.

33. P. Lake, *Anglicans and Puritans? Presbyterianism and English Conformist thought from Whitgift to Hooker* (London: Unwin Hyman, 1988). A. Milton, *Catholic and Reformed. The Roman and Protestant churches in English Protestant thought, 1600–1640* (Cambridge: Cambridge University Press, 1995).

34. 'La Discipline Ecclesiastique des Eglises Reformées de France selon qu'elle a este arrestée aux Synodes nationaux par les deputes des provinces et ratifiée par toutes les Eglises, revue et confermee par le dernier Synode tenu a La Rochelle le 12 Avril 1571 et a Nismes le 7 May 1572' (ed.) G. S. Sunshine, *French History* 4 (1990), 365–8.

35. Jean Morély, *Traicté de la discipline et police Chrestienne* (Lyon, 1562), 185, 200, 286, 300–1. *Reformed Confessions of the 16th Century* (ed.) Cochrane (1966), 155.

36. *Actes Ecclesiastiques et civiles de tous les synodes nationaux des eglises reformées de France* (ed.) J. Aymon (2 vols) (The Hague, 1710), vol. 1, 29, 32. R. M. Kingdon, *Geneva and the consolidation of the French Protestant movement, 1564–1572* (Geneva: Droz 1967), 48–137, 73.

37. C. Kooi, *Liberty and religion. Church and State in Leiden's Reformation, 1572–1620* (Leiden: Brill, 2000), 212. W. Bergsma, 'Calvinismus in Friesland um 1600 am Beispiel der Stadt Sneek', *AFR* 80 (1989), 270.

38. 'Memorie uth Acten Synodael tho Middelborch' (ed.) van't Spijker (1981), 81.

39. Gerard Brandt, *History of the Reformation in the Low-Countries* (ed.) Michael de la Roche (London, 1725), 212–15. B. J. Kaplan, 'Dutch particularism and the Calvinist quest for 'holy uniformity', *AFR* 82 (1991), 239–56.

40. B. J. Kaplan, *Calvinists and Libertines. Confession and community in Utrecht, 1578–1620* (Oxford: Clarendon, 1995). C. C. Hibben, *Gouda in Revolt. Particularism and pacifism in the revolt of the Netherlands, 1572–1588* (Utrecht: Hes, 1983). S. A. Lamet, 'The vroedschap of Leiden, 1550–1600: the impact of tradition and change on the governing elite of a Dutch city', *SCJ* 12 (1981), 15–42.

41. D. G. Mullan, *Episcopacy in Scotland: The history of an idea, 1560–1638* (Edinburgh: John Donald, 1986), 47.

42. *The Second Book of Discipline* (ed.) J. Kirk (Edinburgh: Saint Andrews Press, 1980).

43. *Acts and Proceedings of the General Assemblies of the Kirk of Scotland from the year MDLX* (2 vols) (Edinburgh: The Maitland Club, 1839–45), vol. 1 (1839), 453.

44. G. Donaldson, *The Scottish Reformation* (Cambridge: Cambridge University Press, 1960). I. B. Cowan, *The Scottish Reformation. Church and society in sixteenth-century Scotland* (London: Weidenfeld and Nicolson, 1982). J. Kirk, *Patterns of reform. Continuity and change in the Reformation kirk* (Edinburgh: T&T Clark, 1989). M. H. B. Sanderson, *Ayrshire and the Reformation. People and change, 1490–1600* (East Linton: Tuckwell Press, 1997). F. D. Bardgett, *Scotland Reformed: The Reformation in Angus and the Mearns* (Edinburgh: John Donald, 1989).

45. *Acts and Proceedings of the General Assemblies of the Kirk of Scotland* vol. 1 (1839), 482, 566. *The Booke of the Universall Kirk of Scotland: wherein the headis and conclusionis devysit be the ministers and commissionaris of the particular kirks thereof, are especially expressed and contained* (ed.) A. Peterkin (Edinburgh: William Blackwood, 1839), 567–74, 601–14. D. Shaw, *The General Assemblies of the Church of Scotland, 1560–1600. Their origins and development* (Edinburgh: Saint Andrew Press, 1964).

46. *Register of St Andrews* vol. 1 (1889), 515, vol. 2 (1890), 837, 846. M. F. Graham, *The Uses of Reform. 'Godly discipline' and popular behavior in Scotland and beyond, 1560–1610* (Leiden: Brill, 1996), 205–20.

47. *The Book of Common Order of the Church of Scotland commonly known as John Knox's liturgy* (ed.) G. W. Sprott (Edinburgh: William Blackwood and Sons, 1901).

48. *Register of St Andrews,* vol. 2 (1890), 804–11. Todd, *The culture of Protestantism in early modern Scotland* (2002), 127–82.

49. *Acts and Proceedings of the General Assemblies of the Kirk of Scotland,* vol. 1 (1839), 159, 161.

50. *Register of St Andrews,* vol. 1 (1889), 204–5, 229.

51. *Register of St Andrews,* vol. 2 (1890), 585, 651.

52. *Register of St Andrews,* vols 1–2 (1889–90), 589–777.

53. *Register of St Andrews,* vol. 2 (1890), 755.

54. *Register of St Andrews,* vol. 2 (1890), 796.

55. *Register of St Andrews,* vol. 2 (1890), 815–16.

56. 'La Discipline Ecclesiastique des Eglises Reformées de France' (ed.) Sunshine (1990), 360–5.

57. 'Le registre consistorial de Coutras, 1582–1584' (ed.) A. Soman *BSHPF* 126 (1980), 193–228.

58. 'Le registre consistorial de Coutras' (ed.) Soman (1980), 206–7. 'La Discipline Ecclesiastique des Eglises Reformées de France' (ed.) Sunshine (1990), 364, 375.

59. *Actes de tous les synodes nationaux de France* (ed.) Aymon vol. 1 (1710), 16, 18, 151–2. Lambert Daneau, *Traite des Danses, auquel est amplement resolue la question, asçavoir s'il est permis aux Chrestiens de danser* (Geneva, 1580).

60. 'Le registre consistorial de Coutras' (ed.) Soman (1980), 209–12.

61. Johannes à Lasco, *Forma ac ratio tota ecclesiastici ministerij, in peregrinorum, potissimum vero Germanorum ecclesia: Institut a Londini in Anglia, per pietissimum principem Angliae etc. regem Eduardum, eius nominis sextum* (1554).

62. Nicolas des Gallars, *Forma Politiae Ecclesiasticae, nuper institutae Londini in coetu Gallorum* (London, 1561), 8–9, 12, 17.

63. *Actes du Consistoire de l'Église Française de Threadneedle Street, Londres* (2 vols) (Publications of the Huguenot Society of London vols 38 and 48); vol. 1 (1560–1565) (ed.) E. Johnston (Frome: Huguenot Society, 1937) and vol. 2 (1571–1577) (ed.) A. M. Oakley (London: Huguenot Society, 1969).

64. *Actes du Consistoire de l'Église Française de Threadneedle Street, Londres,* vol. 1 (1937), 90, 98, 100–1, 114–15, 118.

65. *Actes du Consistoire de l'Église Française de Threadneedle Street, Londres* vol. 2 (1969), 95–6, 115–16.

66. *Les Actes des Colloques des Églises Françaises et des Synodes des Églises Étrangères Refugiées en Angleterre, 1581–1654* (Publications of the Huguenot Society 2) (ed.) A. C. Chamier (Lymington, 1890), 68.

67. *Les Actes des Colloques des Églises Françaises* (ed.) Chamier (1890), 80, 82, 105–9.

68. A. Pettegree (ed.), *The Reformation of the parishes* (Manchester: Manchester University Press, 1993), 189. W. R. Foster, *The Church before the covenants. The Church of Scotland, 1596–1638* (Edinburgh: Scottish Academic Press, 1975).

69. G. Bonet-Maury, 'John Cameron: A Scottish Protestant theologian in France', *Scottish Historical Review* 7 (1910), 328.

70. *A xvi. században tartott magyar református zsinatok végzései* (ed.) Á. Kiss (Budapest, 1882), 1577 article no. 15.

71. E. W. Monter, 'Women in Calvinist Geneva (1500–1800)', *Signs* 6 (1980), 191. R. M. Kingdon, 'The control of morals in Calvin's Geneva', in L. P. Buck, J. W. Zophy (eds), *The Social history of the Reformation* (Columbus [OH]: Ohio State University Press, 1972),

3–16. E. W. Monter, 'The consistory of Geneva, 1559–1569', *BHR* 38 (1976), 467–84. R. A. Mentzer, 'Marking the taboo: Excommunication in French Reformed churches', in Mentzer (ed.), *Sin and the Calvinists. Morals control and the consistory in the Reformed tradition* (Kirksville [MO]: Sixteenth Century Journal Publishers, 1994), 125. C. H. Parker, 'Pilgrim's progress: Narratives of penitence and reconciliation in the Dutch Reformed church', *Journal of Early Modern History* 5 (2001), 239. B. J. Kaplan, ' "Remnants of the Papal Yoke": Apathy and opposition in the Dutch Reformation', *SCJ* 25 (1994), 660.

72. Graham, *The uses of Reform* (1996), 167.

73. M. Lynch, *Edinburgh and the Reformation* (Aldershot: Gregg Revivals, 1993), 38–9. R. A. Mentzer, 'Ecclesiastical discipline and communal reorganization among the Protestants of southern France', *European History Quarterly* 21 (1991), 163–84. H. Schilling, *Civic Calvinism in northwestern Germany and the Netherlands. Sixteenth to nineteenth centuries* (Kirksville [MO]: Sixteenth Century Journal Publishers, 1991), 105–61.

74. M. F. Graham, 'Equality before the kirk? Church discipline and the elite in reformation-era Scotland', *AFR* 84 (1993), 289–310.

75. C. H. Parker, *The Reformation of community. Social welfare and Calvinist charity in Holland, 1572–1620* (Cambridge: Cambridge University Press, 1998). C. H. Parker, 'Moral supervision and poor relief in the Reformed church of Delft, 1579–1609', *AFR* 87 (1996), 334–61. R. A. Mentzer, 'Organizational endeavour and charitable impulse in sixteenth-century France: the case of Protestant Nîmes', *French History* 5 (1991), 26.

76. J. R. Watt, 'Women and the consistory in Calvin's Geneva', *SCJ* 24 (1993), 429–39.

77. B. Vogler, J. Estèbe, 'La genèse d'une société protestante: Étude comparée de quelques registres consistoriaux Languedociens et Palatins vers 1600', *Annales* 31 (1976), 362–88. R. A. Mentzer, 'Le consistoire et la pacification du monde rural', *BSHPF* 135 (1989), 385–6.

78. R. A. Mentzer, '*Disciplina nervus ecclesiae.* The Calvinist reform of morals at Nîmes', *SCJ* 18 (1987), 89–115. Vogler, Estèbe, 'La genèse d'une société protestante', *Annales* (1976), 362–88. Schilling, *Civic Calvinism in northwestern Germany and the Netherlands* (1991), 58.

79. M. F. Graham, 'Social discipline in Scotland, 1560–1610' in Mentzer (ed.), *Sin and the Calvinists* (1994), 136.

80. *Acts and Proceedings of the General Assemblies of the Kirk of Scotland,* vol. 1 (1839), 377, 536, 746, 748, 772.

81. M. Spufford, 'Puritanism and social control?', in A. Fletcher, J. Stevenson (eds), *Order and disorder in early modern England* (Cambridge: Cambridge University Press, 1985), 41–57. M. Ingram, 'Puritans and the church courts, 1560–1640' in C. Durston, J. Eales (eds), *The culture of English Puritanism, 1560–1700* (Basingstoke: Macmillan 1996), 58–91.

82. J. Pollmann, 'Off the record: Problems in the quantification of Calvinist church discipline', *SCJ* 23 (2002), 426. J. Pollmann, *Religious choice in the Dutch Republic. The Reformation of Arnoldus Buchelius* (Manchester: Manchester University Press, 1999). Todd, *The Culture of Protestantism in early modern Scotland* (2002), 16–19. P. Benedict, *Christ's Churches Purely Reformed. A social history of Calvinism* (New Haven [CT]: Yale University Press, 2002), 484–9.

83. For these records, see Tiszáninnen Reformed Church Province library manuscript collection (Sárospatak); vols 16–18, 'Zempléni Egyházmegye Protocolluma' (1629–45), (1638–51) and (1653–72).

Chapter 5: Religious Life and Culture

1. W. Naphy, 'Baptisms, church riots and social unrest in Calvin's Geneva', *SCJ* 26 (1995), 87–97. W. G. Naphy, *Calvin and the consolidation of the Genevan Reformation* (Manchester: Manchester University Press, 1994), 144–5. J. R. Watt, 'Calvinism, childhood and education: the evidence from the Genevan consistory', *SCJ* 33 (2002), 439–56. E. W. Monter, 'Historical demography and religious history in sixteenth-century Geneva', *Journal of Interdisciplinary History* 9 (1979), 412–14. P. Benedict, *Christ's churches purely Reformed. A social history of Calvinism* (New Haven [CT]: Yale University Press, 2002), 505–6.

2. 'La Discipline Ecclesiastique des Eglises Reformées de France selon qu'elle a este arrestée aux Synodes nationaux par les deputes des provinces et ratifiée par toutes les Eglises, revue et confermee par le dernier Synode tenu a La Rochelle le 12 Avril 1571 et a Nismes le 7 May 1572' (ed.), Glen S. Sunshine, *French History* 4 (1990), 352–77, 368. *Actes Ecclesiastiques et civiles de tous les synodes nationaux des eglises reformées de France* (2 vols) (ed.) J. Aymon (The Hague, 1710), vol. 1, 27, 140.

3. P. Benedict, *Rouen during the wars of religion* (Cambridge: Cambridge University Press, 1981).

4. *Acta van de Nederlandsche Synoden der Zestiende Eeuw* (ed.) F. L. Rutgers (Utrecht: Kemink and Zoon, 1889), 250. G. Marnef, *Antwerp in the*

age of Reformation. Underground Protestantism in a commercial metropolis, *1550–1577* (Baltimore [PA]: The Johns Hopkins University Press, 1996), 199–201.

5. *Les Actes des Colloques des Églises Françaises et des Synodes des Églises Étrangères Refugiées en Angleterre, 1581–1654* (ed.) A. C. Chamier (Lymington: Huguenot Society, 1890), 8.

6. Richard Bancroft, *Dangerous positions and proceedings, published and practised within this iland of Brytaine, under pretence of Reformation, and for the Presbyteriall discipline* (1640), 104. N. Tyacke, 'Popular Puritan mentality in late Elizabethan England', in Tyacke, *Aspects of English Protestantism, c. 1530–1700* (Manchester: Manchester University Press, 2001), 91–6. P. Collinson, 'Cranbrook and the Fletchers: Popular and unpopular religion in the Kentish Weald', in P. N. Brooks (ed.), *Reformation principle and practice. Essays in honour of Arthur Geoffrey Dickens* (London: Scolar, 1980), 197.

7. *Catechism of the Church of Geneva* (1541) in *Tracts relating to the Reformation by John Calvin* (3 vols) (ed.) H. Beveridge (Edinburgh: Calvin Translation Society, 1844–51), vol. 2 (1849), 36.

8. E. W. Monter, *Calvin's Geneva* (London: Wiley, 1967), 97.

9. *Reformed Confessions of the 16th Century* (ed.) A. C. Cochrane (London: SCM Press, 1966), 305–31.

10. R. Mentzer, 'The printed catechism and religious instruction in the French Reformed churches', in R. B. Barnes, R. A. Kolb, P. L. Presley (eds), *Books have their own destiny. Essays in honor of Robert V. Schnucker* (Kirksville [MO]: Sixteenth Century Essays and Studies, 1998), 93–101.

11. G. Murdock, 'Calvinist catechizing and Hungarian Reformed identity', in M. Crăciun, O. Ghitta, G. Murdock (eds), *Confessional identity in east-central Europe* (Aldershot: Ashgate, 2002), 81–98. János Siderius, *Kisded gyermekeknek való katechizmus, azaz a keresztyéni hitnek fő ágazatairúl rövid kérdések és feleletek által való tanitás* (Debrecen, 1597). Dávid Huszár, *A keresztyén hitről való tudománynak rövid kérdésekben foglaltatott summája* (Pápa, 1577). Ferenc Szárászi, *Catechesis, azaz: Kérdések és feleletek a kerestyéni tudománynak ágairól* (Debrecen, 1604). Albert Szenczi Molnár, *Kis katekizmus… szedetött az haidelbergai öreg katekizmusból* (Herborn, 1607).

12. I. Green, *The Christian's ABC. Catechisms and catechizing in England, c. 1530–1740* (Oxford: Clarendon, 1996). I. Green, ' "For Children in yeeres and children in understanding": The emergence of the English catechism under Elizabeth and the early Stuarts', *JEH* 37 (1986), 397–425.

13. *Traité d'Éducation de la Jeunesse de Marnix de Sainte-Aldegonde* (ed.) J. Catrysse (Brussels: Arscia, 1959), 52.

14. R. Gawthorp, G. Strauss, 'Protestantism and literacy in early modern Germany', *PP* 104 (1984), 31–55. J. Kittleson, 'Successes and failures in the German Reformation: The Report from Strasbourg', *AFR* 73 (1982), 153–75. S. Ozment, *When fathers ruled. Family life in Reformation Europe* (Cambridge [MA]: Harvard University Press, 1983), 176.

15. A. C. Duke, G. Lewis, A. Pettegree (eds), *Calvinism in Europe, 1540–1610* (Manchester: Manchester University Press, 1992), 114.

16. Duke *et al.* (eds), *Calvinism in Europe, 1540–1610* (1992), 51–3.

17. John Calvin, *Epistle to the reader of the Genevan Psalter* in C. Garside (ed.), 'The Origins of Calvin's theology of music', *Transactions of the American Philosophical Society* 69 (1979), 31. A. Spicer, ' "*Qui est de Dieu, oit la parole de Dieu*": the Huguenots and their temples', in Spicer, R. A. Mentzer (eds), *Society and culture in the Huguenot world, 1559–1685* (Cambridge: Cambridge University Press, 2001), 175–92.

18. *Forms of Prayers* (1542) in *Tracts relating to the Reformation by John Calvin* (3 vols) (ed.) H. Beveridge (Edinburgh: Calvin Translation Society, 1844–51), vol. 2 (1849), 95–113. Nicolas des Gallars, *Forma Politiae Ecclesiasticae, nuper institutae Londini in coetu Gallorum* (London, 1561), 7–8.

19. *John Knox's Genevan Service Book, 1556. The liturgical portions of the Genevan Service Book used by John Knox while a minister of the English congregation of Marian exiles at Geneva, 1556–1559* (ed.) W. D. Maxwell (London: The Faith Press, 1965), 23. *The Book of Common Order of the Church of Scotland commonly known as John Knox's liturgy* (ed.) G. W. Sprott (Edinburgh: William Blackwood and Sons, 1901). J. Dawson, 'Calvinism and the Gaidhealtachd in Scotland', in A. C. Duke, G. Lewis, A. Pettegree (eds), *Calvinism in Europe, 1540–1620* (Cambridge: Cambridge University Press, 1994), 231–53.

20. *The Geneva Bible* (ed.) L. E. Berry (Madison [WI]: University of Wisconsin Press, 1969), iv, 14. D. G. Danner, 'Anthony Gilby: Puritan in exile – a biographical approach', *Church History* 40 (1971), 412–22. D. G. Danner, 'The contribution of the Genevan Bible of 1560 to the English Protestant tradition', *SCJ* 12 (1981), 5–18. Thanks to Diarmaid MacCulloch for pointing out how the 'Breeches Bible' got its name.

21. *Form of celebrating Communion* in *Tracts relating to the Reformation by John Calvin* (ed.) Beveridge, vol. 2 (1849), 119–22. 'La Discipline

Ecclesiastique des Eglises Reformées de France' (ed.) Sunshine, *French History* (1990), 370–1. *Les Actes des Colloques des Églises Françaises et des Synodes des Églises Étrangères Refugiées en Angleterre, 1581–1654* (ed.) A. C. Chamier (Lymington: Huguenot Society, 1890), 14.

22. *The Book of Common Order* (ed.) Sprott (1901), 123.

23. *Acta van de Nederlandsche Synoden der Zestiende Eeuw* (ed.) F. L. Rutgers (Utrecht: Kemink and Zoon, 1889), 251.

24. *An Admonition to the Parliament* (1572).

25. *A Seconde Admonition to the Parliament* (1573), 11, 36.

26. *Puritan Manifestoes. A study of the origin of the Puritan revolt* (2nd edn) (eds) W. H. Frere, C. E. Douglas (London: SPCK, 1954), 153–4.

27. Martin Bucer, *De Regno Christi* (1550) in *Melanchthon and Bucer* (ed.) W. Pauck (London: SCM Press, 1969), 253.

28. John Calvin, *Institutes of the Christian Religion* (Geneva, 1559) (ed.) H. Beveridge (2 vols) (Edinburgh: Calvin Translation Society, 1845), 3/3/17.

29. Theodore Beza, *Confession de Foi du Chrétien* (Geneva, 1558) (ed.) J. Clarke (Lewes: Focus Christian Ministries Trust, 1992), 107. *Reformed Confessions* (ed.) Cochrane (1966), 292. 'La Discipline Ecclesiastique des Eglises Reformées de France' (ed.) Sunshine (1990), 352–77, 363.

30. *Die Kirchenratsprotokolle der Reformierten Gemeinde Emden, 1557–1620* (eds) H. Schilling, K-D. Schreiber (2 vols) (Cologne: Böhlau, 1989–92), vol. 1 (1989), 151, 198, 249, 347.

31. *Les Actes des Colloques des Églises Françaises en Angleterre* (ed.) Chamier (1890), 20, 22. *Actes du Consistoire de l'Église Française de Threadneedle Street, Londres* (2 vols), vol. 2 (1571–1577) (ed.) A. M. Oakley (London: Huguenot Society, 1969), 169, 189.

32. *Acts and Proceedings of the General Assemblies of the Kirk of Scotland from the year MDLX* (2 vols) (Edinburgh: The Maitland Club, 1839–45), vol. 1 (1839), 99, 138–9, 252, 312, 390, 407, 727, 730, 747. *Register of the minister, elders and deacons of the Christian congregation of St Andrews. Comprising the proceedings of the kirk session and of the court of the superintendent of Fife, Fothrik and Strathearn, 1559–1600* (2 vols) (ed.) D. H. Fleming (Edinburgh: Edinburgh University Press, 1889–90), vol. 1 (1889), 339, 348, 371, 393, vol. 2 (1890), 861, 862, 884, 896, 902.

33. *The Book of Common Order* (ed.) Sprott (1901), 148–53.

34. C. Garside, *Zwingli and the arts* (New Haven [CT]: Yale University Press, 1966). G. Ehrstine, *Theater, culture, and community in Reformation Bern, 1523–1555* (Leiden: Brill, 2002), 248, 288.

35. Calvin, *Epistle to the reader of the Genevan Psalter*, (ed.) Garside (1979), 33. H. P. Clive, 'The Calvinist attitude to music, and its literary aspects and sources', *BHR* 19 (1957), 80–102.

36. Theodore Beza, *The Psalmes of David, truely opened and explained by Paraphrasis, according to the right sense of every Psalme with large and ample arguments before every psalme, declaring the true use thereof,* (tr.) Anthony Gilby (London, 1580).

37. *The historie of the lyff of James Melvill* (ed.) J. G. Fyfe (Edinburgh: Oliver and Boyd, 1948), 23. M. Patrick, *Four centuries of Scottish Psalmody* (Oxford: Oxford University Press, 1949). W. S. Reid, 'The battle hymns of the Lord. Calvinist Psalmody of the sixteenth century', *Sixteenth Century Essays and Studies* 2 (1971), 36–54.

38. B. Diefendorf, 'The Huguenot Psalter and the faith of French Protestants in the sixteenth century', in Diefendorf, C. Hesse (eds), *Culture and identity in early modern Europe (1500–1800)* (Ann Arbor [MI]: University of Michigan Press, 1993), 41–63. D. Nicholls, 'Social change and early Protestantism in France: Normandy, 1560–1562', *European Studies Review* 10 (1980), 279–308. J. Estèbe, *Protestants du Midi, 1559–1598* (Toulouse: Privat, 1980), 279.

39. H. Slenk, 'Jan Utenhove's Psalms in the Low Countries', *Nederlands Archief voor Kerkgeschiedenis* 49 (1968–69), 155–68. B. J. Kaplan, *Calvinists and Libertines. Confession and community in Utrecht, 1578–1620* (Oxford: Clarendon, 1995), 51.

40. György Gönczi Kovács, *Keresztyéni énekek* (Debrecen, 1592).

41. Albert Szenczi Molnár, *Psalterium Ungaricum* (Herborn, 1607).

42. E. A. Gosselin, 'David *in Tempore Belli*: Beza's David in the service of the Huguenots', *SCJ* 7 (1976), 31–54. I. B. Cowan (ed.), *Blast and counterblast. Contemporary writings on the Scottish Reformation* (Edinburgh: Saltire Society, 1960), 19.

43. G. Murdock, 'Dressed to repress?: Protestant clergy dress and the regulation of morality in early modern Europe', *Fashion Theory. The Journal of Dress, Body and Culture* 2 (2000), 179–99. P. Romane-Musculus, 'Histoire de la robe pastorale et du rabat', *BSHPF* 115 (1969), 307–38.

44. *Original letters relative to the English Reformation written during the reigns of King Henry VIII, King Edward VI, and Queen Mary: Chiefly from the Archives of Zurich. Parker Society vols 23 and 28* (ed.) H. Robinson (2 vols) (Cambridge: Cambridge University Press, 1846–7), vol. 1 (1846), 87.

45. *Miscellaneous writings and letters of Thomas Cranmer. Parker Society vol. 24* (ed.) J. Cox (Cambridge: Cambridge University Press, 1846), 428.

C. Hopf, *Martin Bucer and the English Reformation* (Oxford: Blackwell, 1946), 131–46.

46. *Original Letters*, vol. 1 (1846), 91–5, vol. 2 (1847), 486–90, 558–62, 584–7. M. Anderson, *Peter Martyr. A Reformer in exile (1542–1562)* (Nieuwkoop: De Graaf, 1975), 113–14.

47. *The works of John Jewel, Bishop of Salisbury. Volume 4. Parker Society vol. 40* (ed.) J. Ayre (Cambridge: Cambridge University Press, 1850), 1268. *The Zurich letters, comprising the correspondence of several English bishops and others, with some of the Helvetian reformers, during the early part of the reign of Queen Elizabeth. The Parker Society, volumes 7 and 18* (ed.) H. Robinson (Cambridge: Cambridge University Press, 1843–45), vol. 7 (1843), 63, 74, 84–5, 100, 142, 145, 248, vol. 18 (1845), 5, 25–7, 32–3, 38–41.

48. *The works of James Pilkington. Parker Society vol. 3* (ed.) J. Scholefield (Cambridge: Cambridge University Press, 1842), 659–60. R. Bauckham, 'Marian exiles and Cambridge Puritanism: James Pilkington's "Halfe a score"', *JEH* 26 (1975), 137–48.

49. *Correspondence of Matthew Parker. Parker Society vol. 49* (eds) T. Perowne, J. Bruce (Cambridge: Cambridge University Press, 1853), 240–1, 267–70, 277–9. P. Collinson, *Archbishop Grindal, 1519–1583. The struggle for a Reformed church* (London: Jonathan Cape, 1979), 98–100, 167–76. P. Collinson, *The Elizabethan Puritan Movement* (Oxford: Clarendon, 1990), 71–97.

50. *A briefe examination for the tyme of a certain declaration* (London, 1566), appendix for correspondence of Bucer and Martyr. *An answer for the tyme, to the examination put in print, without the authors name, pretending to mayntayne the apparell prescribed against the declaration of the mynisters of London* (London, 1566). *A briefe discourse against the outwarde apparell and ministring garmentes of the popishe church* (London, 1566).

51. *Acts and Proceedings of the General Assemblies of the Kirk of Scotland*, vol. 1 (1839), 85–6.

52. *Zurich Letters*, vol. 7 (1843), 134, 151–2, 153–5, 157–63.

53. *Zurich Letters*, vol. 7 (1843), 341–3, 345–55, 356–7.

54. *Zurich Letters*, vol. 7 (1843), 157–63, 162.

55. *Zurich Letters*, vol. 7 (1843), 357–60, 360–2, vol. 18 (1845), 136–40.

56. *Zurich Letters*, vol. 18 (1845), 121–4.

57. *Zurich Letters*, vol. 18 (1845), 127–36, 131.

58. *Zurich Letters*, vol. 18 (1845), 144.

59. *Zurich Letters*, vol. 18 (1845), 128, 140.

60. *Zurich Letters*, vol. 18 (1845), 152–6, 244.

61. *The remains of Edmund Grindal* (ed.) W. Nicholson (Cambridge: Cambridge University Press, 1843), 207–11, 339–42. *Zurich Letters*, vol. 18 (1845), 156–64, 339–53.

62. John Whitgift, *The defence of the answer to the admonition agains the reply of Thomas Cartwright* (London, 1574) in *The works of John Whitgift, Volume 2. Parker Society vol. 48* (ed.) J. Ayre (Cambridge: Cambridge University Press, 1852), 1–76.

63. C. H. Parker, 'French Calvinists as the children of Israel: An Old Testament self-consciousness in Jean Crespin's "Histoire des martyrs" before the wars of religion', *SCJ* 24 (1993), 227–48.

64. Gáspár Károlyi, *Két könyv minden országoknak és királyoknak jó és gonosz szerencséjeknek okairól, melyből megérthetni, mi az oka a magyarországnak is romlásának és miczoda ielensegekből esmerhettiuc meg, hogy az istennec iteleti közel vagion* (Debrecen, 1563), 77. K. Benda, 'La réforme en Hongrie', *BSHPF* 122 (1976), 30–53.

65. Lambert Daneau, *Traite de l'estat honneste des Chrestiens en leur accoustrement* (Geneva, 1580), 186.

66. L. P. Fairfield, *John Bale. Mythmaker for the English Reformation* (West Lafayette [IN]: Purdue University Press, 1976).

67. S. A. Burrell, 'The Covenant idea as a revolutionary synbol: Scotland, 1596–1637', *Church History* 27 (1958), 348.

68. G. Groenhuis, 'Calvinism and national consciousness: The Dutch Republic as the New Israel', in A. C. Duke, C. A. Tamse (eds), *Church and State since the Reformation: Britain and the Netherlands 7* (The Hague: Nijhoff, 1981), 118–34. P. Regan, 'Calvinism and the Dutch Israel thesis', in B. Gordon (ed.), *Protestant History and Identity in Sixteenth–Century Europe, Volume 2. The Later Reformation* (Aldershot: Scolar, 1996), 91–107. E. H. Kossmann, *In Praise of the Dutch Republic: some seventeenth–century attitudes* (London: H. K. Lewis, 1963), 11–12.

69. M. Greengrass, D. Ogier, 'A French Reformation on English soil: religious change in the Channel Islands', *PHS* 26 (1994–97), 173–85.

70. John Dane, 'A Declaration of remarkabell provedenses in the corse of my lyfe' in D. Cressy, 'Books as totems in seventeenth–century England and New England', *Journal of Library History* 21 (1986), 100.

71. W. D. Bailie, *The Six Mile Water Revival of 1625* (2nd edn) (Belfast: Presbyterian Historical Society of Ireland, 1984). W. F. Graham, 'The religion of the first Scottish settlers in Ulster', in J. Friedman (ed.), *Regnum, Religio et Ratio. Essays presented to Robert M. Kingdon* (Kirksville [MO]: Sixteenth Century Journal Publishers, 1987), 53–68. R. B. Knox, *James Ussher, Archbishop of Armagh* (Cardiff: University of

Wales Press, 1967), 167–94. N. Canny, 'Protestants, Planters and apartheid in early modern Ireland', *Irish Historical Studies* 25 (1986), 105–15. R. F. G. Holmes, 'Ulster Presbyterianism and Irish Nationalism', in S. Mews (ed.), *Studies in Church History 18. Religion and National Identity* (Oxford: Blackwell, 1982), 535–48.

72. Albert Szenczi Molnár, *Dictionarium Latino–Ungaricum* (1604) in *Szenci Molnár Albert válogatott művei* (eds) J. Vásárhelyi, G. Tolnai (Budapest: Magvető, 1976), 177–8.

73. A. du Toit, '"No chosen people": The myth of the Calvinist origins of Afrikaner nationalism and racial ideology', *AHR* 88 (1983), 920–52. A du Toit, 'The construction of Afrikaner chosenness', in W. R. Hutchinson, H. Lehmann (eds), *Many are chosen. Divine election and western nationalism* (Minneapolis [MN]: Fortress Press, 1994), 115–39.

74. Calvin, *Institutes* (1559), 3/25.

75. *Reformed Confessions* (ed.) Cochrane (1966), 218–19.

76. Károlyi, *Két könyv* (1563), f6. G. Kathona, *Károlyi Gáspár történelmi világképe* (Debrecen, 1943).

77. I. Révész, 'Debreceni lelki válsága, 1561–1571', *Értekezések a Történelmi Tudományok Köréből, vol. 25/6* (Budapest, 1936), 76.

78. K. R. Firth, *The Apocalyptic tradition in Reformation Britain, 1530–1645* (Oxford, 1979). B. W. Ball, *A Great Expectation. Eschatological thought in English Protestantism* (Leiden: Brill, 1975). J. Dawson, 'The apocalyptic thinking of the Marian exiles', in M. Wilks (ed.), *Prophecy and Eschatology. Studies in Church History Subsidia 10* (Oxford: Blackwell, 1994), 75–91.

79. R. G. Clouse, 'John Napier and apocalyptic thought', *SCJ* 5 (1974), 101–14. R. Kyle, 'John Knox and apocalyptic thought', *SCJ* 15 (1984), 449–69.

80. J. L. Farthing, 'Christ and the Eschaton: The Reformed eschatology of Jerome Zanchi', in W. F. Graham (ed.), *Later Calvinism. International perspectives. Sixteenth-century essays and studies* (Kirksville [MO]: North East Missouri State University, 1994), 333–54. E. Le Roy Ladurie, *The peasants of Languedoc* (Urbana [IL]: University of Illinois Press, 1976), 269–86.

81. S. Åkerman, 'The Rosicrucians and the great conjunctions', in J. C. Laursen, R. H. Popkin (eds), *Continental millenarians: Protestants, Catholics, Heretics* (Dordrecht: Kluwer, 2001), 1–8. H. Hotson, *Johann Heinrich Alsted 1588–1638. Between Renaissance, Reformation, and universal reform* (Oxford: Clarendon, 2000).

82. *Reformed Confessions* (ed.) Cochrane (1966), 245–6.

83. R. G. Clouse, 'The rebirth of millenarianism', in P. Toon (ed.), *Puritans, the millennium and the future of Israel: Puritan Eschatology 1600 to 1660* (Cambridge: James Clarke, 1970), 42–65. H. Hotson, *Paradise postponed. Johann Heinrich Alsted and the birth of Calvinist millenarianism* (Dordrecht: Kluwer, 2000).

84. Jan Amos Comenius, *A Reformation of schooles* (London, 1642). Comenius, *Panglottia or Universal language* (ed.) A. M. O. Dobbie, (Shipston-on-Stour, Drinkwater, 1989). Comenius, *Panorthosia, or Universal reform* (ed.) A. M. O. Dobbie (Sheffield: Sheffield Academic Press, 1995). J. E. Sadler, *J. A. Comenius and the concept of universal education* (London: Allen & Unwin, 1966). D. Murphy, *Comenius. A Critical assessment of his life and work* (Dublin: Irish Academic Press, 1995).

Select Bibliography

Printed Sources

Acts and Proceedings of the General Assemblies of the Kirk of Scotland From the year MDLX (2 vols), (Edinburgh: The Maitland Club, 1839–45).

The Politics of Johannes Althusius [Politica methodice digesta, atque exemplis sacris et profanis illustrata] (ed.) F. S. Carney (London: Eyre and Spottiswoode, 1964).

Aylmer, John, *An Harborowe for faithfull and trewe subiectes, agaynst the late blowne Blaste, concerninge the government of women, wherein be confuted all such reasons as a straunger of late made in that behalfe, with a briefe exhortation to obedience* (Strasburg, 1559).

The Vocacyon of Johan Bale (eds) P. Happé, J. King (Binghamton [NY]: Medieval and Renaissance Texts and Studies, 1990).

Bancroft, Richard, *A Survay of the Pretended Holy Discipline. Contayning the beginninges, successe, parts, proceedings, authority, and doctrine of it: with soem of the manifold, and material repugnances, varieties and uncertainties in that behalfe* (1593).

—— *Dangerous Positions and Proceedings, published and practised within this iland of Brytaine, under pretence of Reformation, and for the Presbyteriall discipline* (1593).

Barnaud, Nicolas, *Le Reveille-Matin des François, et de leurs Voisins par Eusebe Philadelphe Cosmopolite* (1574).

Beza, Theodore, *Confession de Foi du Chrétien* (Geneva, 1558) (ed.) J. Clarke (Lewes: Focus Christian Ministries Trust, 1992).

—— *The Life of John Calvin* (Geneva, 1564) in *Tracts and Treatises on the Reformation of the Church* (3 vols) (ed.) T. F. Torrance (Edinburgh: Oliver & Boyd, 1958) vol. 1, lvi–cxxxviii.

Beza, Theodore, *Du droit des magistrats sur leurs subjects* (Heidelberg, 1574) in *Consitutionalism and Resistance in the sixteenth century. Three treatises by Hotman, Beza and Mornay* (ed.) J. H. Franklin (New York: Pegasus, 1969), 101–35.

—— *The Psalmes of David, truely opened and explained by Paraphrasis, according to the right sense of every Psalme with large and ample arguments before every Psalme, declaring the true use thereof* (tr.) Anthony Gilby (London, 1580).

Bilson, Thomas, *The true difference between Christian subjection and unchristian rebellion: wherein the princes lawful power to command for truth, and indepriveable right to beare the sword, are defended against the Popes censures and the Iesuits sophisme* (London, 1586).

Bolsec, Jerome, *Histoire de la vie, moeurs, actes, doctrine, constance et mort de Iean Calvin iadis ministre de Geneve recueilly par Hierosme Hermes Bolsec* (1577) (ed.) L-F. Chastel (Lyon: Scheuring, 1875).

The Booke of the Universall Kirk of Scotland: wherein the headis and conclusionis devysit be the ministers and commissionaris of the particular kirks thereof, are especially expressed and contained (ed.) A. Peterkin (Edinburgh: William Blackwood, 1839).

Bucer, Martin, *De Regno Christi* (1550) in *Melanchthon and Bucer* (ed.) W. Pauck (London: SCM Press, 1969), 174–394.

Buchanan, George, *De Iure Regni apud Scotos, Dialogus* (Edinburgh, 1579).

Bullinger, Heinrich, *The Second Helvetic Confession* (1566) in *Reformed Confessions of the 16th Century* (ed.) A. C. Cochrane (1966), 224–301.

Calvin, John, *Catechism of the Church of Geneva* (1541) in *Tracts relating to the Reformation by John Calvin* (3 vols) (ed.) H. Beveridge (Edinburgh: Calvin Translation Society, 1844–51) vol. 2 (1849), 33–94.

—— *Forms of Prayers* (1542) in *Tracts relating to the Reformation by John Calvin* (3 vols) (ed.) H. Beveridge (Edinburgh: Calvin Translation Society, 1844–51), vol. 2 (1849), 95–113.

—— *Excuse de Jehan Calvin, a Messieurs les Nicodemites, sur la complaincte qu'ilz sont de sa trop grand rigeur* (Geneva, 1544) in *Three French Treatises* (ed.) F. Higman (London: Athlone Press, 1970), 131–53.

—— *De aeterna praedestinatione Dei* (Geneva, 1552) (ed.) J. K. S. Reid *Concerning the Eternal Predestination of God* (London: James Clarke, 1961).

—— *Institutes of the Christian Religion* (Geneva, 1559) (2 vols) (ed.) H. Beveridge (Edinburgh: Calvin Translation Society, 1845).

Coras, Jean de, *Question Politique: s'il est licite aux subjects de capituler avec leur prince* (1570) (ed.) R. M. Kingdon (Geneva: Droz, 1989).

'Le registre consistorial de Coutras, 1582–1584' (ed.) A. Soman *BSHPF* 126 (1980), 193–228.

Coverdale, Miles, *Certain most godly, fruitful, and comfortable letters of such true Saintes and holy Martyrs of God, as in the late bloodye persecution here within this Realme, gave their lyves for the defense of Christes holy gospel: written in the tyme of theyr affliction and cruell imprysonment* (London, 1564).

Crespin, Jean, *Histoire des martyrs persecutez et mis a mort pour la verité de l'Evangile, depuis le temps des Apostres jusques à l'an 1597* (1597).

Daneau, Lambert, *Traite des Danses, auquel est amplement resolue la question, asçavoir s'il est permis aux Chrestiens de danser* (Geneva, 1580).

—— *Traite de l'estat honneste des Chrestiens en leur accoustrement* (Geneva, 1580).

Dent, Arthur, *The Plaine Mans Path-Way to Heaven* (London, 1601).

'La Discipline Ecclesiastique des Eglises Reformées de France selon qu'elle a este arrestée aux Synodes nationaux par les deputes des provinces et ratifiée par toutes les Eglises, revue et confermee par le dernier Synode tenu a La Rochelle le 12 Avril 1571 et a Nismes le 7 May 1572' (ed.) G. S. Sunshine, *French History* 4 (1990), 352–77.

The Iudgement of the Synode holden at Dort, concerning the five articles: as also their sentence touching Conradus Vorstius (London, 1619).

Duplessis-Mornay, Philippe, *Vindiciae contra tyrannos, sive de principis in populum et populi in principem legitima potestate, Stephano Junio Bruto Celta auctore* (1579) in *Constitutionalism and Resistance in the sixteenth century* (ed.) J. H. Franklin (1969), 142–99.

Erastus, Thomas, *An Examination of that most grave question, whether excommunication, or the debarring from the sacraments of professing Christians, because of their sins, be a divine ordinance or a human invention* (ed.) R. Lee (Edinburgh: MacPhail, 1844).

Farel, Guillaume, *Du Vray Usage de la Croix de Iesus Christ, et de l'abus et de l'idolatrie commise autour d'icelle, et de l'authorité de la parole de Dieu, et des traditions humaines* (1560).

The First Book of Discipline (ed.) J. K. Cameron (Edinburgh: Saint Andrews Press, 1972).

Foxe, John, *Actes and monuments of these latter and perillous dayes: touching matters of the church, wherein are described the great persecutions ... practised by the Romish prelates* (1583).

Les Actes des Colloques des Églises Françaises et des Synodes des Églises Étrangères Refugiées en Angleterre, 1581–1654 (ed.) A. C. Chamier (Lymington: Huguenot Society, 1890).

Actes Ecclesiastiques et civiles de tous les synodes nationaux des eglises reformées de France (2 vols) (ed.) J. Aymon (The Hague, 1710).

A Brief Discourse of the troubles begun at Frankfort in Germany, anno domini 1554, about the Book of Common Prayer and Ceremonies; and continued by the Englishmen there to the end of Queen Mary's reign (1575).

Gallars, Nicolas des, *Forma Politiae Ecclesiasticae, nuper institutae Londini in coetu Gallorum* (London, 1561).

Registers of the Consistory of Geneva in the time of Calvin. Volume 1: 1542–1544 (gen ed.) R. M. Kingdon (Grand Rapids [MI]: Eerdmans, 2000).

Gentillet, Innocent, *Discours, sur les moyens de bien gouverner et maintenir en bonne paix un Royaume ou autre Principauté... contra Nicolas Machiavel Florentin* (1576) in C. E. Rathé (ed.), *Anti-Machiavel* (Geneva: Droz, 1968).

Goodman, Christopher, *How Superior powers ought to be obeyed of their subjects: and wherein they may lawfully by Gods worde be disobeyed and resisted, wherein also is declared the cause of all this present misery in England, and the onely way to remedy the same* (Geneva, 1558).

The Heidelberg Catechism (1563) in *Reformed Confessions of the 16th Century* (ed.) Cochrane (1966), 305–31.

Hotman, François, *A Patterne of Popish Peace, or a peace of Papists with Protestants. Beginning in articles, leagues, oathes, and a marriage. And ending in a bloudy massacre of many thousand Protestants* (London, 1644).

—— *Francogallia: or, an account of the ancient free state of France* (London, 1711).

Articles of Religion agreed upon by the Archbishops and Bishops, and the rest of the cleargie of Ireland, in the convocation holden at Dublin in... 1615 (Dublin, 1615).

Károlyi, Gáspár, *Két könyv minden országoknak és királyoknak jó és gonosz szerencséjeknek okairól, melyből megérthetni, mi az oka a magyarországnak is romlásának és miczoda ielensegekből esmerhettiuc meg, hogy az istennec iteleti közel vagion* (Debrecen, 1563).

John Knox. On Rebellion (ed.) R. A. Mason (Cambridge: Cambridge University Press, 1994).

John Knox's Genevan Service Book, 1556. The liturgical portions of the Genevan Service Book used by John Knox while a minister of the English congregation of Marian exiles at Geneva, 1556–1559 (ed.) W. D. Maxwell (London: The Faith Press, 1965).

Lasco, Johannes à, *Forma ac ratio tota ecclesiastici ministerij, in peregrinorum, potissimum vero Germanorum ecclesia: Institut a Londini in Anglia, per pietissimum principem Angliae etc. regem Eduardum, eius nominis sextum* (1554).

Actes du Consistoire de l'Église Française de Threadneedle Street, Londres (2 vols), vol. 1 (1560–1565) (ed.) E. Johnston (Frome: Huguenot Society, 1937); vol. 2 (1571–1577) (ed.) A. M. Oakley (London: Huguenot Society, 1969).

A xvi. században tartott magyar református zsinatok végzései (ed.) Á. Kiss (Budapest, 1882).

Marnix van St Aldegonde, Philip, *The Bee Hive of the Romishe Churche. Wherein the author a zealous Protestant, under the person of a superstitious Papist, doth so driely repell the grose opinions of Popery, and so divinely defend the articles of Christianitie, that (the sacred Scriptures excepted) there is not a booke to be founde, either more necessarie for thy profite, or sweeter for thy comfort* (London, 1579).

The Political Thought of Peter Martyr Vermigli. Selected Texts and Commentary (ed.) R. M. Kingdon (Geneva: Droz, 1980).

Morély, Jean, *Traicté de la discipline et police Chrestienne* (Lyon, 1562).

Texts Concerning the Revolt of the Netherlands (eds) E. H. Kossman, A. F. Mellink (Cambridge: Cambridge University Press, 1974).

Original letters relative to the English reformation written during the reigns of King Henry VIII, King Edward VI, and Queen Mary: Chiefly from the Archives of Zurich. Parker Society vols 23 and 28 (2 vols) (ed.) H. Robinson (Cambridge: Cambridge University Press, 1846–47).

Pareus, David, *Irenicum, sive de unione et synodo evangelicorum concilianda, votivus paci ecclesiae et desideriis pacificorum dicatus* (Heidelberg, 1614).

The Work of William Perkins (ed.) I. Breward (Abingdon: Sutton Courtenay Press, 1970).

Ponet, John, *A short treatise of politike power, and of the true obedience which subiectes owe to kynges and other civile governours, with an exhortacion to all true naturall Englishe men* (1556).

Puritan Manifestoes. A study of the origin of the Puritan revolt (2nd edn) (eds) W. H. Frere, C. E. Douglas (London: SPCK, 1954).

Reformed Confessions of the 16th century (ed.) A. C. Cochrane (London: SCM Press, 1966), 185–219.

Register of the minister, elders and deacons of the Christian congregation of St Andrews. Comprising the proceedings of the kirk session and of the court of the superintendent of Fife, Fothrik and Strathearn, 1559–1600 (2 vols) (ed.) D. H. Fleming (Edinburgh: Edinburgh University Press, 1889–90).

Salvard, Jean-François, *An harmony of the confessions of the faith of the Christian and Reformed Churches, which purelie professe the holy doctrine of the Gospell in all the chiefe kingdomes, nations, and provinces of Europe* (Cambridge, 1586).

The Book of Common Order of the Church of Scotland commonly known as John Knox's liturgy (ed.) G. W. Sprott (Edinburgh: William Blackwood and Sons, 1901).

Scots Confession, 1560, and Negative Confession, 1581 (ed.) G. D. Henderson (Edinburgh: Church of Scotland Publications, 1937).

The Second Book of Discipline (ed.) J. Kirk (Edinburgh: Saint Andrews Press, 1980).

Siderius, János, *Kisded gyermekeknek való katechizmus, azaz a keresztyéni hitnek fő ágazatairúl rövid kérdések és feleletek által való tanitás* (Debrecen, 1597).

Sutcliffe, Matthew, *A treatise of Ecclesiasticall Discipline: Wherein that confused forme of government, which certeine under false pretence, and title of reformation, and true discipline do strive to bring into the Church of England is examined and confuted* (London, 1590).

Szenci Molnár Albert válogatott művei (eds), J. Vásárhelyi, G. Tolnai (Budapest: Magvető, 1976).

Le Tocsin, Contre les Massacreurs et auteurs des confusions en France. Par laquel, la source et origine de tous les maux, qui de long temps travaillent le France, est decouverte (1579).

Travers, Walter, *A full and plaine declaration of Ecclesiasticall Discipline, out of the word of God and of the declininge of the Churche of England from the same* (London, 1574).

Utenhove, Jan, *Simplex et fidelis narratio de instituta ac demum dissipata Belgarum, aliorumque peregrinorum in Anglia, ecclesia: et potissimum de susceptis postea illius nomine itineribus, quaeque eis in illis evenerunt* (1560).

Viret, Pierre, *Du Vray Usage de la Salutation faite par l'ange a la vierge Marie, et de la source des chadelets, et de la maniere de prier par conte, et de l'abus qui y est: et du vray moyen par laquel la vierge Marie peut estre honorée* (1556).

Whitgift, John, *The defence of the answer to the admonition agains the reply of Thomas Cartwright* (London, 1574).

The apologie of Prince William of Orange against the Proclamation of the King of Spaine (1581) (ed.) H. Wansink (Leiden: E. J. Brill, 1969).

The Zurich Letters, comprising the correspondence of several English bishops and others, with some of the Helvetian reformers, during the early part of the reign of Queen Elizabeth. The Parker Society, volumes 7 and 18 (ed.) H. Robinson (Cambridge: Cambridge University Press, 1843–45).

Secondary Literature

L. J. Abray, *The People's reformation. Magistrates, clergy, and commons in Strasbourg, 1500–1598* (Oxford: Blackwell, 1985).

M. Anderson, *Peter Martyr. A reformer in exile (1542–1562). A chronology of Biblical writings in England and Europe* (Nieuwkoop: De Graaf, 1975).

B. G. Armstrong, *Calvinism and the Amyraut heresy: Protestant scholasticism and humanism in seventeenth-century France* (Madison [WI]: University of Wisconsin Press, 1969).

M. Aston, *England's Iconoclasts* (Oxford: Clarendon 1988).

M. F. Backhouse, *The Flemish and Walloon communities of Sandwich during the reign of Elizabeth I* (Brussels: Koninklijke Academie van België, 1985).

J. W. Baker, *Heinrich Bullinger and the Covenant: The other Reformed tradition* (Athens [OH]: Ohio University Press, 1980).

W. Balke, *Calvin and the Anabaptist radicals* (Grand Rapids [MI]: William Eerdmans, 1981).

B. W. Ball, *A Great expectation – Eschatological thought in English Protestantism to 1660* (Leiden; Brill, 1975).

C. Bangs, *Arminius. A study in the Dutch Reformation* (Nashville [TN]: Abingdon, 1971).

J. R. Beeke, *Assurance of faith. Calvin, English Puritanism and the Dutch Second Reformation* (New York: Peter Lang, 1991).

K. Benda, 'A kálvini tanok hatása a magyar rendi ellenállás ideológiájára', *Helikon* 17 (1971), 322–30.

P. Benedict, *Rouen during the wars of religion* (Cambridge: Cambridge University Press, 1981).

—— *The Huguenot population of France, 1600–1685: The demographic fate and customs of a religious minority* (Philadelphia: American Philosophical Society, 1991).

—— *The faith and fortunes of France's Huguenots, 1600–1685* (Aldershot: Ashgate, 2001).

—— *Christ's churches purely reformed. A social history of Calvinism* (New Haven [CT]: Yale University Press, 2002).

P. Benedict, G. Marnef, H. van Nierop, M. Venard (eds), *Reformation, revolt and civil war in France and the Netherlands, 1555–1585* (Amsterdam: Royal Netherlands Academy, 1999).

L. D. Bierma, *German Calvinism in the confessional age. The covenant theology of Caspar Olevianus* (Grand Rapids [MI]: Baker Brooks, 1996).

—— *The Doctrine of the sacraments in the Heidelberg Catechism: Melanchthonian, Calvinist or Zwinglian?* (Princeton [NJ]: Princeton Theological Seminary, 1999).

W. J. Bouwsma, 'The quest for the historical Calvin', *AFR* 77 (1986), 47–57.

—— *John Calvin. A sixteenth-century portrait* (Oxford: Oxford University Press, 1988).

T. A. Brady, *Ruling class, regime and reformation at Strasbourg, 1520–1555* (Leiden: Brill 1978).

J. S. Bray, *Theodore Beza's doctrine of predestination* (Nieuwkoop: B de Graaf, 1975).

Q. Breen, *John Calvin: a study in French humanism* (London: Archon, 1968).

I. Breward, 'The significance of William Perkins', *Journal of Religious History* 4 (1966–67), 113–28.

M. Bucsay, *Der Protestantismus in Ungarn, 1521–1798. Ungarns Reformationskirchen in Geschichte und Gegenwart. 1. Im Zeitalter der Reformation, Gegenreformation und katholischen Reform* (Vienna: Böhlau, 1977).

A. N. Burnett, *The yoke of Christ: Martin Bucer and Christian discipline* (Kirksville [MO]: Sixteenth Century Journal Publishers, 1994).

P. Collinson, 'The Elizabethan puritans and the foreign Reformed churches in London', *PHS* 20/5 (1962–63), 528–55.

—— *The religion of Protestants. Church in English society, 1559–1625* (Oxford: Clarendon, 1982).

—— *The Puritan character. Polemics and polarities in early seventeenth-century English culture* (Los Angeles[CA]: University of California, 1987).

—— *The Elizabethan Puritan movement* (Oxford: Clarendon, 1990).

B. Cottret, *The Huguenots in London. Immigration and settlement, c. 1550–1700* (Cambridge: Cambridge University Press, 1991).

I. B. Cowan, *The Scottish Reformation. Church and society in sixteenth-century Scotland* (London: Weidenfeld and Nicolson, 1982).

P. M. Crew, *Calvinist preaching and iconoclasm in the Netherlands, 1544–69* (Cambridge: Cambridge University Press, 1978).

D. G. Danner, *Pilgrimage to Puritanism. History and theology of the Marian exiles at Geneva, 1555–1560* (New York: Peter Lang, 1999).

N. Z. Davis, 'The rites of violence: Religious riot in sixteenth-century France', *PP* 59 (1973), 51–91.

J. Dawson, 'The two John Knoxes: England, Scotland and the 1558 tracts', *JEH* 42 (1991), 555–76.

—— 'The apocalyptic thinking of the Marian exiles', in M. Wilks (ed.), *Prophecy and Eschatology. Studies in Church History Subsidia 10* (Oxford: Blackwell, 1994), 75–91.

P. Denis, *Les Églises d'étrangers en pays Rhénans (1538–1564)* (Liège: L'Université de Liège, 1984).

B. B. Diefendorf, *Beneath the cross: Catholics and Huguenots in sixteenth-century Paris* (New York: Oxford University Press, 1991).

—— 'The Huguenot Psalter and the faith of French Protestants in the sixteenth century', in Diefendorf, C. Hesse (eds), *Culture and identity in early modern Europe (1500–1800)* (Ann Arbor [MI]: University of Michigan Press, 1993), 41–63.

G. Donaldson, *The Scottish Reformation* (Cambridge: Cambridge University Press, 1960).

J. P. Donnelly, *Calvinism and Scholasticism in Vermigli's doctrine of man and grace* (Leiden: Brill, 1976).

A. C. Duke, G. Lewis, A. Pettegree (eds), *Calvinism in Europe, 1540–1610. A collection of documents* (Manchester: Manchester University Press, 1992).

—— (eds), *Calvinism in Europe, 1540–1620* (Cambridge: Cambridge University Press, 1994).

C. M. N. Eire, *War against the idols. The Reformation of worship from Erasmus to Calvin* (Cambridge: Cambridge University Press, 1986).

J. Estèbe, *Protestants du Midi, 1559–1598* (Toulouse: Privat, 1980).

R. J. W. Evans, *The making of the Habsburg monarchy, 1550–1700* (Oxford: Clarendon, 1979).

T. G. Fehler, *Poor relief and Protestantism. The Evolution of social welfare in sixteenth-century Emden* (Aldershot: Ashgate, 1999).

K. R. Firth, *The Apocalyptic tradition in reformation Britain, 1565–1645* (Oxford: Oxford University Press, 1979).

A. Ford, *The Protestant reformation in Ireland* (Frankfurt: Lang, 1987).

W. R. Foster, *The Church before the covenants. The Church of Scotland, 1596–1638* (Edinburgh: Scottish Academic Press, 1975).

A. Ganoczy, *The young Calvin* (Edinburgh: T&T Clark, 1988).

C. H. Garrett, *The Marian exiles. A study in the origins of Elizabethan Puritanism* (Cambridge: Cambridge University Press, 1938).

C. Garside, *Zwingli and the arts* (New Haven [CT]: Yale University Press, 1966).

M. van Gelderen, *The Political thought of the Dutch revolt, 1555–1590* (Cambridge: Cambridge University Press, 1992).

R. E. Giesey, 'The monarchomach *triumvirs*: Hotman, Beza and Mornay', *BHR* 32 (1970), 41–56.

B. Gordon, *Clerical discipline and the rural reformation. The synod in Zurich, 1532–1580* (Bern: Lang, 1992).

—— (ed.), *Protestant history and identity in sixteenth-century Europe, volume 2. The Later Reformation* (Aldershot: Scolar 1996).

—— *The Swiss Reformation* (Manchester: Manchester University Press, 2002).

T. H. Gräf, 'The Collegium Mauritianum in Hesse-Kassel and the making of Calvinist diplomacy', *SCJ* 28 (1997), 1167–80.

M. F. Graham, *The Uses of Reform. 'Godly discipline' and popular behavior in Scotland and beyond, 1560–1610* (Leiden: Brill, 1996).

W. F. Graham (ed.) *Later Calvinism. International perspectives. Sixteenth century essays and studies* (Kirksville [MO]: North East Missouri State University, 1994).

I. Green, *The Christian's ABC. Catechisms and catechizing in England, c.1530–1740* (Oxford: Clarendon, 1996).

M. Greengrass, 'The anatomy of a religious riot in Toulouse in May 1562', *JEH* 34 (1983), 367–91.

—— 'Protestant exiles and their assimilation in early modern England', *Immigrants and Minorities* 4 (1985), 68–81.

—— 'Samuel Hartlib and international Calvinism', *PHS* 25/5 (1993), 464–75.

O. P. Grell, *Dutch Calvinists in early Stuart London. The Dutch church in Austin Friars, 1603–1642* (Leiden: Brill, 1989).

—— *Calvinist exiles in Tudor and Stuart England* (Aldershot: Scolar, 1996).

B. Hall, 'Calvin against the Calvinist', in G. E. Duffield (ed.), *John Calvin* (Abingdon: Sutton Courtenay Press, 1966), 19–37.

—— *John à Lasco, 1499–1560. A Pole in Reformation London* (London: Dr William's Trust, 1971).

H. Heller, *The conquest of poverty. The Calvinist revolt in sixteenth–century France* (Leiden: Brill, 1986).

C. C. Hibben, *Gouda in Revolt. Particularism and pacifism in the revolt of the Netherlands, 1572–1588* (Utrecht: Hes, 1983).

P. C. Holtrop, *The Bolsec controversy on predestination, from 1551 to 1555* (2 vols) (Lewiston [NY]: Edwin Mellen Press, 1993).

C. Hopf, *Martin Bucer and the English Reformation* (Oxford: Blackwell, 1946).

H. Höpfl, *The Christian polity of John Calvin* (Cambridge: Cambridge University Press, 1982).

H. Hotson, *Johann Heinrich Alsted 1588–1638. Between Renaissance, Reformation, and Universal Reform* (Oxford: Clarendon, 2000).

—— *Paradise postponed. Johann Heinrich Alsted and the birth of Calvinist millenarianism* (Dordrecht: Kluwer, 2000).

W. S. Hudson, *John Ponet (1516?–1556). Advocate of limited monarchy* (Chicago [IL]: University of Chicago Press, 1942).

B. J. Kaplan, 'Dutch particularism and the Calvinist quest for "holy uniformity"', *AFR* 82 (1991), 239–56.

—— ' "Remnants of the Papal Yoke": Apathy and opposition in the Dutch Reformation', *SCJ* 25 (1994), 653–69.

—— *Calvinists and Libertines. Confession and community in Utrecht, 1578–1620* (Oxford: Clarendon, 1995).

D. R. Kelley, *François Hotman. A revolutionary's ordeal* (Princeton [NJ]: Princeton University Press, 1973).

—— *The beginning of ideology. Consciousness and society in the French Reformation* (Cambridge: Cambridge University Press, 1981).

R. T. Kendall, *Calvin and English Calvinism to 1649* (Oxford: Oxford University Press, 1981).

Robert M. Kingdon, 'The first expression of Theodore Beza's political ideas', *AFR* 46 (1955), 88–100.

—— *Geneva and the coming of the wars of religion in France, 1555–1563* (Geneva: Droz, 1956).

—— *Geneva and the consolidation of the French Protestant movement, 1564–1572* (Geneva: Droz, 1967).

—— 'Social welfare in Calvin's Geneva', *AHR* 76 (1971), 50–69.

—— *Myths about the St. Bartholomew's Day massacres, 1572–1576* (Harvard [MA]: Harvard University Press, 1988).

—— 'Calvin and the establishment of consistory discipline in Geneva: the institutions and the men who directed it', *Nederlands Archief voor Kerkgeschiedenis* 70 (1990), 158–72.

—— 'International Calvinism', in Tracy *et al.* (eds), *Handbook of European History, 1400–1600* (Leiden: Brill, 1995), 229–47.

J. Kirk (ed.), *Patterns of reform. Continuity and change in the Reformation kirk* (Edinburgh: T&T Clark, 1989).

J. M. Kittelson, *Toward an established church. Strasbourg from 1500 to the dawn of the seventeenth century* (Mainz: von Zabern, 2000).

S. J. Knox, *John Knox's Genevan congregation* (London: Presbyterian Historical Society, 1956).

—— *Walter Travers: Paragon of Elizabeth Puritanism* (London: Methuen, 1962).

C. Kooi, *Liberty and Religion. Church and State in Leiden's Reformation, 1572–1620* (Leiden: Brill, 2000).

M. Kosman, 'Programme of the Reformation in the Grand Duchy of Lithuania and how it was carried through (c. 1550–c. 1650)', *Acta Poloniae Historica* 35 (1977), 21–50.

E. I. Kouri, *England and the attempts to form a Protestant alliance in the late 1560s: a case study in European diplomacy* (Helsinki: Suomalainen Tiedeakatemia, 1981).

P. Lake, 'The significance of the Elizabethan identification of the Pope as Antichrist', *JEH* 31 (1980), 161–78.

—— *Moderate Puritans and the Elizabethan church* (Cambridge: Cambridge University Press, 1982).

P. Lake, 'Calvinism and the English church, 1570–1635', *PP* 114 (1987), 32–76.

—— *Anglicans and Puritans? Presbyterianism and English Conformist thought from Whitgift to Hooker* (London: Unwin Hyman, 1988).

M. H. Lesnoff, *The Spirit of capitalism and the Protestant ethic. An enquiry into the Weber thesis* (Cambridge: Edward Elgar, 1994).

J. Lindeboom, *Austin Friars. History of the Dutch Reformed church in London, 1550–1950* (The Hague: Nijhoff, 1950).

R. D. Linder, *The Political ideas of Pierre Viret* (Geneva: Droz, 1964).

Th. H. Lunsingh Scheurleer, G. H. M. Posthumus Meyjes (eds), *Leiden university in the seventeenth century. An exchange of learning* (Leiden: Brill, 1975).

M. Lynch, *Edinburgh and the Reformation* (Aldershot: Gregg Revivals, 1993).

K. Maag, *Seminary or university? The Genevan academy and Reformed higher education, 1560–1620* (Aldershot: Scolar, 1995).

—— (ed.), *The Reformation in eastern and central Europe* (Aldershot: Scolar, 1997).

D. MacCulloch, *Reformation. Europe's house divided, 1490–1700* (London: Penguin, 2003).

A. R. MacDonald, *The Jacobean kirk, 1567–1625. Sovereignty, polity and liturgy* (Aldershot: Ashgate, 1998).

L. Makkai, *A magyar puritánusok harca a feudálizmus ellen* (Budapest: MTA, 1952).

G. Marnef, *Antwerp in the age of Reformation. Underground Protestantism in a commercial metropolis, 1550–1577* (Baltimore [PA]: The Johns Hopkins University Press, 1996).

E. A. McKee, *John Calvin on the diaconate and liturgical almsgiving* (Geneva, Droz: 1984).

J. C. McLelland (ed.), *Peter Martyr Vermigli and Italian Reform* (Waterloo [ON]: Wilfrid Laurier University Press, 1980).

P. McNair, *Peter Martyr in Italy. An anatomy of apostasy* (Oxford: Clarendon, 1967).

R. A. Mentzer, '*Disciplina nervus ecclesiae*. The Calvinist reform of morals at Nîmes', *SCJ* 18 (1987), 89–115.

—— 'Le consistoire et la pacification du monde rural', *BSHPF* 135 (1989), 373–89.

—— 'Ecclesiastical discipline and communal reorganization among the Protestants of southern France', *European History Quarterly* 21 (1991), 163–84.

—— (ed.), *Sin and the Calvinists. Morals control and the consistory in the Reformed tradition* (Kirksville [MO]: Sixteenth Century Journal Publishers, 1994).

—— *Blood and Belief. Family Survival and confessional identity among the provincial Huguenot nobility* (West Lafayette [IN]: Purdue University Press, 1994).

J. P. Meyer, *Reformation in La Rochelle. Tradition and change in early modern Europe, 1500–1568* (Geneva: Droz, 1996).

S. Michalski, *The Reformation and the visual arts. The Protestant image question in western and eastern Europe* (London: Routledge, 1993).

B. C. Milner, *Calvin's Doctrine of the Church* (Leiden: Brill, 1970).

A. Milton, *Catholic and Reformed. The Roman and Protestant churches in English Protestant thought, 1600–1640* (Cambridge: Cambridge University Press, 1995).

J. Moltmann, *Christoph Pezel (1539–1604) und der Calvinismus in Bremen* (Bremen: Forschungen zur Bremischen Kirchengeschichte, 1958).

—— *Calvin's Geneva* (London: Wiley, 1967).

E. W. Monter, 'Crime and punishment in Calvin's Geneva', *AFR* 64 (1973), 281–7.

—— 'The Consistory of Geneva, 1559–1569', *BHR* 38 (1976), 467–84.

—— *Judging the Reformation. Heresy trials by sixteenth-century parlements* (Cambridge [MA]: Harvard University Press, 1999).

N. Mout, 'The International Calvinist church of Prague, the Unity of Brethren and Comenius, 1609–1625', *Acta Comeniana* 4 (1979), 65–77.

D. G. Mullan, *Episcopacy in Scotland: The history of an idea, 1560–1638* (Edinburgh: John Donald, 1986).

—— *Scottish Puritanism, 1590–1638* (Oxford: Oxford University Press, 2000).

R. A. Muller, *Christ and the decree. Christology and predestination in Reformed theology from Calvin to Perkins* (Durham [NC]: Labyrinth Press, 1986).

—— *The unaccommodated Calvin. Studies in the foundation of a theological tradition* (Oxford: Oxford University Press, 2000).

G. Murdock, 'The importance of being Josiah: An image of Calvinist identity', *SCJ* 29 (1998), 1043–59.

—— *Calvinism on the frontier, 1600–1660. International Calvinism and the Reformed Church in Hungary and Transylvania* (Oxford: Clarendon, 2000).

—— 'Dressed to repress?: Protestant clergy dress and the regulation of morality in early modern Europe', *Fashion Theory. The Journal of Dress, Body and Culture* 2 (2000), 179–99.

G. Murdock, M. Crăciun, O. Ghitta (eds), *Confessional identity in east-central Europe* (Aldershot: Ashgate, 2002).

W. G. Naphy, *Calvin and the consolidation of the Genevan reformation* (Manchester: Manchester University Press, 1994).

B. Nischan, 'The second reformation in Brandenburg: aims and goals', *SCJ* 14 (1983), 173–87.

—— *Prince, people and confession. The second reformation in Brandenburg* (Philadelphia: University of Philadelphis Press, 1994).

F. A. Norwood, *The Reformation refugees as an economic force* (Chicago: The American Society of Church History, 1942).

H. Oberman, 'The "extra" dimension in the theology of Calvin', *JEH* 21 (1970), 43–64.

—— '*Europa afflicta*: The reformation of the refugees', *AFR* 83 (1992), 91–111.

—— 'Calvin and Farel: the dynamics of legitimation in early Calvinism', *Journal of Early Modern History* 2 (1998), 32–60.

O. Odlozilík, 'A church in a hostile state: The unity of Czech Brethren', *Central European History* 6 (1973), 111–27.

J. E. Olson, *Calvin and social welfare. Deacons and the Bourse Française* (Cranbury [NJ]: Associated University Presses, 1989).

S. Ozment, *The reformation in the cities. The appeal of Protestantism to sixteenth-century Germany and Switzerland* (New Haven [CT]: Yale University Press, 1980).

C. H. Parker, 'French Calvinists as the children of Israel: An Old Testament self-consciousness in Jean Crespin's 'Histoire des martyrs' before the wars of religion', *SCJ* 24 (1993), 227–48.

—— *The Reformation of community. Social welfare and Calvinist charity in Holland, 1572–1620* (Cambridge: Cambridge University Press, 1998).

—— 'Pilgrim's progress: Narratives of penitence and reconciliation in the Dutch Reformed church', *Journal of Early Modern History* 5 (2001), 222–40.

D. Parker, *La Rochelle and the French monarchy: conflict and order in seventeenth-century France* (London: Royal Historical Society, 1980).

K. L. Parker, *The English Sabbath: a study of doctrine and discipline from the Reformation to the Civil War* (Cambridge: Cambridge University Press, 1988).

T. H. L. Parker, *Calvin's doctrine of the knowledge of God* (Edinburgh: Oliver Boyd, 1969).

—— *Calvin's preaching* (Edinburgh: T&T Clark, 1992).

K. A. Parrow, *From defense to resistance: Justification on violence during the French wars of religion* (Philadelphia [PA]: American Philosophical Society, 1993).

K. Péter, 'Az 1608 évi vallásügyi törvény és a jobbágyok vallásszabadsága', *Századok* 111 (1977), 93–113.

—— *Papok és nemesek. Magyar művelődéstörténeti tanulmányok a reformációval kezdődő másfél évszázadból* (Budapest, 1995).

A. Pettegree, *Foreign Protestant communities in sixteenth-century London* (Oxford: Clarendon Press, 1986).

—— 'The Exile churches and the churches "under the cross": Antwerp and Emden during the Dutch revolt', *JEH* 38 (1987), 187–209.

—— *Emden and the Dutch revolt. Exile and the development of Reformed Protestantism* (Oxford: Clarendon, 1992).

—— *Marian Protestantism. Six studies* (Aldershot: Scolar, 1996).

—— (ed.), *The Reformation World* (London: Routledge, 2000).

J. Pollmann, *Religious choice in the Dutch Republic. The Reformation of Arnoldus Buchelius* (Manchester: Manchester University Press, 1999).

—— 'Off the record: Problems in the quantification of Calvinist church discipline', *SCJ* 23 (2002), 428–38.

G. R. Potter, *Zwingli* (Cambridge: Cambridge University Press, 1976).

V. Press, *Calvinismus und Territorialstaat. Regierung und Zentralbehörden der Kurpfalz, 1559–1619* (Stuttgart: Klett, 1970).

M. Prestwich (ed.), *International Calvinism, 1541–1715* (Oxford: Clarendon, 1985).

J. Raitt, *The Eucharistic theology of Theodore Beza* (Chambersburg [PA]: American Academy of Religion, 1972).

—— *The Colloquy of Montbéliard. Religion and politics in the sixteenth century* (Oxford: Oxford University Press, 1993).

W. S. Reid, *Trumpeter of God. A biography of John Knox* (New York: Scribner, 1974).

I. Révész, *Társadalmi és politikai eszmék a magyar puritánizmusban* (Budapest, 1948).

—— *A history of the Hungarian Reformed church* (Washington: Hungarian Reformed Federation of America, 1956).

P. Roberts, *A city in conflict: Troyes during the French wars of religion* (Manchester: Manchester University Press, 1996).

N. L. Roelker, *Queen of Navarre. Jeanne d'Albret, 1528–1572* (Cambridge [MA]: Harvard University Press, 1968).

—— 'The role of noblewomen in the French reformation', *AFR* 63 (1972), 168–95.

P. Rorem, *Calvin and Bullinger on the Lord's Supper* (Nottingham: Grove Books, 1989).

H. Schilling, 'Innovation through migration: The settlements of Calvinistic Netherlanders in sixteenth- and seventeenth-century central and western Europe', *Histoire Sociale-Social History* 16 (1983), 7–33.

—— (ed.), *Die Reformierte Konfessionalisierung in Deutschland- Das Problem der 'Zweiten Reformation'* (Gütersloh: Mohn, 1985).

—— 'Die Konfessionalisierung im Reich. Religiöser und gesellschaftlicher Wandel in Deutschland zwischen 1555 und 1620', *Historische Zeitschrift* 246 (1988), 1–45.

—— *Civic Calvinism in northwestern Germany and the Netherlands. Sixteenth to nineteenth centuries* (Kirksville [MO]: Sixteenth Century Journal Publishers, 1991).

—— *Religion, political culture and the emergence of early modern society. Essays in German and Dutch history* (Leiden: Brill, 1992).

—— 'Confessional Europe', in Tracy *et al.* (eds), *Handbook of European History, 1400–1600* (Leiden: Brill, 1995), 641–81.

H. R. Schmidt, 'Sozialdisziplinierung? Ein Plädoyer für das Ende des Etatismus in der Konfessionalisierungsforschung', *Historische Zeitschrift* 265 (1997), 639–82.

R. V. Schnucker (ed.), *Calviniana. Ideas and influence of Jean Calvin: Sixteenth century essays and studies, volume 10* (Kirksville [MO]: Sixteenth Century Journal Publishers, 1988).

P. Seaver, *Wallington's world. A Puritan artisan in seventeenth-century London* (London: Methuen, 1985).

D. Shaw, *The General Assemblies of the Church of Scotland, 1560–1600. Their origins and development* (Edinburgh: Saint Andrew Press, 1964).

A. Soman (ed.), *The Massacre of St. Bartholomew. Reappraisals and documents* (The Hague: Nijhoff, 1974).

A. Spicer, *The French–speaking Reformed community and their church in Southampton, c. 1567–1620* (Stroud: Sutton Publishing, 1999).

—— ' "Qui est de Dieu, oit la parole de Dieu": the Huguenots and their temples', in Spicer, R. A. Mentzer (eds), *Society and culture in the Huguenot world, 1559–1685* (Cambridge: Cambridge University Press, 2001), 175–92.

K. L. Sprunger, *The learned Doctor William Ames: Dutch backgrounds of English and American Puritanism* (Urbana [IL]: University of Illinois Press, 1972).

—— *Dutch Puritanism: a history of English and Scottish churches of the Netherlands in the sixteenth and seventeenth centuries* (Leiden: Brill, 1982).

—— *Trumpets from the tower. English Puritan printing in the Netherlands 1600–1660* (Leiden: Brill, 1994).

J. Stachniewski, *The persecutory Imagination. English Puritanism and the literature of religious despair* (Oxford: Clarendon Press, 1991).

R. Stauffer, 'Calvinism and the universities', in L. Grane (ed.), *University and Reformation. Lectures from the University of Copenhagen symposium* (Leiden: Brill, 1981), 76–98.

D. Steinmetz, *Calvin in context* (Oxford: Oxford University Press, 1995).

W. R. Stevenson, *Sovereign Grace. The place and significance of Christian freedom in John Calvin's political thought* (Oxford: Oxford University Press, 1999).

N. M. Sutherland, *The Massacre of St. Bartholomew and the European conflict, 1559–1572* (London: Macmillan, 1973).

—— 'The Marian exiles and the establishment of the Elizabethan regime', *AFR* 78 (1987), 253–86.

M. Todd, *The culture of Protestantism in early modern Scotland* (New Haven [CT]: Yale University Press, 2002).

P. Toon (ed.), *Puritans, the millennium and the future of Israel: Puritan Eschatology 1600 to 1660* (Cambridge: James Clarke, 1970).

C. P. Venema, 'Heinrich Bullinger's correspondence on Calvin's doctrine of predestination, 1551–1553', *SCJ* 17 (1986), 435–50.

B. Vogler, 'Le rôle des Électeurs palatins dans les guerres de religion en France (1559–1592)', *Cahiers d'Histoire* 10 (1965), 51–85.

—— 'Les contacts culturels entre Huguenots français et protestants palatins au 16e siècle', *BSHPF* 115 (1969), 29–42.

—— *Le Clergé Protestant Rhénan au Siècle de la Réforme (1555–1619)* (Paris: Editions Ophrys, 1976).

B. Vogler, J. Estèbe, 'La genèse d'une société protestante: Étude comparée de quelques registres consistoriaux Languedociens et Palatins vers 1600', *Annales* 31 (1976), 362–88.

A. Walsham, *Providence in early modern England* (Oxford: Oxford University Press, 1999).

L. P. Wandel, *Always among us. Images of the poor in Zwingli's Zurich* (Cambridge: Cambridge University Press, 1990).

—— *Voracious idols and violent hands. Iconoclasm in reformation Zurich, Strasbourg, and Basel* (Cambridge: Cambridge University Press, 1995).

J. R. Watt, 'Women and the consistory in Calvin's Geneva', *SCJ* 24 (1993), 429–39.

—— 'Calvinism, childhood and education: the evidence from the Genevan consistory', *SCJ* 33 (2002), 439–56.

M. Weber, *The Protestant ethic and the spirit of capitalism* (1930) (London: Harper Collins, 1996).

F. Wendel, *Calvin. The origins and development of his religious thought* (London: Collins, 1963).

J. Wormald, *Court, Kirk, and Community. Scotland, 1470–1625* (Edinburgh: Edinburgh University Press, 1991).

D. F. Wright (ed.), *Martin Bucer. Reforming church and community* (Cambridge: Cambridge University Press, 1994).

E. W. Zeeden, *Konfessionsbildung. Studien zur Reformation, Gegenreformation und Katholischen Reform* (Stuttgart: Klett-Cotta, 1985).

J. Zoványi, *Puritánus mozgalmak a magyar református egyházban* (Budapest, 1911).

—— *A reformáczió Magyarországon 1565-ig* (Budapest: Genius, 1921).

—— *A magyarországi protestántizmus 1565-től* (Budapest: Akadémiai Kiadó, 1977).

Index